'This book will become the definitive resource on the physical, social, and cognitive development of advanced learners. It provides an honest accounting of how they are unique, where they are not, and what questions remain unanswered.'

Scott J. Peters, Ph.D.,
Professor of Assessment and Research Methodology,
University of Wisconsin-Whitewater

'This book takes the most in-depth look at the field of developmental psychology applied to the study of children with high ability of any book on the market. This is a must read for folks interested in the psychology of high ability.'

Anne N. Rinn, Ph.D.,
Professor of Educational Psychology,
University of North Texas

The Development of the High Ability Child

This valuable text will help readers to understand the physical, social, and cognitive development of high ability children. Written by experts in the fields of education and psychology, each chapter applies core principles of psychology to the development of gifted and talented children. Through the content, readers will be shown how these children are like all children as well as the ways in which their development is unique.

Covering the psychology of learning and learners, personality differences, language and physical development, problem solving, and motivation of high ability children, this book provides readers with a strong foundation for supporting and developing advanced learners. The text also includes Field Note and Eye for Diversity sections to enable readers to put into practice, and recognize, important issues being discussed.

Throughout, the editors blend discussions of research with practical advice for individuals charged with nurturing children with advanced cognitive potential. It is an essential read for students, counsellors, administrators, therapists, and parents seeking to support high ability children and their needs.

Erin M. Miller has a doctorate in Educational Psychology with a specialization in gifted and talented children from the University of Virginia. She has been active in the field of gifted education for 15 years, presenting at the National Association for Gifted Children (NAGC) each of those years. She has held multiple leadership positions for NAGC and American Educational Research Association (AERA) and is currently the Associate Editor for the *Journal of Advanced Academics*. She holds an Associate Professor of Psychology position at Bridgewater College where she teaches General Psychology, Memory and Cognition, Biology of the Mind, Creativity and Problem-Solving, and Measurement and Statistics courses.

Michael S. Matthews is a Professor and Program Director for the Academically/ Intellectually Gifted graduate programs at UNC Charlotte where he teaches courses related to various aspects of gifted education. He is a co-editor of *Gifted Child Quarterly* and has served as a Board Member of the National Association for Gifted Children. He is also past Chair of the Research on Giftedness, Creativity, and Talent group of the AERA, and a former board member for the Metrolina Scholars Academy charter school and the North Carolina Association for the Gifted & Talented. He is the author or editor of five books, around 45 peer reviewed articles, and over a dozen book chapters. He presents regularly at state, national, and international conferences, and his scholarship has been recognized with the Early Scholar Award (NAGC), the Pyryt Collaboration Award (AERA), and the Legacy Book Award from the Texas Association for the Gifted and Talented in the category of "Best Scholarly Work."

Dante D. Dixson is an Assistant Professor of School and Educational Psychology at Michigan State University. He currently serves on the editorial boards of *Gifted Child Quarterly*, the *Journal for the Education of the Gifted, School Psychology Review*, and the *Journal of Black Psychology*. In addition, he is a board member for the Roeper Institute and the Michigan Association of Gifted Children. Dr. Dixson's areas of expertise include the role of hope in the educational and psychological functioning of children and adolescents, psychosocial precursors of achievement, and the underrepresentation of minority and disadvantaged youth in gifted education.

The Development of the High Ability Child

Psychological Perspectives on Giftedness

Edited by Erin M. Miller, Michael S. Matthews, and Dante D. Dixson

Routledge
Taylor & Francis Group

LONDON AND NEW YORK

Cover image: © Getty Images

First published 2022
by Routledge
2 Park Square, Milton Park, Abingdon, Oxon OX14 4RN

and by Routledge
605 Third Avenue, New York, NY 10158

Routledge is an imprint of the Taylor & Francis Group, an informa business

British Library Cataloguing-in-Publication Data
A catalogue record for this book is available from the British Library

Library of Congress Cataloging-in-Publication Data
Names: Miller, Erin M., editor. | Matthews, Michael S., 1968- editor. | Dixson, Dante D., 1989- editor.
Title: The development of the high ability child : psychological perspectives on giftedness / edited by Erin M. Miller, Michael S. Matthews and Dante D. Dixson.
Description: Abingdon, Oxon ; New York, NY : Routledge, 2022. | Includes bibliographical references and index.
Identifiers: LCCN 2021030168 (print) | LCCN 2021030169 (ebook) | ISBN 9780367458010 (hardback) | ISBN 9780367458027 (paperback) | ISBN 9781003025443 (ebook)
Subjects: LCSH: Gifted children—Education. | Child psychology. | Educational psychology.
Classification: LCC LC3993 .D48 2022 (print) | LCC LC3993 (ebook) | DDC 371.95—dc23
LC record available at https://lccn.loc.gov/2021030168
LC ebook record available at https://lccn.loc.gov/2021030169

ISBN: 978-0-367-45801-0 (hbk)
ISBN: 978-0-367-45802-7 (pbk)
ISBN: 978-1-003-02544-3 (ebk)

DOI: 10.4324/9781003025443

Typeset in Sabon
by KnowledgeWorks Global Ltd.

Contents

Figures

Tables

Contributors

Camelia Birlean is a lecturer in the Department of Educational and Counselling Psychology at McGill University where her primary teaching responsibilities are within the field of special education, specifically in gifted education, and in differentiated assessment in inclusive education.

Camelia Birlean
McGill University
Canada

Emma Margaret Birlean is a grade 9 student at Royal West Academy (RWA) in Montreal and has represented her schools at McGill's Let's Talk Science Competition, Battle of the Books Competition, and Kids Lit Quiz, and RWA's Science Fair Competition where she was the recipient of the bronze medal.

Emma Margaret Birlean
Royal West Academy
Canada

James Bishop is a Licensed Professional Counselor (LPC) and National Certified Counselor (NCC) serving children and adults in Texas, USA. James earned his Ph.D. in Educational Psychology with a focus on giftedness and talent from the University of North Texas.

James Bishop
Blank Slate Therapy
United States of America

Julia Hujar is a doctoral student and graduate research assistant in the Educational Research, Measurement, and Evaluation program at UNC Charlotte where she also received her M.Ed. in Special Education (AIG). Previously, she worked as a 6–8th grade mathematics and social studies teacher at a magnet school for gifted students.

Julia Hujar
University of North Carolina-Charlotte
United States of America

Jennifer L. Jolly is the director of the Gifted Education and Talent Development Office at the University of Alabama and a professor in the College of Education. She holds an Honorary Associate Professor at the University of New South Wales.

Jennifer L. Jolly
University of Alabama
United States of America

Andrea Esperat Lein holds a Ph.D. in Clinical & School Psychology and an M.Ed. in Educational Psychology, specializing in giftedness, from the University of Virginia. Over the last 20 years, she has served as a school administrator, clinician, researcher, and educator, focused on helping gifted/2e students and their families.

Andrea Esperat Lein
United States of America

Sakhavat Mammadov is an assistant professor at Valdosta State University. He received his MA. from Boğaziçi University and Ph.D. in Gifted Education from William & Mary University. His primary research interest is to examine and explore issues dealing with social and emotional needs of children with gifts and talents.

Sakhavat Mammadov
Valdosta State University
United States of America

Matthew McBee is a data scientist and educational psychologist. He has spent the last fifteen years trying to draw inferences from data and sometimes succeeding. He has worked as an applied statistician, a faculty member in a department of psychology, and most recently as a machine learning engineer.

Matthew T. McBee
Eastman Chemical Company
United States of America

Bruce M. Shore is a licensed teacher and psychologist in Quebec, elected Fellow of the American Educational Research Association, and Professor Emeritus of Educational Psychology at McGill University where he continues to serve as a supervisor of graduate students and as an accreditation site-visit chair for the American and Canadian Psychological Associations.

Bruce M. Shore
McGill University
Canada

Mary Slade is a professor in the Department of Early Childhood Education in the College of Education at Towson University. Mary's teaching includes early childhood education as well as gifted, talented, and creative education. Mary is one of the inaugural FACET teaching fellows for the university with a focus in online learning.

Mary Slade
Towson University
United States of America

Hope E. Wilson is an associate professor at University of North Florida and the graduate program director for the department of Teaching, Learning, and Curriculum. She earned her Ph.D. in Gifted Education from the University of Connecticut. She is the co-author of Letting Go of Perfect (Prufrock Press).

Hope Elisabeth Wilson
University of North Florida
United States of America

Introduction

Erin M. Miller and Michael S. Matthews

Teachers, administrators, and counsellors are often tasked with making decisions about how to best nurture children's intellectual development; however, many have had limited experience and typically no formal coursework regarding advanced cognitive development. Current books about parenting intellectually advanced children are limited because they either present opinions that are not supported by empirical evidence or rely on now-outdated information. Parents and teachers turn to school psychologists and administrators for assistance in nurturing their child's talents. The goal of this book is to apply core developmental psychology principles to the nurturing of children with high cognitive ability.

The idea for this book arose from observations of sessions at psychology and educational conferences that did not seem to be supported by what we know of current psychological research. We also noticed when speaking at schools about students with exceptional cognitive ability that the attendees often did not seem to understand that these children were generally normal psychologically, apart from their advanced academic abilities. These misconceptions were also evident in discussions on the U.S. and international social media accounts. The need for the book was further supported by discussions with our research colleagues, who had observed that many parents, teachers, administrators, and even school psychologists and other scholars sometimes expressed misconceptions about how basic psychology applies to intellectually advanced children. These experiences led us to the idea to gather scholars in the field of gifted education to address this issue through preparation of an edited volume on these topics.

One of the biggest challenges when discussing the research that is relevant to what is called the gifted education field is the issue of defining the terms used to label and describe individuals. We think that using the label "gifted" as the way of indicating the need for more challenging educational programming and curriculum is likely doing more harm than good. Beyond the fact that the connotation of the word "gifted" is loaded with value judgments that obfuscate the application of the term to only a few students, there is considerable debate regarding what "giftedness" even means (Brown et al., 2020). As of now, there is no common operational definition that is used by the majority of researchers or programs. The United States federal definition is:

> Students, children, or youth who give evidence of high achievement capability in areas such as intellectual, creative, artistic, or leadership capacity, or in specific

DOI: 10.4324/9781003025443-1

academic fields, and who need services and activities not ordinarily provided by the school in order to fully develop those capabilities.

Title IX, Part A, Definition 22 (2002)

The Kaveri Gifted Education and Research Center in India (KGERC, n.d.) also defines giftedness as "exceptional potential or high capacity in intellectual, creative, artistic areas, leadership capacity, or in specific fields" but then notes the importance of socio-cultural context. They link the concept of giftedness to ancient Indian philosophy regarding spirituality and the unlimited capacity of humans that has been a part of Indian culture since ancient times. Giftedness in the Kingdom of Saudi Arabia is also described in terms similar to the U.S. federal definitions while also being part of the overarching national vision based on Islamic, educational, social, and professional foundations (Al Nafa'a et al., 2000; Saudi Vision, 2030, 2021).

In a study of the effect of teacher training in Belgium, Vreys et al. (2018) describe gifted children as:

children who are either labeled gifted based on a valid IQ-test, or who are considered above average ability children without being labeled as gifted, but according to the teachers' sound judgment, could benefit from enrichment activities in one or more curriculum areas (around 10–20% of the children in Flemish schools). (p. 5)

Differences in definitions of giftedness from nation to nation often reflect what that nation values as important human traits as well as attitudes towards education. For example, Finland does not have a national policy for labeling gifted students likely due to an egalitarian approach to education, rather there is a focus on differentiation and services for these students in the regular classroom (Laine & Tirri, 2015). In Japan, the focus has been on domain-specific services most often in science and math (Basister & Kawai, 2018; Sumida, 2013). And as national priorities change so often does the conception of giftedness, an example of which is described by Pang (2012) in a change in focus in China from serving college-age gifted students through more open-ended services to focusing more on efficiency and utility.

Dai and Chen (2013) outlined three major perspectives regarding definitions of giftedness: (1) the Gifted Child, (2) the Talent Development, and (3) the Differentiation paradigms. For each paradigm, Dai and Chen describe *what* does gifted mean, *why* does it exist, *who* is labeled, and *how* participants are served. From the Gifted Child perspective, giftedness is a general trait in humans that is best measured through traditional intelligence (IQ) tests. This IQ factor is thought to influence all aspects of an individual's life resulting in a qualitative difference in how one relates to the world. Decisions about identification are based on comparisons to the normal distribution of intellectual ability. Theories that focus on asynchronous development reflect the Gifted Child perspective (e.g., Neville et al., 2013). The purpose of the label is to help facilitate development across the lifespan based on the individual's idiosyncratic conception of self-actualization.

The Talent Development paradigm focuses on specific domains of performance rather than a holistic trait and includes both formal selection through assessments of performance and self-selection into programming depending on interest and motivation. The goal of identification is to help the individual reach excellence in a certain domain. Within this paradigm are both multifactorial/mechanistic models such as Renzulli's three-ring conception of giftedness (Renzulli, 1978; 1986), Gagné's Differentiated Model of Giftedness and Talent (Gagné, 2004) and Sternberg's WICS model (Sternberg, 2003) and systems models in which giftedness is an emergent behavior such as the Actiotope Model (Ziegler, 2005; Ziegler & Phillipson, 2012). The difference between the two types of models can be subtle and a matter of inter-pretation, but regardless, talent development research seeks to define – the cognitive abilities, personality traits, and sociological factors that are specific to different domains of talent with the goal of developing these abilities and traits as well as building programs that reflect the necessary sociological factors.

The Differentiation approach focuses on the match or mismatch between the current educational environment and the specific child at any one moment of time. Permanent labels are not relevant and the goal is to meet the dynamic needs of any child who needs a more challenging experience in school. There is little to no focus on national norms of performance in identification, but rather a focus on local norms for the particular school system (Peters et al., 2019). Examples of this perspective can be seen in the work of Carol Tomlinson (2017) and the Advanced Academics model (Peters et al., 2014). The goal is meeting the current needs rather than concern about future performance in a particular domain of adult achievement.

These three different perspectives lead to a range of possible types of individuals being described as gifted in the research literature. In order to provide clarity, the following terms are used to describe individuals in the chapters of this text. The phrases "gifted students/children" and "students identified for gifted programming" are used to refer to students who were identified for advanced services, likely based on exceptional performance on aptitude or achievement tests. If the authors are referring to both those students who are formally identified and all other students who would benefit from advanced academic services even if not formally identified, then the terms advanced learners, cognitively advanced learners, or academically advanced students is used. The phrase "individuals with exceptional IQ scores" is used to refer to both children and adults when describing the results of studies that involved participants who were chosen based on psychometric assessments of intelligence.

Across all of these different models, perspectives and descriptors are also a recognition of specific populations who merit additional consideration or attention. None of the conceptions discussed earlier preclude the possibility of students also benefiting from additional educational labels such as those associated with specific learning disabilities/differences or psychological diagnoses such as ADHD in order to facilitate the best learning environment for those students. Those students are often referred to as twice-exceptional or 2e students. Where relevant, the chapter authors will discuss how these additional exceptionalities can affect the application of research presented in the chapter. An additional factor to consider is the effect of the students' socio-cultural and socio-economic backgrounds on their education and development. Of particular concern is the underrepresentation of racial, ethnic, or other minority groups in programming for cognitively advanced students. Any inequities of health, environment, and opportunity will be reflected in a society's educational system and other societal structures.

A consistent theme through the chapters is that there is a large range of behaviors that are within the normal range. Most individuals are familiar with the idea of the normal range. It is often presented when discussing physical traits such as the normal range of heights. There is an average human height (162 cm for U.S. women) but also a large range (one of the editors is only 154 cm). Most women are around 162 cm but some are more or less while still being within the norm. Erin has always been short, but not so much that doctors would be concerned for her health. There are a smaller number of people with highly superior cognitive abilities but there is no reason to think they are not part of the expected range. Further, the range is a continuous measure, meaning there are no distinct markers. For example, it would be difficult to tell the difference between an individual who scored a 98.5% versus a 99% on a 600 point test just by observing their classroom behavior. Students with advanced academic potential are not average as far as cognitive ability is concerned, but are likely as variable as any other group of people in other human traits. Individual characteristics such as personality and motivation likely vary independently of cognitive ability. However, cognitive ability can interact with other human characteristics such as personality and motivation. For example, a child with high cognitive abilities who is motivated by academic rewards from teachers would be very concerned with their grades. A child with high cognitive abilities who is more motivated by self-initiated creative production would care more about their projects outside of the classroom. Every child has their own individual profile making them a unique person.

Throughout the text there are sidebars that extend and enrich the content in several different ways. There are reflections from students, parents, teachers, and counselors called "Field Notes." These provide insight into real-world experiences that illustrate one or more of the issues and ideas discussed in this chapter. These vary in length and number depending on the content of the specific chapter. The one exception is the Problem-Solving chapter. Here, you will find a practical example built into this chapter from the perspective of a gifted teenager rather than discrete "Field Notes." Some of the Field Notes have the full name of the author and others include only the first names depending on whether the individual wanted to be fully identified. There are also sidebars labeled "Eye for Diversity" each of which were written by Dante Dixson. These will address, when necessary, how the information or advice in the chapter might be affected by differences in cultural norms, values, or beliefs.

The chapters included in the book roughly follow the order that these topics are presented in many General Psychology textbooks beginning with research methods.

In "Key Methodological Issues in Researching Gifted Education and Advanced Academics" Matthew McBee guides the reader through the complexities of studying this small subgroup of children. Most of the topics, such as how to be a critical consumer of information, are applicable to research in general and others such as issues of studying small populations are more specific to studying groups such as gifted and advanced learners. McBee also effectively summarizes several overarching concerns such as the replication crisis in the field of psychology and the push towards more open science practices.

Chapters 2–4 cover the fundamental topics of physical development, the psychology of learning, and memory. These chapters form a foundation as the concepts discussed in these chapters are applied though the remaining chapters of the book. Gifted education researcher and historian, Jennifer Jolly tackles the complicated and often controversial topic of physical development and advanced cognitive ability. This is a challenging area of study due to the emeshing of legitimate scientific studies such as longitudinal studies of the relationship between IQ scores and health with less reputable endeavors such as the snake oil of pseudoscience all the way to the horrors of eugenics. Jolly separates the trustworthy from the fictions and myths in her review of this topic.

The chapter, "Understanding Cognitively Advanced and Gifted Learners Through the Psychology of Learning," by James Bishop and Julia Hujar, describes the application of Behaviorism, Social Cognitive Theory and Constructivism to understanding the actions and reactions of cognitively advanced learners. Although the basic principles of these theories apply to all individuals equally, how the principles are applied and the outcomes vary for advanced learners. Understanding these core systems of learning is the key to understanding psychology in general.

An exploration of the cognitive processes of memory also involves aspects that are universal to all learners and aspects that are specific to advanced learners. This chapter is written by one of the editors, Erin Morris Miller. Memory is an overarching term for multiple processes related to the acquisition, storage, and retrieval of information of all kinds. As superior memory is a key ability that is assessed when determining which students would be identified as needing gifted education services, this chapter provides critical knowledge regarding how to recognize and serve these students. These superior memory abilities would then be applied in the two other major topics of cognitive psychology in the chapters, "Language Development and Education of Gifted Learners and Precocious Readers," by Mary Slade and "Problem Solving Characteristics in Gifted and Advanced Learners," by Camelia Birlean, Emma Margaret Birlean, and Bruce M. Shore. Sophisticated language and problem-solving skills are two more areas that are often noted as characteristics of gifted and cognitively advanced students.

The final three chapters address several non-cognitive factors that are important in the actualization of the learning and cognitive abilities into academic achievement and professional success. Hope Wilson lives up to her name with a chapter, "Motivation and Achievement in Gifted and Advanced Learners," describing the drives that determine in what direction individuals will apply their abilities and whether they will persevere in those endeavors. Another factor affecting direction and perseverance is personality. Although there is no single definition of personality the chapter, "Individual Differences in Personality Among Gifted and Cognitively Advanced Learners," by Sakhavat Mammadov focuses on the trait approach and specifically applies the Big Five factors to understanding behavior and decision making. These major factors (Openness to Experience, Conscientiousness, Extraversion, Agreeableness, and Neuroticism) are correlated with multiple characteristics of lifespan development and provide a reliable lens through which to view cognitively advanced individuals. The final chapter addresses mental health. In her chapter, "The Psychological Adjustment of Gifted Children and Cognitively Advanced Learners," clinical psychologist Andrea Esperat Lein describes the biological, learning, cognitive and non-cognitive factors that facilitate positive mental health as well as the factors that can lead to mental health struggles.

In the final chapter, we share possible directions for future research to understand students with advanced academic abilities and potential. We hope that this text will become a resource for counselors, teachers, and parents as well as facilitate the education of those who like to learn more about gifted and academically advanced students.

REFERENCES

Al Nafa'a, A., Al Gateai, A., Al Dudiban, S., Al Hazmi, M., & Al Saleem, A. (2000). *Disclosure program for talented and caring*. King Abdulaziz City for Science and Technology.

Basister, M. P. & Kawai, N. (2018). Japan's educational practices for mathematically gifted students. *International Journal of Inclusive Education, 22*(11), 1213–1241. https://doi.org/10.1080/13603116.2017.1420252

Brown, M., Peterson E. R., & Rawlinson, C. (2020) Research with gifted adults: What international experts think needs to happen to move the field forward. *Roeper Review, 42*(2), 95–108. https://doi.org/10.1080/02783193.2020.1728797

Dai, D. Y. & Chen, F. (2013). Three paradigms of gifted education. *Gifted Child Quarterly, 57*(3), 151–168. https://doi.org/10.1177/0016986213490020

Gagné, F. (2004). Transforming gifts into talents: the DMGT as a developmental theory. *High Ability Studies, 15*(2), 119–147. https://doi.org/10.1080/1359813042000314682

KGERC (n.d.) *About Us*. Retrieved February 23, 2021 from https://kaveri.edu.in/kgec/about-us/

Laine, S. & Tirri, K. (2015). How Finnish elementary school teachers meet the needs of their gifted students. *High Ability Studies, 27*(2), 149–164. https://doi.org/10.1080/13598139.2015.1108185

Neville, C. S., Piechowski, M. M., & Tolan, S. S. (2013). *Off the charts: asynchrony and the gifted child*. Royal Fireworks Press.

Pang, W. (2012). The Actiotope Model of Giftedness: a useful model for examining gifted education in China's universities. *High Ability Studies, 23*(1), 89–91. https://doi.org/10.1080/13598139.2012.679101

Peters, S. J., Matthews, M. S., McBee, M. T., & McCoach, D. B. (2014). *Beyond gifted education: Designing and implementing advanced academic programs*. Prufrock Press.

Peters, S. J., Rambo-Hernandez, K., Makel, M. C., Matthews, M. S., & Plucker, J. A. (2019). Effect of local norms on racial and ethnic representation in gifted education. *AERA Open*, 5(2), 233285841984844. https://doi.org/10.1177/2332858419848446

Renzulli, J. S. (1978). What makes giftedness? Re-examining a definition. *Phi Delta Kappan*, 60, 180–184, 261.

Renzulli, J. S. (1986). The three ring conception of giftedness: A developmental model for creative productivity. In R. J. Sternberg & J. E. Davidson (Eds.), *Conceptions of giftedness* (pp. 53–92). Cambridge University Press.

Saudi Vision 2030 https://www.vision2030.gov.sa/en

Sternberg, R. J. (2003). *Wisdom, intelligence, and creativity synthesized*. Cambridge University Press.

Sumida, M. (2013). Emerging trends in Japan in education of the gifted. *Journal for the Education of the Gifted*, 36(3), 277–289. https://doi.org/10.1177/0162353213493534

Tomlinson, C. A. (2017). *How to differentiate instruction in academically diverse classrooms*. ASCD.

Vreys, C., Ndanjo Ndungbogun, G., Kieboom, T. & Venderickx, K. (2018) Training effects on Belgian preschool and primary school teachers' attitudes towards the best practices for gifted children. *High Ability Studies*, 29(1), 3–22. https://doi.org/10.1080/1359813 9.2017.1312295

Ziegler, A. (2005). *The Actiotope Model of Giftedness*. In R. J. Sternberg & J. E. Davidson (Eds.), *Conceptions of giftedness* (p. 411–436). Cambridge University Press. https://doi-org/10.1017/CBO9780511610455.024

Ziegler, A. & Phillipson, S. N. (2012) Towards a systemic theory of gifted education. *High Ability Studies*, 23(1), 3–30. https://doi-org/10.1080/13598139.2012.679085

Key methodological issues in researching gifted education and advanced academics

Matthew T. McBee

Winston Churchill famously observed that "democracy is the worst form of government, except for all the others" (Langworth, 2009). This chapter has a similar thesis: research is the worst way of knowing things, except for every other way. I will not offer platitudes such as "believe science" or provide inviolable rules to differentiate trustworthy science from science fiction (McBee & Field, 2017). Indeed, my position may seem excessively skeptical, or perhaps excessively bearish on the reliability of research and its ability to differentiate truth from falsity. This is so. But my critiques of research can be made simply because research exposes itself, by definition, to the possibility of being wrong. Every other way of knowing – induction from one's own experiences, adherence to unsupported theories that "feel true," adoption of sociopolitical worldviews, or embracing the opinions of experts – is just as (or more) capable of going astray. The problem with these methods is that they fail silently. Research, though flawed, is superior to these methods precisely because it repeatedly is made to crash against reality.

This chapter is not a substitute for rigorous study of research methods, the history and philosophy of social science, or statistics. Instead, it is a survey of issues to consider when delving into the diverse body of research and pseudo-research on gifted students; it is a meditation on applied epistemology. What constitutes knowledge pertaining to gifted students? Who produces it, and how do I know if it is reliable? What is evidence, and what should be my standard for accepting it? There are no consistent rules that definitively can distinguish reliable from unreliable work (though there are clues that will be discussed later in this chapter). Instead, offered here are background knowledge and a set of heuristics to assist in judging claims about giftedness and gifted children. As statistician George Box observed, "Since all models are wrong the scientist must be alert to what is importantly wrong. It is inappropriate to be concerned about mice when there are tigers abroad" (Box, 1976, p. 792). Let us seek to avoid the "tigers" – ideas and concepts which are damagingly wrong, leading to the adoption of harmful practices or the discarding of helpful ones. I am less concerned about the "mice."

DOI: 10.4324/9781003025443-2

THE BIG PICTURE: WHO DOES GIFTED EDUCATION RESEARCH, AND WHERE DO I FIND IT?

For a claim about giftedness or gifted children to qualify for the hallowed status of **supported by research,** there must at some point be data – the records of careful and systematic observation – at the end of the chain of reasoning. Observations derived from other sources – for example, intuition, informal observation, expert opinion, tradition, folk psychology, or even reasonable-sounding armchair theorizing – simply do not achieve the same status as those derived from data. These are potent fodder for hypothesis formation, but cannot themselves qualify as evidence. This is because human cognition is notoriously unreliable, and it is exceptionally prone to noticing patterns that actually do not exist (see Friedman, 2017 for review). We can almost always find *ex post facto* explanations for the phenomena we observe, and even worse: the patterns we notice are biased by our preconceived notions and self-interest. Absent the structure imposed by the *careful study* requirement phrase in the definition of research, it would be all too easy for multiple observers to disagree about even the observation itself, to say nothing of its interpretation, implication, or meaning.

One must also bear in mind the distinction between *primary sources* and *secondary sources* when interacting with the gifted education literature. Primary sources are those that reference data directly – in the form of statistical summaries of quantitative data or the quotes, field notes, or other primary artifacts of qualitative data. As the *open science* movement (McBee et al., 2018) continues to gather steam in the social sciences, we can increasingly expect research articles to link to the raw data itself. In the United States, the majority of gifted education primary-source research is published in the field's specialty journals, which include *Gifted Child Quarterly*, *Journal of Advanced Academics* (formerly called the *Journal of Secondary Gifted Education*), *Journal for the Education of the Gifted*, and *Roeper Review*. There are also two international gifted education journals, *Gifted and Talented International* and *High Ability Studies* (formerly known as the *European Journal of High Ability*). Most original research in gifted education is published in one of these outlets.

Secondary sources are those that do not describe data *per se*, but instead describe, synthesize, or translate primary research documents into a more orderly, readable, or comprehensive form. Such is the case with textbooks as well as many other books, periodicals, and websites. For example, *Teaching for High Potential* and *Parenting for High Potential* seek to translate research findings into a form that can be consumed by teachers and parents, respectively. Most people who interact with the research in our field do it through the secondary source literature. One reason is that the primary source literature is more technical. But more importantly, nearly all of the primary research outlets mentioned in the previous paragraph are **paywalled.** This means that most non-university readers have no reasonable access to primary research on gifted students. And although extra-legal means of free access to paywalled articles have appeared, not everyone knows about them or is comfortable using them. One hopeful development on this front is the recent appearance of preprint servers such as http://psyarxiv.com and https://edarxiv.org/ which host free pre-publication versions of published articles. Unfortunately, only a small proportion of new work is being uploaded there, and there is no prospect for liberating access to the back catalog of already-published work via this mechanism.

FIELD NOTE 1.1 USING RESEARCH TO INFORM CURRICULUM & INSTRUCTION: A SCHOOL ADMINISTRATOR'S PERSPECTIVE

Dina Brulles

Director of Gifted Education for Paradise Valley Unified School District and Coordinator of the Gifted Master's Program at Arizona State University

As the director of gifted education for a large school district with a well-supported gifted program, I recognize the importance of relying on information that is guided by research when making decisions about the curriculum and instructional approaches. In schools, the reality is that research is not always considered when making decisions that impact school practices. These decisions are oftentimes guided by educators' observations, interpretation, opinions, traditions and informal interactions, such as those obtained from teachers' professional learning opportunities and experiences, which are not always supported by empirical data.

Another factor that hinders reliance on research-based decision making is that those making decisions rarely have access to much of the educational research available. One method for addressing this imbalance is to invite the researchers into the school system. I have participated in several partnerships with researchers by collaborating with them to bring data collection and resulting analyses into the school district in ways that support my goals toward gifted program development and support. The collaboration with researchers and publishers provides: 1) guidance and oversight by experts in the field, which strengthens efforts in building exemplary curriculum, instruction and assessment methods; 2) systems for exploring new resources and opportunities that support or guide gifted program development and evaluation; and 3) free resources, such as curriculum, assessment tools, and opportunities to learn from experts in the field.

A few examples of these interactions with universities and publishers include participation with the following institutions and publishers:

- Baylor University – Participation in a Screening Assessment for Gifted Elementary and Middle School Students (SAGES-2) validation study
- College of William & Mary Curriculum validation study
- Purdue University – Depth and Complexity Gifted Program Evaluation
- University of Connecticut – School Imagination, Creativity, and Innovation (ICI) Index
- Devareuax Student Strength Assessment (DESSA) & Arizona State University.

In all of these collaborations curriculum, assessments, training, and data from the studies were donated to the district. This participation yielded data used to evaluate and revise gifted programs, to design curriculum, and to guide future professional learning opportunities. Most importantly, the teachers and administrators involved gained first-hand knowledge of the expertise provided during the processes.

Perils of reliance on secondary sources

It is perilous to rely on secondary sources alone. The description of primary research can degrade like in a "game of telephone" in which multiple layers of summarizing and translation render the original author's description nearly unrecognizable. Primary literature always describes the details of the design, sample size, and other features, which can help readers to determine how much weight to give to the conclusion. Further, every research article must include a *limitations* section disclosing the known flaws of the research and how they might jeopardize the conclusion. These often are the first details to disappear when summaries of primary research are written. The summary of the research sometimes reads like a set of claims and counterclaims that all have the same implicit weight (for example, X and Y found that gifted students had higher satisfaction in cluster grouping, while Z did not) even when these studies might vary in rigor. Perhaps X's claim was based on a sample of 4,000 students from five states, while Z's was a convenience sample of 30 students in his own classroom.

Another issue is that sometimes secondary sources do not lead to a primary source bearing data or evidence. Secondary sources can become a recursive train to nowhere in which the original source is based on theory or expert opinion with no actual data or evidence at the basis. My colleague Matthew Makel has coined the phrase "handbooks all the way down" to describe this lack of grounding. I want to emphasize this issue because it is so common and, in my opinion, destructive to the intellectual foundation of the field. Once a person injects an evidence-free claim into the research literature, it can easily receive the credibility of actual evidence. Subsequent citations of that claim in secondary sources may not adequately indicate the questionable basis. Over time, the claims may become accepted as factual and may reach the same status as those findings supported by actual research. A perfect case study for this phenomenon is Silverman's (1997) paper entitled "The Construct of Asynchronous Development," which was published in the *Peabody Journal of Education*. This is an important and influential paper in our field which advances an alternative conceptualization of giftedness. But it is critical to realize that this paper is a theoretical piece which does not present any empirical data in support of its arguments. Though intriguing and stimulating to read, it is not an empirical research. Simply appearing in an academic journal or a book does not make something *research*. Theorizing is just as important as verification in the scientific process, but making a claim is not the same as supporting it. I will pick on myself as well – a book I co-authored (*Beyond Gifted Education*; Peters et al., 2013) similarly is not research. The evidence that both of these pieces offer in terms of supporting their core arguments is logical, rhetorical, and in some cases based on anecdote – each of which is thin gruel in comparison to verified data derived from structured observation.

A distressing number of concepts in gifted education have been laundered into research through this or similar mechanisms. One example is the *Bright Versus Gifted* checklist that one often encounters in the field, which I shall not reproduce here out of fear of further spreading a misguided idea. For an example of the influence this conception retains in our field, see Taibbi's (2012) *Psychology Today* piece. Scott Peters (2017) traced the origin of this idea to a 1989 article in *Challenge* magazine, which is not a research journal. This idea – that there is a meaningful distinction between the truly *gifted* child, as opposed to the mere *high achiever* – and that our field should be interested in the former but not the latter, is commonly described as *research based* when it is not. So, one of the most important ideas of this chapter is the following.

There is no need to be a nihilist, but a little skepticism goes a long way. I recognize that this task is made far more difficult by the paywalls restricting access to journal articles for non-university-based individuals. Tools, such as Google Scholar, can help trace references back to their sources. Further, there are resources, such as Plucker and Callahan's (2020) *Critical Issues in Gifted Education: What the Research Says*, which do a nice job of identifying the empirically supported ideas in our field. But unfortunately, this is not a job that can be completely outsourced. We must all be responsible for our own conceptions and our duty to align them ever more closely to reality.

Who does gifted education research?

Most gifted education research is performed by university faculty, graduate students, and K-12 personnel with university affiliation (perhaps during a degree program). These researchers tend to be found in education, educational psychology, or psychology departments, though recently some economists have become interested in the field. Unfortunately, most of the research output produced by these individuals – which is the highest quality and most reliable of all the content produced in this area of inquiry – disappears behind the paywall where its influence and reach is greatly limited. Most of the *writing* on giftedness, as found all over the internet in blog posts, websites, social media groups, and other such sources, is performed by laypersons with seemingly much lower evidentiary standards. The sad fact is that only a small percentage of the concepts, ideas, or perspectives one encounters in lay writing on the subject have any scientific or research-based validity whatsoever. There is an exceptional amount of nonsense flourishing in the wild under the rubric of giftedness.

Why do university types publish their work in paywalled journals? To understand that requires consideration of the incentives they confront. Writing accessible pieces for non-university audiences, engaging in public discussion and debate about giftedness and gifted education, and other types of what might be called "outreach" or "science communication" are not only not rewarded but also actively punished. A researcher who spent their research time on those things rather than preparing and submitting work to academic journals would fall behind in the competition for publication productivity and grant funding – and thus run the risk of losing their position. Even tenured professors, whose jobs are not in jeopardy, would risk losing professional status ("retiring in place"), competitiveness for other positions, or future success gaining grants if they chose to allocate their effort away from status-generating activities. There is almost no incentive to engage in activities that do not promote career development.

For historical and now largely anachronistic reasons, private publishing companies provide the structure for typesetting, publishing, and distributing research work. When publishing transitioned from the intrinsically limited, bound printing model to online distribution during the first decade of the 2000s, publishers erected paywalls to protect their revenue streams. From the perspective of a university-based researcher, nothing had changed. After all, one would have needed library access to read printed and bound research journals; restricting online articles to the same audience of people was no different. But the transition to online dissemination presented an opportunity to radically democratize access to scholarly research; an opportunity that was largely not taken.

SETTING EXPECTATIONS ABOUT RESEARCH ON GIFTEDNESS

There are four critically important issues to bear in mind when one evaluates the literature on giftedness. They initially may seem somewhat disconnected, but together they provide a critical background for reading and understanding the literature.

The replication crisis

In the early 2010s, a confluence of events in the social and biomedical sciences collectively demonstrated that the usual methods of "doing research" in these fields were producing a much higher than expected rate of false positive claims. This was demonstrated most clearly by a paper on parapsychology published by social psychologist Daryl Bem (2011) in the *Journal of Personality and Social Psychology*. It was only Bem's status as an eminent and legitimate scholar that made this publication possible; Bem secured an arrangement with the journal's editors to subject this submission to the same peer review process as other, more topical submissions would receive. The editors agreed to publish the paper if the peer reviewers were satisfied (Judd & Gawronski, 2011).

Bem's paper was published. It reported the results of nine experiments, involving over 1,000 subjects, testing for the effect of time-reversed responses to classic social-cognitive psychological phenomena. The participants' responses were observed *prior* to the presentation of the stimuli and found to be significantly different, at or beyond the customary $p = .05$ statistical threshold, in eight of the nine experiments. The mean effect size – a measure of the magnitude, and thus the real-world importance, of the difference between the "treatment" and "control" subjects – across all the experiments was 0.22 standard deviations. This paper created a sensation in psychology because it demonstrated that the usual standards for scientific and statistical work in the field could utterly fail. And if these methods could be used to support a claim that "the future causes the past," how many other false ideas might have received similar scientific support?

The answer, as it turned out, was quite a lot. One might initially think that the publication of a false claim would not be a huge problem because replications of that study would inevitably reveal it to be in error. This is precisely what happened when Pons and Fleishman claimed to have achieved cold fusion in the 1980s; within weeks multiple teams of physicists reported being unable to replicate cold fusion, and the idea was quickly abandoned (Browne, 1989). But the social and biomedical sciences do not have a culture of replication, which has historically been viewed as a waste of time and resources, or as low-status make-work for insufficiently innovative researchers. Makel et al. (2012) analyzed the psychology literature and discovered that only 1–2% of published work was a replication of a previous study. The same analysis on education research revealed even worse findings. Only 0.13% of the research published in the top 100 education journals was identified as a replication of previous work (Makel and Plucker, 2014). Thus, erroneous research conclusions in these fields have a good chance of remaining unchallenged and uncorrected.

When psychologists began to invest in replication studies in the mid-2010s, they made a series of alarming discoveries. Many social psychology findings, which had previously been understood as well-established, began to fall apart under replication. These included such phenomena as ego depletion (Hagger et al., 2016), the facial feedback hypothesis (Wagenmakers et al., 2016), and social priming (Doyen et al., 2012). Table 1.1 summarizes the results of some recent large-scale replication efforts in the social and biomedical sciences. Overall, only 35% of the replicated studies have successfully produced evidence in line with the original claims. An excellent timeline of the replication crisis through 2016 was compiled by Gelman (2016b). A discussion of the causes of the replication crisis, and some proposed reforms, are given by McBee et al. (2018), van der Zee and Reich (2018), and Makel et al. (2019).

The observant reader will note the absence of any education replication projects in the table. We do not know what the replication rate of education research in general (or giftedness research specifically) might be, but since it relies on the same methods, norms, and incentives as general social science work, we might expect a similar degree of replicability. Educational studies are much harder to replicate than simple lab studies involving undergraduate volunteers because it is difficult to collect data in K-12 settings. Further, educational researchers have not yet faced a Bem-like situation, and are largely aware of the replication crisis as something that has occurred elsewhere rather than something truly threatening to the status quo. However, there are signs that education research will face the same issues. A replication of Steele and Aronson's (1995) stereotype threat effect, which purports to explain race and gender differences in academic performance, found no evidence that it accounted for disparities in math achievement by gender (Flore et al., 2019).

TABLE 1.1 Summary of Large-Scale Social and Biomedical Science Replication Efforts

Study	Field	Replicability
Prinz et al. (2011)	Biomedical	13/52 = 25%
Begley and Ellis (2012)	Biomedical	6/59 = 11%
RP: Psychology (2015)	Psychology	35/97 = 36%
Camerer et al. (2016)	Economics	11/18 = 61%
Camerer et al. (2018)	Social science	13/21 = 62%
Many Labs 1 (Klein et al., 2014)	Psychology	10/13 = 77%
Many Labs 2 (Klein et al., 2018)	Psychology	14/28 = 54%
Many Labs 3 (Ebersole et al., 2016)	Psychology	3/10 = 30%
Registered Replication Reports	Psychology	1/9 = 11%
RP: Cancer Biology (preliminary)	Biomedical	7/16 = 44%

Note: **Overall replication rate: 35%.** RP stands for "Reproducibility Project." PR: Psychology refers to Open Science Collaboration (2015). RP: Cancer Biology refers to Errington et al. (2014). Registered Replication Reports refers to the series of articles published in *Perspectives on Psychological Science* and includes Alogna et al. (2014); Haggar et al. (2016); Eerland et al. (2016); Cheung et al. (2016); Wagenmakers et al. (2016); Bouwmeester et al. (2017); O'Donnell et al. (2018); McCarthy et al. (2018), and Verschuere et al. (2018).

A recent large-scale, high-profile replication of Dweck's *growth mindset* theory (Yeager et al., 2019) found that a mindset intervention had no effect for average or high-achieving students, but did increase the average achievement of low-achieving students by 0.1 GPA units. By comparison, websites, such as MindsetWorks.com, claim that growth mindset research started a revolution that "changed education forever." It would not be unreasonable to expect that only a third to two thirds of educational research is trustworthy.

Most educational interventions have modest effects

The previous section attempted to bracket expectations about the trustworthiness of published research. Even if only a third of published educational research holds up, that is, (in my estimation) at least ten to one hundred times better reliability than what one might find in a random parenting blog or gifted education Facebook group. And at least it exposes the details of the reasoning chain to scrutiny.

Another type of adjustment of expectations needs to occur in order for readers to establish appropriate expectations about the effect of educational interventions, that is, most interventions do not work. And the ones that do work tend to exhibit weak effect sizes. I highly recommend spending some time browsing the studies compiled by the Institute for Education Sciences *What Works Clearinghouse* (WWC, https://ies.ed.gov/ncee/wwc/) in the United States. The WWC reports results from a carefully curated set of education studies which meet certain standards of rigor (e.g., randomized experiment or quasi-experiment). The studies are organized by topic and presented in a standard format. The effect sizes for the studies are expressed on a common metric for ease of comparability; for many studies, this is an *improvement index* value, computed as the expected percentile improvement for treated versus control students. So, for example, an intervention with an improvement index of 10 would be expected to increase the average achievement of treated students by 10 percentile units relative to untreated students.

There are a few striking aspects about the WWC. First is that so few studies qualify. The WWC has reviewed over 10,741 studies, but only 204 (about 1.9%) of these were deemed rigorous enough for inclusion in the Clearinghouse. Many of the topic areas summarized do not include any studies at all. Second is that the effect sizes tend to be so small. Most positive effects reported by the WWC are small; the largest ones tend to be in the 8–12 percentile range. A little time with the WWC can help to establish reasonable expectations for the impact of educational interventions in general. Educational outcomes are resistant to improvement.

Weaker studies tend to show stronger effects

Another pattern that is crucial to understand is that, when examining studies published in peer-reviewed academic journals, weaker studies tend to show larger and stronger effects than stronger studies do. One easy-to-measure aspect of a study's strength is its sample size (n). Figure 1.1 plots the sample size against the meta-analytic effect size, in this example, for studies in three areas of biomedical science. The relationship is striking; small-n studies generally reported effect sizes in the 0.6–1.0 range, whereas large-n studies reported effect sizes in the 0.15–0.25 range.

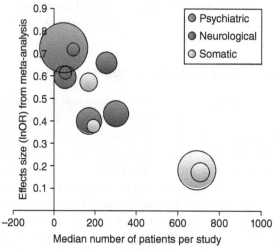

FIGURE 1.1 The Relationship between Sample Size and the Reported Effect Size in Biomedical Science, as Presented by Dumas-Mallet et al. (2017)

Note: This figure was presented as Figure 4a in the original publication. Published by the Royal Society under the terms of the Creative Commons Attribution License http://creativecommons.org/licenses/by/4.0/

Perhaps you are thinking, "Wait a minute. Maybe scientists reserve large sample sizes to study phenomena that they expect to be weak or subtle." This is absolutely a reasonable hypothesis, and there may be some truth to it – but it cannot be the whole story of what is happening here. This pattern is so consistent as to almost be a physical law. It is observed even within the same phenomenon. For example, the growth mindset work discussed earlier showed strong effects on achievement in small studies (see Yeager & Dweck, 2012, for review). Because initial studies tend to be small, and follow-up studies larger, this pattern makes it appear that effects are weakening over time. In a piece for *New Yorker* magazine, Jonah Lehrer (2010) used the phrase "the truth wears off" to describe this pattern. But the truth isn't wearing off. It is rather that a mirage disappears when you look at it more closely.

More on incentives

Absent any filtering, one would expect there to be no relationship between estimated effect size and study rigor; at least not within a particular topic area. Small studies would produce more variable results, to be sure, but when averaging over these effect sizes (as in meta-analysis), size/rigor should be independent of effect size. In reality, there are multiple aspects of filtering that are linked to incentives operating at different levels of the system.

- There are at least two ways for a study to be interesting: rigor and findings. A large, rigorous study that finds nothing can be interesting, as can a small study that produces an exciting finding. But a small, null study is not very exciting.
- "Interesting" articles get read and cited more than uninteresting articles.
- Academic journals print only a small proportion of the submitted articles, ranging from a ~50% acceptance rate for low-prestige journals to <5% for the most prestigious journals.
- A journal's prestige is measured by the *impact factor*, which is calculated on the basis of citations. High-prestige journals will attract more interesting studies, leading to higher prestige. There is a positive feedback loop with selection pressure.
- Researchers need to amass publications in high-prestige journals.
- Researchers are rewarded much more thoroughly for making new discoveries than for running rigorous studies that find nothing. The former is a path to scientific fame and celebrity, with all its attendant rewards (plum jobs, grants, editorships, speaking and book contracts, the best graduate students, etc.).

So journals need a steady supply of interesting (as defined above) research to publish. This is why it is, even now, quite difficult to publish replication studies in many fields (and why replications have been so historically underutilized). Null findings are largely uninteresting unless they result from extremely rigorous investigations with high prior probability. So null findings are rarely published (Ferguson & Heene, 2012). Large effect sizes are interesting. And they are much easier to generate in small studies rather than large ones.

Most quantitative research in gifted education is analyzed using frequentist statistical methods. These methods have built-in compensation for variability as a function of sample size. The standard for judging an estimate (e.g., a mean, a treatment effect, and a correlation) as statistically significant adjusts with the sample size such that a larger value is required for significance in small samples than in large ones. This standard is set such that only 5% of observed results would cross this threshold by chance when there is no effect. These *false positives* are known as Type-I errors in statistics. Figure 1.2 displays the results of a large set of simulated studies when there is no underlying effect. Each dot represents the absolute value of the effect size estimated from the study. The curved line shows the threshold for statistical significance. Only 5% of the dots lie above this threshold, even though the dots have much more vertical dispersion in small samples than in large ones.

Thus far, there is no reason to expect any relationship between sample size and effect size. Sure, smaller samples are more variable, therefore, having a higher chance of yielding a large estimated effect, but this is cancelled out perfectly by the higher threshold they must reach to trigger statistical significance. The problem occurs when a selection mechanism is applied to the results.

Journals are incentivized to publish interesting results. Results that show no effect are generally not considered very interesting (unless they are surprising).

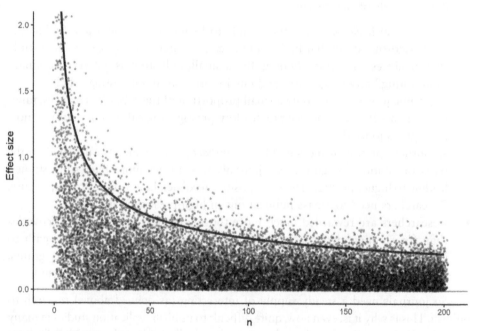

FIGURE 1.2 Relationship between Sample Size and the Effect Size When the True Effect is Zero

Note: Based on 5,000 simulated studies generated under a condition of no true effect. The results vary due to statistical noise. Each dot represents one study's result. The line displays the threshold absolute effect size for statistical significance; points above the line would be deemed significant at or beyond the .05 level. The figure illustrates how (a) results from small studies have a much larger spread of effect size estimates, and (b) the small-sample statistically significant studies would have much larger effect sizes than the large-sample significant studies.

Therefore, journals tend to be filled with statistically significant results (van Zwet & Cator, 2020). Look again at Figure 1.2, but imagine only seeing the dots above the curved significance threshold line. The significant results from small samples have much larger effect sizes than those from large samples. When you examine only significant results, you will induce a negative relationship between sample size and effect size.

Gelman and Carlin (2014) coined the term *Type-M error* to refer to this inflation of effect sizes in studies that have been selected for significance (the "M" standard for "magnitude"). The smaller the study, the larger the Type-M error is likely to be. This implies that the published literature overestimates effect sizes, sometimes severely. Unfortunately, this overestimation also contaminates summaries of the literature. For example, meta-analysis is a technique for computing the average weighted effect size over a set of studies. A meta-analysis of a set of inflated effect sizes yields an inflated meta-analytic estimate. There is what is known as a *garbage-in, garbage-out* problem. When large-scale multi-lab replication results have been compared to meta-analytic estimates, the replication effect size is typically one third of its meta-analytic counterpart (Kvarven et al., 2020).

Selection effects bias the literature

The selection of statistically significant articles for publication is often called the *file drawer* problem (Rosenthal, 1979). It is important to note that the selection process happens at multiple levels, not just at the level of journal publication. In fact, selection bias operates at every level of the system. For an individual researcher operating within a competitive academic culture, a non-publishable study represents an enormous waste of effort. Studies with null results may not be completed if an interim analysis shows little hope of positive findings. If data collection is complete, the research paper may never be written. (After all, writing the paper takes time and effort that would better be spent on a new study.) In both cases, the record of the study ever having been attempted disappears. This pressure also affects the way researchers allocate their time and resources. If a researcher has the resources to collect data from 1,000 students in a year, they could choose to do one study of $n = 1,000$ or 20 studies of $n = 50$. Running a large set of small studies maximizes the probability of producing a few publishable studies. If the one large study fails, the researcher (and his or her students) will have no research output for the year, imperiling their ability to continue doing research. The incentives strongly contradict the notion of putting "all the eggs in one basket," even though scientific progress would be greatly improved by running fewer studies with higher quality.

Worse yet, researchers may apply selection methods *within* the study itself to attempt to achieve significance. Such efforts are known as *questionable research practices* (QRPs; Simmons et al., 2011) or *p-hacking*, and include practices such as collecting additional data to try to push a marginal result over the line or trying out different statistical analysis methods until a significant result is obtained. The influence of these methods is much stronger on small studies, because they have a high degree of variability in their results due to their inherent instability. Because statistical significance and effect size are linked, any p-hacking motivated to achieve statistical significance also inflates effect sizes. This is a serious problem that is worthy of deep consideration for anyone who wishes to read or (especially) do research. Beyond these within-study selection methods there is even yet another type of post-publication selection bias – studies making positive claims are cited at much higher rates (Murray et al., 2019; de Vries, 2019).

The end result of all of these complementary biases is a poor replicability rate for the published literature, such as the 35% overall value reported in Table 1.1. When interested readers turn to the primary literature to assess, for example, the evidence base for growth mindset interventions, they will find study after study reporting positive effects. What they do not see are the studies that might have been done that did not find benefits for these interventions. If I show you five studies that all support mindset interventions, you are likely to form the impression that research supports their effectiveness. If I show you the same five positive studies, along with twenty-five studies with null results, you would likely reach a different conclusion. Your overall estimate of both the probability of existence as well as the magnitude of the effect should hinge on how many null or near-zero results are in the set. But this is precisely the information that is hidden when each stakeholder in the academic research system follows its own private incentives.

What should we do?

In summary, there are multiple types of selection effects that make it so research results are not readily interpretable at face value. These effects not only bias the primary literature toward false positives, but also inflate the reported effect sizes for true positive effects.

1. Researchers who allocate effort to many small studies instead of fewer large studies.
2. Researchers who select for positive results within a study (e.g., via QRPs or p-hacking).
3. Researchers who fail to write up or submit null results for publication.
4. Journals that reject papers reporting null results.

It might appear that researchers bear nearly all the blame for this tragic state of affairs, but it is crucial to understand that the underlying driving factor actually is market demand. Consumers of research (the market) conflate entertainment value with scientific worth. The artificial scarcity of publishing capacity, which is necessary to create a status hierarchy among researchers, means that only the "best" articles are selected for publication. And since readers generally find "something" to be more interesting than "nothing," journals that publish affirmative content are rewarded with increased subscriptions, downloads, and citations. This pressure is passed down to researchers, who create the interesting content; if they don't create it, they are replaced by other researchers who will. The missing null literature, which renders

EYE FOR DIVERSITY 1.1 GENERALIZING TO STUDENTS FROM DIVERSE BACKGROUNDS

Dante D. Dixson

Many quantitative study designs within gifted education, and psychosocial science in general, do not adequately account for the multitude of disadvantages that participants from diverse backgrounds commonly experience. Specifically, researchers either do not control for detrimental forces like poverty, racism, and sexism in their quantitative studies, or they discount the influence of these forces on the lived experiences of their research participants. Relatedly, even if a quantitative study design does attempt to account for the various detrimental forces that participants from diverse backgrounds commonly endure, quantitative research has the huge drawback of being limited by measurement. Researchers can only control for what they are able to measure. Although there are respectable research measures of some detrimental forces (e.g., measures of socioeconomic status), many of these measures are imprecise at best (e.g., self-report measures of being racist or sexist). Moreover, due to financial and practical limitations, even the best indicators of detrimental forces are not perfect, as obtaining verified information about all study participants is usually impractical. As a result of these common limitations that are pervasive in gifted education research, interested parties should always: (a) examine the diversity of a study's sample (e.g., is it 25% African American and 30% Asian American?), (b) evaluate how extensively the study's design took into account the disadvantages of its sample (e.g., did the researchers control for race and gender? How accurately did they measure socioeconomic status?), and (c) make a judgement of how adequately the study's design accounted for the diversity of its sample. This process is important because even studies that are considered to have acceptable technical rigor, procedural rigor, and transparency may not generalize to those from diverse backgrounds. This process should provide a rough idea of how likely a study's results generalize to students from diverse backgrounds.

those interesting, positive findings interpretable, is a tragedy of the commons. Until recently, its harm has been too diffuse and abstract to elicit a strong reform response from any part of the system. Even now, reformers appear to be only a small (but vocal) minority of scholars.

Taken together, the issues discussed in this section paint a somewhat dismal picture of the status quo of education research. Obviously, findings from primary research filter down into secondary sources, such as textbooks, so these latter sources cannot be any more reliable than their foundational material. Even though academic journal articles have gone through a gatekeeping process involving editors and peer reviewers, outsourcing one's sceptical discernment to any third party is still a bad idea.

I believe that one can derive insight, knowledge, and wisdom from published academic research, by treating it carefully. The first and most important consideration is simply understanding that the literature is strongly biased toward affirmative claims; that some uncomfortably large proportion of what is published likely would not replicate, and that effect size estimates are inflated. With this knowledge, one can apply some basic heuristics to try to "de-bias" the research base. The easiest one is to mentally divide the claimed effect size by three. Would this effect still be interesting if it were one-third as large? As discussed, many true effect sizes are zero, and most of the others are modest. Educational outcomes are strongly resistant to change. So when reading about some type of quick, minimal intervention that claims to have a strong effect on student achievement, weigh the relative likelihood of two possible explanations in your mind:

1. The actual effect is either zero or quite modest, but the results reported in this study are inflated.
2. This is actually one of the few, the proud, the strong educational effects.

Bear in mind that strong effects usually require a large, meaningful intervention that differs substantially from the status quo and that is delivered over a sustained period of time with high dosage. For example, the Knowledge is Power Program (KIPP, Tuttle et al., 2015) dramatically increases the time students spend in school over multiple academic years. According to the WWC, its effect on language arts, math, science, and social studies are 8, 12, 11, and 5 improvement index points, respectively.

IDENTIFYING CREDIBLE RESEARCH

Simine Vizire, a personality psychologist and leader in the open science movement, has asked, "do we want to be incredible or credible?" (Vizire, 2020). This framing cleverly captures both the appeal and the harm caused by the many biasing factors discussed in the previous section. The literature is *incredible* in the sense that it presents surprising finding after surprising finding that all appear to have the potential to revolutionize education. For example, growth mindset researchers suggested that just a subtle change from praising effort instead of ability can cause students to develop a growth mindset and thereby increase their achievement (Yeager and Dweck, 2012). But it is also *incredible* in the sense that it is *not credible*. When investigated rigorously, growth mindset interventions have no benefits for most students (Yeager et al. 2019). And if *credibility* is the opposite of untrustworthiness, it is also the opposite of the whiz-bang, one-weird-trick, low-effort/high-reward promises that have seduced so many educators and educational researchers. Credible research usually isn't very surprising, but it can be counted on. One can implement credible interventions and expect them to work. And one can build on credible research to identify new principles and applications. Addressing the critique that credible science is boring, Andrew Gelman (2016a) wrote:

> Daryl Bem claimed that Cornell students had ESP abilities. *If true*, this would indeed be interesting, given that it would cause us to overturn so much of what we thought we understood about the world. On the other hand, **if false, it's pretty damn boring,** just one more case of a foolish person believing something he wants to believe. (no page, emphasis original)

Research isn't supposed to be exciting. It's just supposed to be true. And Gelman is right; it is hard to see much value in counterintuitive, surprising, clever, but ultimately incorrect research findings. Science fiction is an enjoyable genre, but it works better with characters and a plot.

Where does credibility come from?

I think of research credibility as arising from three fundamental sources: technical rigor, procedural rigor, and transparency. Technical rigor comprises those elements that are typically taught in research methods courses, for example, the design of the study, the constraining or elimination of threats to validity, blinding procedures, ethics, measurement, sampling process and sample size, and data analysis. Technical rigor is often the only area in which people receive any training. Textbooks often treat it as if it is the only type of rigor needed. In doing so, they ignore the human element of the research process.

Procedural rigor involves creating and closely following a workable plan for the research. It involves data management, version control of data and analysis files, training of research staff, and coding of data. It also involves clearly thinking through and preemptively solving problems that may arise during the study – or designing the study such that those problems do not occur. Procedural rigor is about constraining the researcher's "degrees of freedom" - the ability to make mid-study alterations in the research plan. These must be limited because once the data start being observed, the researchers' decision-making process becomes suspect. There is a definite chance that the researcher will either consciously or unconsciously make decisions to enhance the probability that the study produces a desired result. The highest level of procedural rigor occurs when researchers produce a detailed preregistration of the study and are able to follow it without deviation (McBee & Field, 2017).

The final aspect of credibility is transparency. Transparency means *showing your work*, allowing for every aspect of the inferential chain to be exposed for verification and criticism. This has been a core scientific value for hundreds of years. The motto of the Royal Society, the world's oldest scientific society, is *Nullius in Verba*, which translates to "take no one's word." Lupia and Elman (2014) wrote:

> The credibility of scientific claims comes, in part, from the fact that their meaning is, at a minimum, available for other scholars to rigorously evaluate [...] Such open access to the origins of others' claims is the hallmark of scientific ways of

knowing. Accordingly, when social scientists fail to document their assumptions, decisions, and actions [...] it limits others' ability to understand the meaning of scientists' claims. (p. 20)

Transparency of data, study materials, and data analysis code are three hallmarks of the open science movement (McBee et al., 2018). But the transparency also encompasses disclosing the true process used in the research, warts and all. For example, imagine how differently you might interpret the conclusions from these two processes:

1. We planned a sample size of 150 students. When data collection was complete, we performed a blinded, pre-planned analysis of the data. Our complete results are presented in the paper. We did not examine any other analysis other than that which was reported.
2. We initially planned a sample size of 70 students. When this was finished, the result was close to significant but not quite there. We began collecting more data and reanalyzing the data in increments of 20 students. Once we hit a sample of 150, the result for our main hypothesis was no longer near significance. However, we noticed another significant effect in the data analysis that we found exciting. We revised the framing of the paper around this finding.

The first situation is fully confirmatory, while the second is completely exploratory. Further, the main finding in the second paper resulted from HARKing ("hypothesizing after results are known;" Kerr, 1998). In the first situation, the confirmatory nature of the data analysis allows the false positive rate of the statistical analysis to be constrained to some tolerably low value. In the second situation, conversely, the false positive risk cannot be controlled (De Groot, 1969). In the long run, it is 100%. That is, given enough unconstrained freedom, one can *always* achieve statistical significance.

Credibility depends on these three aspects, all of which are necessary but not sufficient conditions. The problem is, typically, only technical rigor can be ascertained from reading a study. This is also the most difficult aspect to judge, as it can require a great deal of expertise to determine whether a particular statistical analysis was properly done or whether the design adequately protects against certain types of confounding. The procedural aspect of rigor is almost impossible to ascertain from a direct reading of a journal article, unless it is a preregistered study – in which case, the publication can be compared to the preregistration document and reviewed for consistency. The best one can do is to amass circumstantial evidence by carefully "reading between the lines" while looking for certain signs that might betray the use of questionable research practices. Transparency can be greatly improved by open data, open code, and open materials. But procedural transparency is essentially totally absent in standard, non-preregistered research articles. Readers have no choice but to take the authors at their word. So much for *nullius in verba*!

There is even a fourth aspect of credibility, outside of the internal validity structure of the research itself that concerns the inference from the study's results to the status of the theoretical propositions being evaluated. Studies provide the strongest evidence when they evaluate *severe tests* of theoretical statements (Mayo, 2018a). Mayo (2018b) wrote that "A claim is severely tested to the extent it has been subjected to and passes a test that probably would have found flaws, were they present" (no page). A severe test is one in which an observation is evaluated that would only be expected to occur under the theory being evaluated, but not other theories. Affirmative study results provide corroborating evidence of theory only to the extent that they are severe tests. This idea connects directly to Karl Popper's (1959) notion that a scientific theory is distinguishable from pseudo-science to the extent that it makes *risky predictions* – predictions that are capable of being contradicted by evidence.

Strategies for learning to "read between the lines" to evaluate credibility

Learning to evaluate the technical rigor of a study requires a substantial understanding of research methods, measurement, and statistics. These skills are well-covered in many other publications and so I will not discuss them here. Instead, I will try to give some insight into some things I look for when evaluating research that has not been preregistered. Altmejd et al. (2019) showed that machine learning algorithms can be trained to identify the replicability of research articles with 70% accuracy. Dreber et al. (2015) found a similar 71% rate using a betting market. Clearly, the signs are there if we know what to look for, these methods are definitely not foolproof. They may fail to detect bogus articles (false negatives) and erroneously flag other trustworthy articles as likely untrue (false positives). But I believe that they likely result in much more highly calibrated judgments than simply accepting every published study's claims at face value.

1. *Does the research question or hypothesis seem like something that was formulated before or after seeing the data?* In his seminal article on HARKing, Kerr (1998) wrote about the "too convenient qualifier" that often distinguishes hypotheses that were formulated after the data were examined. This can often manifest as a hypothesized effect for one subgroup but not another, or an interaction between variables but not an overall effect (e.g., a main effect). Is it truly reasonable to expect that the effect would manifest for only a specific subset of the participants? Is it believable that the researchers would have been able to identify this specific subgroup in advance of seeing the data? One way to tell is by the sample size – detecting subgroup effects or interactions takes much larger samples than detecting main effects. A possible example of this type of HARKing is from Bem's (2011) precognition study. In the first experiment, there were three types of stimuli presented to subjects. The "psi effect" was observed only for one of the three classes of stimuli.

2. *Do the researchers seem like they would have taken "no" for an answer?* Given that researcher degrees of freedom are ubiquitous in research that is not preregistered, readers need to understand how much they were used. One "tell" I look for is *spin*. This is most readily observed in the discussion section of the article. If the authors engage in a discussion of how their theory is probably true (or of how the intervention they evaluated is probably effective) in the face of underwhelming findings, I discount my appraisal of the likely truth-value of the findings they reported. I am much more impressed by a straightforward appraisal of evidence (e.g., "we thought this would work, but it didn't") rather than "it didn't work so well this time, but here's why we still believe in it." In other words, if the authors don't believe their own negative results, why should I believe their positive results? This is also why I can find qualitative research using grounded theory to be persuasive, but I am not very moved by qualitative work performed under theoretical perspectives that seem founded on strong worldview commitments.

3. *Is there evidence of outcome switching?* Where the presence of "spin" gives you information about the researchers' potential preference for a certain set of results, assessing researcher degrees of freedom gives you information about their opportunity to bias the conclusion (either consciously or unconsciously) toward some preferred result. One manifestation of these degrees of freedom occurs when researchers have a large set of outcome variables available for reporting, and selectively report the ones that "worked." For example, if the researchers are assessing academic achievement, how many different measures were available to them, and how many of these did they report? Do they report results only for the state mathematics achievement test, but not other subjects or other tests? Other times, the researchers may report a primary outcome on something other than the logical variable one would expect to assess given the research question. For example, the paper may report a significant increase in student or teacher satisfaction, but not report any achievement outcomes. You might ask yourself, "if I was studying this intervention, would I really care more about satisfaction than achievement?" If the answer is not "yes," you might correctly surmise that the achievement outcome is not being reported because it was a null effect. And further, the satisfaction outcome being reported may well be a secondary outcome that would not even have been examined if the achievement outcome had been successfully impacted by the intervention.

4. *Does the finding have high prior probability?* Ioannidis (2005) showed that not all statistically significant p-values have the same interpretation – even those with exactly the same value. The most important determinant of whether a significant p-value is likely to correspond with a true effect is the prior probability of that effect. Is the effect plausible? Do you find it surprising? Does the effect have a clear mechanism of action? Is the magnitude of its benefit commensurate with the intensity and dosage of its delivery? I am much more inclined to believe that grade-skipping (a full-time intense academic intervention whose dosage amounts

to over a thousand hours per year) produces large effects on achievement than I am to believe the same for a one-hour per month pull-out enrichment program. This is also why I think so-called "nudge" interventions are completely bogus. I am not saying that we should discount any scientific finding that clashes with our preexisting beliefs. I am merely stating that extraordinary claims require extraordinary evidence.

5. *Are the numbers internally consistent?* The numbers reported in quantitative research papers follow certain regularities. For example, the sample sizes for subgroups should sum to the total sample size. The weighted mean of subgroup means should equal the overall mean. The test statistic equals the point estimate divided by its degrees of freedom. The p-value is directly calculable from the test statistic and degrees of freedom. Nuitjen et al. (2016) analyzed 250,000 psychology papers and found that 50% contain at least one reported p-value that is inconsistent with its test statistic and degrees of freedom, with 12% containing a gross error. Nick Brown (2017, 2019, 2020) has uncovered numerous examples of scientific misconduct (or fraud) by examining reported numbers for internal consistency.

6. *Do the authors have a conflict of interest?* One might expect the originator of a theory or model under study to have a higher stake in how research results turn out than a third party. After all, their reputation and professional status is at stake. And indeed, "first party replications" (those that involve the original progenitors of an idea) succeed at higher rates (Makel et al., 2012). I am much more apt to believe claims after they are replicated by a third party.

7. *Are the key p-values barely significant?* One telltale sign of p-hacking is a pattern of barely significant p-values. When effects are real, p-values should follow a right-skewed distribution. There should be many more small values than large ones (Simonsohn et al, 2014). This even applies to the "significant" range of values between 0 and .05. For example, there should be more p-values in the [0,.025] range than in the [.025,.05] range. There should be more p-values in [0,.01] than in [.04,.05]. A natural pattern of p-values might look like: .001, .005, .01, .0004, .034. An unnatural pattern of p-values might look like: .043, .021, .035, .047, .039. Once you understand this, you might be amazed how often you see this pattern in classic social psychology papers – most of which have not replicated.

8. *Are the results too good to be true?* If the results seem too good to be true, they probably aren't true. Social science research is inherently noisy. The constructs are often vaguely defined. Manipulations or interventions may not be delivered with perfect fidelity. Measurement is imperfect. And humans are incredibly variable. We should expect this messiness to manifest itself in research results. Schimmack (2012) described how excess success diminishes the credibility of research papers. For example, if a study reports six experiments, where each one is powered at 60%, the probability that all six would succeed *even if their underlying hypothesis is true* is less than 5%. It is far more likely that some of

these experiments would fail by chance. So, ironically we should find four out of six or five out of six successful experiments more convincing than six out of six. The latter is so unlikely that it should make you suspect that it is the result of some chicanery. Having reason to believe that researchers would not hide their failures should bolster your confidence when they show you their successes. This also applies to effect sizes that are too large to be believable. Often the blame does not lie with researchers themselves. Peer reviewers and editors are notorious for demanding that non-successful studies or hypothesis tests be removed. This is scientific malpractice that is typically justified for reasons of "space" (even though publication is online and electrons are free) or of "telling a clear story." But as we have discussed, you cannot interpret successes without seeing the failures.

9. *Do we see the deadly "small n, big effect size" combination?* Large effect sizes may be inherently suspicious given everything that has been discussed thus far. I am far more willing to entertain the possibility when they come from large, rigorous studies than from small ones. For example, if the Yeager et al. (2019) pre-registered national experiment on mindset had found a moderate or large effect size for the intervention, I would have been willing to update my beliefs. When an $n = 60$ study finds a large effect, it does not move my belief in the slightest.

CONCLUSION AND CODA

As I write this chapter, a movement toward abandoning testing on the grounds of equity is ascendent in the United States. Graduate programs are abandoning the GRE; colleges are making the SAT optional. Racial and socioeconomic inequities are easily observable in test scores. The rationale for eliminating them is to increase the fairness of admissions. But I fear that this effort will backfire. In the absence of tests, universities will become more reliant on letters of recommendation, personal statements, research experience, and prior academic performance. It seems self-evident to me that disparities also exist in all of these things, and that they will probably be much more severe than those seen in test scores. After all, which students will be able to get professional help crafting personal statements, intern in well-known laboratories, secure recommendation letters from famous academics, or attend elite universities? Tests make disparate outcomes visible, and for that they are being shunned in favor of admissions criteria whose biases are much harder to evaluate.

In the same manner, research is the worst way of knowing (except for all the others). Research is far from perfect, but at least we can see and evaluate its flaws. Some research is misleading, but some of it is trustworthy. And some flawed research is right in spite of itself. While I am bearish on the present state of social research and education research, I am optimistic about its future. Science is self-correcting. It may not happen quickly enough for our taste, but it is happening. The replication crisis has blossomed into a credibility revolution (Vizire, 2020). Someday soon, the revolution will begin in earnest in educational research; the new generation of researchers demands it (see McBee et al., 2018; van der Zee and Reich, 2018; Makel et al., 2019). I am certain that the quality of research in 2030 will be better than it is now (2020), and in 2040 better still. I cannot say the same about the opinions of self-appointed gifted consultants, memes in Facebook groups, or opinions espoused in parenting blogs. What will never, ever change is the responsibility of each consumer of research to critically evaluate claims made about reality, and the necessity of adopting a high standard of evidence before accepting those claims.

REFERENCES

Alogna, V. K., Attaya, M. K., Aucoin, P., Bahník, Š., Birch, S., Birt, A. R., … Brown, C. (2014). Registered replication report: Schooler & Englster-Schooler (1990). *Perspectives on Psychological Science, 9*(5), 556–578. http://dx.doi.org/10.1177/1745691614545653

Altmejd, A., Dreber, A., Forsell, E., Huber, J., Imai, T., Johannesson, M., et al. (2019) Predicting the replicability of social science lab experiments. *PLoS ONE 14*(12): e0225826. http://dx.doi.org/10.1371/journal.pone.0225826

Begley, C. G., & Ellis, L. M. (2012). Raise standards for preclinical cancer research. *Nature, 483*(7391), 531–533. http://dx.doi.org/10.1038/483531a

Bem, D. J. (2011). Feeling the future: Experimental evidence for anomalous retroactive influences on cognition and affect. *Journal of Personality and Social Psychology, 100*(3), 407–425. http://dx.doi.org/10.1037/a0021524

Bouwmeester, S., Verkoeijen, P. P. J. L., Aczel, B., Barbosa, F., Bègue, L., Brañas-Garza, P., … Espín, A. M. (2017). Registered replication report: Rand, Greene, and Nowak (2012). *Perspectives on Psychological Science, 12*(3), 527–542. http://dx.doi.org/10.1177/1745691617693624

Box, G. E. P. (1976). Science and statistics. *Journal of the American Statistical Association, 71*(356), 791–799, http://dx.doi.org/10.1080/01621459.1976.10480949.

Brown, N. (2017, March 22). Strange patterns in some results from the Food and Brand Lab. [blog post]. https://steamtraen.blogspot.com/2017/03/strange-patterns-in-some-results-from.html

Brown, N. (2019, February 19). Just another week in real-world science [blog post]. https://steamtraen.blogspot.com/2019/02/just-another-week-in-real-world-science.html

Brown, N. (2020, April 21). Some issues in recent gaming research [blog post]. https://steamtraen.blogspot.com/2020/04/some-issues-in-recent-gaming-research.html

Browne, M. (1989, May 3). Physicists Debunk claim of a new kind of fusion. *The New York Times*. Retrieved December 12, 2020

Camerer, C. F., Dreber, A., Forsell, E., Ho, T.-H., Huber, J., Johannesson, M., & … Wu, H. (2016). Evaluating replicability of laboratory experiments in economics. *Science, 351*(6280), 1433–1436. http://dx.doi.org/10.1126/science.aaf0918

Camerer, C. F., Dreber, A., Holzmeister, F., Ho, T.-H., Huber, J., Johannesson, M., … Wu, H. (2018). Evaluating the replicability of social science experiments in Nature and Science between 2010 and 2015. *Nature Human Behaviour*. http://dx.doi.org/10.1038/s41562-018-0399-z

Cheung, I., Campbell, L., LeBel, E. P., Ackerman, R. A., Aykutoğlu, B., Bahník, Š., … Yong, J. C. (2016). Registered replication report: Study 1 from Finkel, Rusbult, Kumashiro, & Hannon (2002). *Perspectives on Psychological Science, 11*(5), 750–764. http://dx.doi.org/10.1177/1745691616664694

De Groot, A. D. (1969). *Methodology: Foundations of inference and research in the behavioral sciences*. Mouton.

De Vries, Y., Roest, A., De Jonge, P., Cuijpers, P., Munafò, M., & Bastiaansen, J. (2018). The cumulative effect of reporting and citation biases on the apparent efficacy of treatments: The case of depression. *Psychological Medicine, 48*(15), 2453–2455. doi:10.1017/S0033291718001873

Doyen, S., Klein, O., Pichon, C. L., & Cleeremans, A. (2012). Behavioral priming: It's all in the mind, but whose mind? *PLoS ONE, 7*(1), e29081. https://doi.org/10.1371/journal.pone.0029081

Dreber, A., Pfeiffer, T., Almenberg, J., Isaksson, S., Wilson, B., Chen, Y., Nosek, B. A., & Johannesson, M. (2015). *Proceedings of the National Academy of Sciences, 112*(50) 15343–15347. http://dx.doi.org/10.1073/pnas.1516179112

Dumas-Mallet, E., Button, K. S., Boraud, T., Gonon, F., & Munafò, M. R. (2017). Low statistical power in biomedical science: A review of three human research domains. *Royal Society Open Science, 4*, 160254. http://dx.doi.org/10.1098/rsos.160254

Ebersole, C. R., Atherton, O. E., Belanger, A. L., Skulborstad, H. M., Allen, J. M., Banks, J. B., ... Brown, E. R. (2016). Many Labs 3: Evaluating participant pool quality across the academic semester via replication. *Journal of Experimental Social Psychology, 67*, 68–82. http://dx.doi.org/10.1016/j.jesp.2015.10.012

Eerland, A., Sherrill, A. M., Magliano, J. P., Zwaan, R. A., Arnal, J. D., Aucoin, P., ... Prenoveau, J. M. (2016). Registered Replication Report: Hart & Albarracín (2011). *Perspectives on Psychological Science, 11*(1), 158–171. http://dx.doi.org/10.1177/1745691615605826

Errington, T. M., Iorns, E., Gunn, W., Tan, F. E., Lomax, J., & Nosek, B. A. (2014). Science forum: An open investigation of the reproducibility of cancer biology research. *E-life, 3*, e04333. http://dx.doi.org/10.7554/eLife.04333

Ferguson, C. J. & Heene, M. (2012). A Vast Graveyard of Undead Theories: Publication Bias and Psychological Science's Aversion to the Null. *Perspectives on Psychological Science, 7*(6), 555–561. http://dx.doi.org/10.1177/1745691612459059

Flore, P. C., Mulder, J., & Wicherts, J. M. (2019). The influence of gender stereotype threat on mathematics test scores of Dutch high school students: a registered report. *Comprehensive Results in Social Psychology*, 1–35. http://dx.doi.org/10.1080/23743603.2018.1559647

Friedman, H. H. (2017), Cognitive biases that interfere with critical thinking and scientific reasoning: A course module. Available at SSRN: https://ssrn.com/abstract=2958800 or http://dx.doi.org/10.2139/ssrn.2958800

Gelman, A. (2016a, 23 June). It comes down to reality and it's fine with me cause I've let it slide. [blog post]. Retrieved from https://statmodeling.stat.columbia.edu/2016/06/23/it-comes-down-to-reality-and-its-fine-with-me-cause-ive-let-it-slide/

Gelman, A. (2016b, 21 September). What has happened down here is that the winds have changed. [blog post]. Retrieved from https://statmodeling.stat.columbia.edu/2016/09/21/what-has-happened-down-here-is-the-winds-have-changed/

Gelman, A. & Carlin, J. (2014). Beyond power calculations: Assessing type-S (sign) and type-M (magnitude) errors. *Perspectives on Psychological Science, 9*, 641–651. http://dx.doi.org/10.1177/1745691614551642

Hagger, M. S., Chatzisarantis, N. L. D., Alberts, H., Anggono, C. O., Batailler, C., Birt, A. R., ... Bruyneel, S. (2016). A multilab preregistered replication of the ego-depletion effect. *Perspectives on Psychological Science, 11*(4), 546–573. http://dx.doi.org/10.1177/1745691616652873

Ioannidis, J. (2005). Why most published research findings are false. *PLoS Med, 2*(8): e124. http://dx.doi.org/10.1371/journal.pmed.0020124

Judd, C. M. & Gawronski, B. (2011). Editorial comment. *Journal of Personality and Social Psychology, 100*(3), 406. http://dx.doi.org/10.1037/0022789

Kerr, N. L. (1998). HARKing: Hypothesizing after the results are known. *Personality and Social Psychology Review*, 2(3): 196–217. http://dx.doi.org/10.1207/s15327957pspr0203_4

Klein, R. A., Ratliff, K. A., Vianello, M., Adams, R. B., Bahník, Š., Bernstein, M. J., ... Nosek, B. A. (2014). Investigating variation in replicability: A "Many Labs" replication project. *Social Psychology*, 45, 142–152. http://dx.doi.org/10.1027/1864-9335/a000178

Klein, R. A., Vianello, M., Hasselman, F., Adams, B. G., Adams, R. B., Alper, S., ... Bahník, Š. (2018). Many Labs 2: Investigating variation in replicability across samples and settings. *Advances in Methods and Practices in Psychological Science*, 1(4), 443–490. http://dx.doi.org/10.1177/2515245918810225

Kvarven, A., Strømland, E., & Johannesson, M. (2020). Comparing meta-analyses and preregistered multiple-laboratory replication projects. *Nature Human Behavior*, 4, 423–434. http://dx.doi.org/10.1038/s41562-019-0787-z

Langworth, R. (2009, June 26). Democracy is the worst form of government... [blog post]. Retrieved from https://richardlangworth.com/worst-form-of-government

Lehrer, J. (2010, December 6). The truth wears off. *New Yorker*. Retrieved from https://www.newyorker.com/magazine/2010/12/13/the-truth-wears-off

Lupia, A. & Elman, C. (2014). Openness in political science: Data access and research transparency. *Political Science & Politics*, 47, 19–42. http://dx.doi.org/10.1017/s1049096513001716

Makel, M. C., & Plucker, J. A. (2014). Facts are more important than novelty. *Educational Researcher*, 43(6), 304–316. https://doi.org/10.3102/0013189x14545513

Makel, M. C., Plucker, J. A., & Hegarty, B. (2012). Replications in psychology research. *Perspectives on Psychological Science*, 7(6), 537–542. https://doi.org/10.1177/1745691612460688

Makel, M. C., Smith, K. N., McBee, M., Peters, S. J., & Miller, E. M. (2019). A path to greater credibility: Large-scale collaborative education research. *AERA Open*. http://dx.doi.org/10.1177/2332858419891963

McBee, M., Makel, M. C., Peters, S. J., & Matthews, M. S. (2018). A call for open science in giftedness research. *Gifted Child Quarterly*, 62(4), 374–388. http://dx.doi.org/10.1177/0016986218784178. Preprint: https://psyarxiv.com/nhuv3/

McBee, M. & Field, S. (2017). Confirmatory study design, data analysis, and results that matter. In Makel, M. C. & Plucker, J. A. (Eds.), *Toward a more perfect psychology: Improving trust, accuracy, and transparency in research* (pp. 59–78). American Psychological Association.

Mayo, D. (2018a). *Statistical inference as severe testing: How to get beyond the statistics wars*. Cambridge University Press.

Mayo, D. (2018b). The meaning of my title 'Statistical Inference as Severe Testing: How to Get Beyond the Statistics Wars' [blog post]. Retrieved from https://errorstatistics.com/2018/05/19/the-meaning-of-my-title-statistical-inference-as-severe-testing-how-to-get-beyond-the-statistics-wars/#:˜:text=That's%20what%20it%20means%20to,foundwe%20flaws%2C%20were%20they%20present.&text=The%20probability%20that%20a%20method,data%20is%20an%20error%20probability.

Murray, S. B., Compte, E. J., Quintana, D. S., Mitchison, D., Griffiths, S., & Nagata, J. M. (2019). Registration, reporting, and replication in clinical trials: The case of anorexia nervosa. *International Journal of Eating Disorders*, 53(1), 138–142. https://doi.org/10.1002/eat.23187

McCarthy, R. J., Skowronski, J. J., Verschuere, B., Meijer, E. H., Jim, A., Hoogesteyn, K., ... Bakos, B. E. (2018). Registered replication report on Srull and Wyer (1979). *Advances in Methods and Practices in Psychological Science*. http://dx.doi.org/10.1177/2515245918777487

O'Donnell, M., Nelson, L. D., Ackermann, E., Aczel, B., Akhtar, A., Aldrovandi, S., ... Babincak, P. (2018). Registered replication report: Dijksterhuis and van Knippenberg (1998). *Perspectives on Psychological Science*, 13(2), 268–294. http://dx.doi.org/10.1177/1745691618755704

Open Science Collaboration. (2015). Estimating the reproducibility of psychological science. *Science*, 349(6251), aac4716–aac4716. http://dx.doi.org/10.1126/science.aac4716

Peters, S. J., Matthews, M. S., McBee., M. T., & McCoach, D. B. (2013). *Beyond gifted education: Designing and implementing advanced academic programs.* Prufrock.

Peters, S. J. (2017, September 5). Bright versus gifted: An unnecessary distinction. [blog post]. Retrieved from https://www.nagc.org/blog/bright-vs-gifted-unnecessary-distinction

Plucker, J. A. & Callahan, C. M. (2020). *Critical issues and practices in gifted education: A survey of current research on giftedness and talent development.* Prufrock Press, Inc.

Popper, K. (1959). *Logic of scientific discovery.* Hutchison.

Prinz, F., Schlange, T., & Asadullah, K. (2011). *Believe it or not: How much can we rely on published data on potential drug targets? Nature Reviews Drug Discovery*, 10(9), 712. http://dx.doi.org/10.1038/nrd3439-c1

Rosenthal, R. (1979). File drawer problem and tolerance for null results. *Psychological Bulletin*, 86(3), 638–641. http://dx.doi.org/10.1037/0033-2909.86.3.638

Schimmack, U. (2012). The ironic effect of significant results on the credibility of multiple-study articles. *Psychological Methods*, 17(4), 551–566. https://dx.doi.org/10.1037/a0029487

Silverman, L. (1997). The construct of asynchronous development. *Peabody Journal of Education*, 72(3–4), 36–58.

Simmons, J. P., Nelson, L. D., & Simonsohn, U. (2011). False-positive psychology: Undisclosed flexibility in data collection and analysis allows presenting anything as significant. *Psychological Science*, 22(11), 1359–1366. https://dx.doi.org/10.1177/0956797611417632

Simonsohn, U., Nelson, L. D., & Simmons, J. P. (2014). P-curve: A key to the file-drawer. *Journal of Experimental Psychology: General*, 143(2), 534–547. https://dx.doi.org/10.1037/a0033242

Taibbi, C. (2012, January 29). "Bright Child" vs. "Gifted Learner": What's the difference? *Psychology Today*. Retrieved from https://www.psychologytoday.com/us/blog/gifted-ed-guru/201201/bright-child-vs-gifted-learner-whats-the-difference

Tuttle, C. C., Gleason, P., Knechtel, V., Nichols-Barrer, I., Booker, K., Chojnacki, G., ... Goble, L. (2015). Understanding the effect of KIPP as it scales: Volume I, impacts on achievement and other outcomes. *Final Report of KIPP's "Investing in Innovation Grant Evaluation."* Mathematica Policy Research, Inc.

van der Zee, T. & Reich, J. (2018). Open education science. *AERA Open*. https://dx.doi.org/10.1177/2332858418787466

van Zwet, E. & Cator, E. (2020). The significance filter, the winner's curse and the need to shrink. *ArXiV*. Retrieved from https://arxiv.org/abs/2009.09440

Vizire, S. (2020, January). Do we want to be credible or incredible? *Association for Psychological Science Observer*. Retrieved from https://www.psychologicalscience.org/observer/do-we-want-to-be-credible-or-incredible

Verschuere, B., Meijer, E. H., Jim, A., Hoogesteyn, K., Orthey, R., McCarthy, R. J., ... Bakos, B. E. (2018). Registered replication report on Mazar, Amir, and Ariely (2008). *Advances in Methods and Practices in Psychological Science*, 1(3), 299–317. http://dx.doi.org/10.1177/2515245918781032

Wagenmakers, E.-J., Beek, T., Dijkhoff, L., Gronau, Q. F., Acosta, A., Adams, R. B., ... Blouin-Hudon, E.-M. (2016). Registered replication report: Strack, Martin, and Stepper (1988). *Perspectives on Psychological Science*, 11(6), 917–928. http://dx.doi.org/10.1177/1745691616674458

Yeager, D. S. & Dweck, C. S. (2012). Mindsets that promote resilience: When students believe that personal characteristics can be developed. *Educational Psychologist*, 47(4), 302–314. http://dx.doi.org/10.1080/00461520.2012.722805

Yeager, D. S., Hanselman, P., Walton, G. M., Murray, J. S., Crosnoe, R., Muller, C., ... Dweck, C. S. (2019). A national experiment reveals where a growth mindset improves achievement. *Nature. 573*. http://dx.doi.org/10.1038/s41586-019-1466-y

Physical development of gifted students

Jennifer L. Jolly

The physical development of gifted and high ability children has not been studied in a systematic or organized fashion in over 100 years. Yet a popular perception is that high cognitive ability must be accompanied by deficits in another area of human development. Contemporary findings regarding the physical development and health of highly intelligent children may appear to be contradictory, but to arrive at an understanding of this area it is essential that the quality of the research be evaluated; many of the studies that suggest high cognitive ability is detrimental to health are of lesser quality than the research pointing to high cognitive ability as advantageous. Research simply does not support some of the public's widely held beliefs regarding the supposed sensitive and fragile nature of children identified as gifted and talented. To address these disparate beliefs, in this chapter I offer an overview of the varied and uneven research related to these students' physical development.

HISTORICAL INFLUENCE OF MYTHS AND STEREOTYPES

Stereotypes held by society and even some scientists at the turn of the 20th century portrayed children who possessed high academic ability as being sickly, bespeckled, mentally unstable, thin, and frail (Borland, 2004; Jolly, 2018; Tannenbaum, 1983; Terman, 1925). The popular media also promulgated these caricatures, with cartoonists drawing large heads in disproportion to the child's body, equating advanced ability with grossly large and unattractive heads. In addition, newspapers produced stories of "young geniuses" who burned bright during their youth and then burned out just as quickly, with these young people failing to achieve adult careers proportionate to their early abilities (Jolly & Bruno, 2010). Early researchers in the field sought to address and eliminate these myths and stereotypes, emphasizing that gifted children were "not likely to be the physical and nervous wreck that some have supposed" (Hollingworth, 1926, p. 100). They suggested that the media stories were just that—stories, created to sell papers, and magazines. The maxim of "early rise, early rot" did not stand up to the systematic inquiry evident in the works of Francis Galton, Lewis Terman, and Leta Stetter Hollingworth.

DOI: 10.4324/9781003025443-3

Galton's influence

Francis Galton engaged in some of the earliest systematic inquiry regarding widely held views of his time regarding the character and talent of eminent men. During the mid and late 19th century, Galton, inspired by his cousin Charles Darwin, began an investigation of intelligence and individual differences, which he fully outlined in *Hereditary Genius* (1869). His hypotheses challenged the pervasive ideas of this time period, including that eminent men were more likely to have stupid children (with the stupidity being inherited from their mother; Jolly, 2018). The prevailing thought was that these children in adulthood then exhibited feeble constitutions and a lack of sociability (Gillham, 2001).

In 1884, Galton established a lab at the University College London to measure physical traits. *Hereditary Genius* and his subsequent writings had brought him fame, so thousands of individuals were amenable to having their anthropomorphic measurements taken in his lab. Galton collected an astonishing amount of data and developed statistical techniques to test his theories regarding genetic inheritance (Gillham, 2001). For example, based on his collection of height measurements from approximately 200 parents and their 900 children, he observed, "regression toward mediocrity," which evidenced that extremely tall or short parents had children who averaged two-thirds as extreme in their height (Goldstein, 2012). Galton's regression toward mediocrity is now referred to as regression toward the mean. While Galton's mathematical analysis was correct, his biological explanation was not; his theory of Ancestral Law, which assigned an amount of genetic inheritance to parents and familial predecessors, was eventually rebutted (Gillham, 2001; Goldstein, 2012). Ancestral Law also aligned with Galton's thoughts about eugenics, where if "talented men were mated with talented women … generation after generation, we might produce a highly-bred human race" (Galton, 1865, p. 318). Galton also considered intelligence to be an inherited characteristic and he proposed using the normal distribution to map the intellectual range in populations. He divided the entire population into 18 classes such that genius could be found in the top classes (Burt, 1962). The contrast between what Galton got right (genetic factors do play a role in predicting adult accomplishments) and what he got terribly wrong (eugenics) presents a tension that scientists struggle with today. There is a clash between applying the science and mathematics approaches developed by men like Galton and Ronald Fisher while condemning the terrible violence against some members of society that their personal beliefs inspired. This is an issue for which there is still no satisfactory solution.

Applications of modern science

Advances in psychology and statistical methods at the beginning of the 20th century brought a number of individuals together to investigate urgent problems facing America's schools. Schools were becoming increasingly more diverse—reflecting shifts in student race and ethnicity, socioeconomic status, population movements from rural to urban centers, child labor laws, and views of academic potential and ability. In an attempt to bring order to schools, Progressive Era reforms capitalized on these new approaches to bring efficiency and systematization to classrooms across the country (Jolly, 2018).

Psychologists such as Lewis Terman and Leta Hollingworth sought to apply the tools of their field to educational problems. One of these tools was the recently developed IQ test, designed to help classify children based on their quantifiable intelligence and academic abilities (Jolly, 2018). Terman was instrumental in translating the Binet-Simon Scales for an American audience. The Binet-Simon, developed for French school children to quantify intellectual capacity, became the Stanford-Binet. In 1906, Terman's dissertation focused on "bright and dull" children; combined with his work on the Stanford-Binet, it was not surprising when in 1921 he commenced a longitudinal study focused on gifted children in California (Terman, 1925).

In addition to aptitude and achievement data, Terman collected physical measurement data on children in the sample. Terman's colleagues at the University of Iowa were responsible for collecting the 37 anthropometric measures, health histories, and medical examinations on 594 of the 1,528 participants in Terman's longitudinal study. Based on these data, a composite portrait of gifted children offered a slightly "upward direction" finding, i.e., that these children scored more highly on nearly all the "desirable" traits measured. This upward trend was not of the same degree across all traits. Even though some types of maladaptive behaviors also were recorded, they were not found at any greater rate than among the general population. These maladaptive behaviors and traits included social maladjustment, physical frailty, and emotional instability (Chapman, 1988; Terman, 1925; Terman & Oden, 1947).

Leta Hollingworth began her work with gifted children while a professor at Teachers College in New York City. In 1916, while teaching a course on mental testing, Hollingworth brought a child into her class to model the administration of an IQ test. This serendipitous encounter began her interest and subsequent decades-long research on gifted children (Jolly, 2018). Hollingworth collected similar types of data as Terman from the students in her longitudinal study. Although a much smaller group, she presented a number of findings that also pushed back against the common stereotypes of the time (Hollingworth, 1926), and she too included data related to physical development. Notably, Hollingworth was one of the first scholars to observe that some educators were fixated on a student's physical development in relation to their grade placement in school. For example, even a practice as esoteric as the ossification of wrist bones had been proposed by some researchers as a way to place children into appropriate grades, despite a lack of any data to actually support this approach (Hollingworth, 1926).

The reality is that all children have varying rates of physical maturation, especially during puberty. These observations by Hollingworth (1926) and Terman

(1925) helped to dispel the idea that academic achievement was tied to physical development. This proved particularly useful when advocating for acceleration and grade skipping, as physical size is not typically a legitimate reason to refuse a child the opportunity to accelerate their academic development. Seventy years later in her work with students who were radically accelerated, Gross found resistance against acceleration that largely was based on unfounded ideas regarding self-esteem and social adjustment rather than physical size (Gross, 2006). In the words of Hollingworth's contemporary, a child's "intellectual work should not be measured by his rate of anatomical development" (Freeman & Carter, 1924 as cited in Hollingworth, 1926, p. 98). This is not to say that physical development is irrelevant, but rather only that it should not be an impediment to academic acceleration. Differences between cognitive and physical development will require accommodations in order to help a child thrive.

FIELD NOTE 2.1

Emily Kircher-Morris, MA, MEd, LPC

My mixed classroom of gifted students consisted of students who were chronologically second and third grade students, but were doing academic tasks designed for upper elementary or middle school students. The curriculum for the upper grade levels required students to show mastery of basic skills, including timed math tests to show fluency of math facts. While my students understood the concept of the math skills and could correctly calculate the answer, they weren't always able to get the answers on the paper within the time expectations set by the curriculum. The uneven development of their fine motor skills versus cognitive skills created a barrier for meeting the expectations of the grade level curriculum they were completing.

Fine motor skills generally develop based on a child's chronological age, and this can cause distress when the discrepancy between what they're able to produce and what they cognitively grasp doesn't align. Now working as a mental health counselor for gifted and twice exceptional kids, I frequently see students struggling in this way and hear them describe the frustration they feel. When writing, verbally gifted kids want to use their advanced vocabulary and complex ideas, but are hindered when they can't get the words written on the page as quickly as their minds go. Visually talented students are frustrated when their artwork doesn't match what they visualize in their mind. Helping kids focus on the process of developing a skill (instead of the final product) and teaching them self-advocacy skills to ask for accommodations when appropriate are two strategies I use to support these learners until their physical skills catch up to their cognitive abilities.

Persistent stereotypes

Despite the findings from these early studies and subsequent confirming research (Hollingworth, 1926; Lubinski, 2016; Terman, 1925; Whipple, 1924), negative stereotypes of gifted and intellectually advanced children and adults have proven stubbornly persistent, particularly in the media. As mainstream media expanded into movies and television shows, the portrayal of gifted individuals has continued to use stereotypical characterizations found in Western culture. For example, the movie *A Beautiful Mind* (2001) is a true story of Nobel Laureate in Economics John Nash that chronicled both his groundbreaking work in mathematics and his struggle with schizophrenia. The movie emphasized the link between giftedness and mental illness, reminiscent of the portrayals of the early 20th century. In 2007, *The Big Bang Theory* debuted and continued over a run of 12 seasons. The show's protagonist, Sheldon Cooper, is a former child prodigy turned theoretical physicist. He is often rude and does not suffer fools gladly. His friends and girlfriend on the show also display exaggerated stereotypical behaviors—nerdy, unathletic, and socially awkward. Although these characterizations include some three-dimensional aspects of their lives, such as romantic relationships and workplace dynamics, it is difficult not to hypothesize that these characters have influenced how the approximately 190 million viewers over the show's history now understand gifted persons. Netflix's hugely successful series, *The Queen's Gambit* (2020), is the story of Beth Harmon, an orphan and chess prodigy during the 1960s. Her exceptional abilities are closely linked to an addiction to tranquilizers. In addition, the series continually raised her mother's mental illness and exceptional ability in mathematics to suggest that Beth may also be mentally unstable. The exploration of her own struggles as resulting from exposure to her mother's erratic behavior and then being orphaned is never undertaken. The orphanage also tranquilized the children to keep them under control, forming an early addiction to the substance for Beth. In addition to these depictions in film, there is also a clear influence of media reports found in the news or in unmoderated discussions on the Internet on people's stereotypes of highly intelligent individuals (Finch, 2017; Hall & Suutamm, 2020).

As negative stereotypes in the media about gifted individuals are often the first exposure to these individuals that people experience, these popular culture examples and others like them are critical to society's understanding of gifted children. Recurring negative reports also serve to reinforce already-developed negative attitudes and stereotypes (Baudson, 2016; Bergold et al., 2021). News reports typically report problematic issues, as well-adjusted bright children are not perceived as newsworthy, and even general stories on topics such as advanced school programming options often fail to support gifted education or gifted students (Bergold et al., 2021; Karnes & Lewis, 1995). Images of gifted students in popular culture still depict these students as androgynous, unathletic, and unpopular (Vialle, 2007), even though the stereotypical view of the sickly, mentally unstable, and nerdy gifted child was dispelled over a century ago (Lubinski, 2016). The persistence of these negative stereotypes is frustrating not only because of the harm it can cause (e.g., via bullying) but also because there is no basis in the research literature to support them.

CONTEMPORARY STUDIES IN INFANCY

Lewis Terman's *Genetic Studies of Genius* project collected data in a number of areas, including from parents. Based on parent reports, study children were found to be one pound heavier on average at birth, and their early acquisition of language and ability to walk were also recorded (Terman, 1925). In general, prenatal health is associated with multiple developmental outcomes. Hollingworth's studies reported similar results regarding the indicators she referred to as vitality (Hollingworth, 1926). However, more current research literature examining the connections between intellect and early motor ability during infancy is not as straightforward. For example, a Swiss study from 2013 found that early walking did not hold strong predictive value for advanced intellect (Jenni et al., 2013).

Vaivre-Douret, a French neuropsychologist, conducted a series of studies regarding developmental characteristics of high ability children beginning in infancy. As the majority of children are identified as gifted once they have already begun elementary school, psychomotor data on very young gifted children is largely retrospective in nature and dependent on parental memory and records, such as baby books. Her research is drawn from these types of data and as such faces the same limitations. These findings documented advanced development in infants, including in characteristics, such as motor and language development, when compared to average milestones (Vaivre-Douret, 2011). In another study, she and her colleagues also investigated preterm infants, looking at a range of factors, including birth weight, gestational age, head circumference, stature, gender, socioeconomic status, and motor development. Their findings suggest that preterm infants from economically advantaged homes evidence a homogeneity in anthropometric variables (e.g., weight, height, and head circumference) and suggest less variance in future motor and intellectual development. The study's main limitation was that middle- and upper-income households were overrepresented among participating families (Vaivre-Douret et al., 2010), suggesting that the developmental characteristics that appear to turn into high potentialities could also result from the families – and thus their children's – relatively advantaged developmental environments (Vaivre-Douret, 2011).

IMMUNE SYSTEM CONCERNS AND HANDEDNESS

There is little evidence to support that immune system issues impact gifted individuals disproportionately or at a higher rate than among the general population. The human immune system, which is complex and impacts the entire body's functioning, works to prevent or limit infection. When the immune system does not function properly, issues such as allergies or autoimmune disorders arise. Environmental allergies such as those associated with pollen and food are caused by either antibodies or T cells. Autoimmune diseases are either specific to an organ, or are systemic and have clear genetic components (National Institute of Allergy and Infectious Disease, 2017).

Benbow (1986) reported that among participants from the Study of Mathematically Precocious Youth who had obtained at least a 630 SAT-V and/or 700 SAT-M before age 13, 80% reported being myopic, left-handed, and/or had asthma/allergies. Approximately 70% of the U.S. child population would have at least one of these traits in the 1980s (Mannino et al., 2002; Platts-Mills, 2015; Theophanous et al., 2018). In addition to Benbow's findings, several other studies have also found a relationship between left-handedness and gifted-level academic ability. For example, a study of Mensa Society members revealed a 20% rate of self-reporting left-handedness (Ehrman & Perelle, 1983) in comparison to the 10% prevalence of left-handedness in the general population. And a study of 150,000 medical college admissions test scores reported an overrepresentation of left handers (Halpern et al., 1998). Based on a sample of American Mensa members, Karpinski et al. (2018) suggested high IQ was a risk factor for autoimmune disorders, allergies, and asthma. However, these studies' results are based on samples that are impacted by self-selection bias and lack of a comparison group.

These handedness findings are part of a long history which links intelligence and handedness and has become the most researched behavioral asymmetry (Papadatou-Pastou & Tomprou, 2015), including psychological and medical issues and neuropsychological functioning. However, this body of research has yet to reach definitive findings due to the measures of handedness used and samples involved (Michel et al., 2013). Right-handedness reflects a left cerebral hemisphere control of language and is the predominant organization among 90% of the population, including across all ethnicities and races. Left-handedness is not simply a mirror of right-handedness, and it is more likely to occur in males (Christman, 2012). The development of handedness and its relations to cognitive and emotional observable characteristics or to phenotypes and psychological development remain an area for additional research (Michel et al., 2013). Despite some evidence to suggest that left-handedness occurs more often in intellectually gifted individuals, the research overall does not support this conclusion. Papadaou-Patou & Tomprou's (2015) meta-analysis of studies included intellectually disabled, typically developing, and gifted individuals. Of the over 16,000 individuals from across five studies (19 data sets), non-right-handedness and/or left-handedness occurred at the same rate for typically developing and gifted individuals, while levels were higher for intellectually disabled individuals than for the typically developing comparison groups. These authors suggested that the cerebral reorganization that accompanied left-handedness may produce cerebral crowding leading to cognitive disability, rather than leading to enhanced brain activity.

Using data from Early Childhood Longitudinal Study-Birth Cohort (ECLS-B), Wilson (2019) found that parents did not report higher incidences of health concerns, including asthma, allergies, and respiratory illnesses, for the gifted population within this early childhood sample. This finding using a nationally representative sample of young children in the United States further supports Hollingworth and Terman's initial findings that gifted children did not experience higher rates of sickness when compared to their chronological peers. Brown et al. (2021), in a sample of 48,558 participants from across multiple longitudinal studies, observed either positive associations or no relationship between health and cognitive ability and this trend did not differ for those participants with high cognitive ability. While there are some findings to suggest that those with high intellectual ability have higher incidences of immune irregularities or characteristics related to handedness, these studies are not based on representative samples or lack comparison groups. This type of research results in biased findings and should not be generalized to gifted children and adults as a population. The preponderance of the research suggests that higher cognitive ability is not associated with specific physical characteristics to any practical extent.

HEALTH OUTCOMES ACROSS THE LIFESPAN

Longitudinal studies play an important role in understanding physical and health outcomes of individuals over their lifetime. These studies have shown correlations between early childhood characteristics and circumstances and outcomes later in life. For example, mental ability differences early in life are associated with inequalities in late-life health (Deary et al., 2003, 2004; Terman & Oden, 1959). Physical activity and healthy diets before the age of five contributed to better cognitive outcomes mid-life, underscoring the neurocognitive developments that take place during early childhood (Tandon et al. 2016). Extending to later-life, those who participated in aerobic physical activity tended to experience less cognitive loss related to neural plasticity (Gomez-Pinilla & Hillman, 2013).

The National Longitudinal Surveys (NLSY79) have also provided data regarding a whole host of subject areas and variables. Children born from 1957 to 1965 were initially interviewed in 1979 (Round 1) when they were 14 to 22 years of age. Round 27 was just completed in 2016. (Wraw et al. (2018) in their follow-up of NLSY79 participants at mid-life (age 50) found that higher IQ in youth correlated to healthier behaviors in mid-life, including being less likely to smoke. Other health-related outcomes measured included greater and more varied physical activity, a greater likelihood to read nutrition labels, and brushing and flossing their teeth twice as often. These behaviors were in contrast to a greater tendency to skip meals and to snack and to drink alcohol more often, compared to their peers with lower IQs who drank less often but in much greater quantity (described as binge-drinking), impacting their health outcomes later in life. Study participants with high IQs in youth were found to be in better overall health at mid-life and had lower risk factors for chronic illnesses (e.g., arthritis and diabetes; Wraw et al., 2015). These findings were largely independent of early life socioeconomic status. However, the authors did acknowledge that individuals with higher IQs tended to earn higher incomes as adults, and therefore, had greater discretionary spending to devote to exercising, seeking out medical treatments and therapies, and accessing a variety of fresh foods and healthier dietary choices. IQs measured early in life strongly correlated to educational outcomes as adults, suggesting a cyclical pattern (Wraw et al., 2015, 2018).

FIELD NOTE 2.2

Scott Lutostanski, LPC

Adapted from Lutostanski (2018)

The impact of asynchronous development on the motor cortex, coupled with social and emotional obstacles, can discourage some gifted children from finding athletic and social outlets. Of course, physical activity is vital to the overall health and well-being of children, and exercise is needed to build muscle tone, maintain a healthy body weight, and strengthen the cardiovascular system. Additionally, exercise can have psychological and mental health benefits. Sports can enhance academically talented teenagers' physical capabilities, physical appearance, emotional stability, self-concept or general sense of self, and peer relationships. The sheer physical nature of many varieties of athletics can be taxing for some gifted children – especially given that academic and cognitive tasks come so easily to them. However, it can be worth the struggle because of the social-emotional benefits. Sports require sharing, working well with others, graciously losing, persisting through challenges, accepting penalties, and publicly displaying ability. You must be thoughtful about what your child will be able to manage – and have fun participating in. It's important to consider sports that gifted children will be most successful in, based on their physical, social, and emotional needs. Luckily, there are plenty of types of sports that can provide the right fit and will allow children to have fun, be active, and interact with others. All it takes is a little bit of research into various options, and some dedicated thought about how to align a child's strengths and weaknesses with the demands of the sport.

One of the most influential longitudinal studies of Western culture outside the United States, the Scottish Mental Survey tested all of the country's 11-year-olds in 1932, capturing an entire birth cohort and following them into old age. In addition to administering the Moray House Test (used as a placement test for British secondary schools), 1,000 children were also administered the Stanford-Binet, which strongly correlated with the Moray House Test. The Stanford-Binet was the same measure administered to the children in Terman's longitudinal study. For the children in this study, high IQ in childhood correlated to living to an older age. Those with lower IQs died younger and more often from stomach and lung cancer. Lower IQs generally were correlated with an adverse impact on later health, while those who had higher IQs led lifestyles resulting in fewer ill health effects (Deary et al., 2003). The only group among which this did not apply was the cohort of young men who died during World War II, in which those with higher IQs experienced greater mortality rates (Whalley & Deary, 2001).

To help understand health outcomes across the lifespan, not only health indices and behaviors but also psychosocial factors that contribute to longevity and the later or late-life health should be considered. Individual differences in personality also appear to help explain outcomes over a lifespan. Personality is "a person's biopsychosocial patterns of reactions and behaviors" (Kern & Friedman, 2011, p. 76). Personality and health are linked as evidenced by health behaviors and habits; the quality and quantity of relationships; regulation and responses to challenges and psychophysiological stress; and recreational choice (Kern & Friedman, 2011).

In the early 20th century, Cannon proposed the idea of psychological homeostasis. In this perspective, the balance between the physical and psychological well-being of a person helps to inform their emotional balance, which is also informed by nerves and hormones (Cannon, 1929) (for a more detailed discussion regarding personality, see Chapter 8 in this volume). These pathways initially were poorly studied and thus became erroneously and stubbornly linked. For example, Type A individuals, those who are often characterized by competitiveness, urgency, hyper-organization, and lack of patience, originally were thought to be at greater risk for heart disease while Type B individuals (whose personality is characterized by being relaxed and easy-going with a greater steadiness applied to tasks) were thought to be the "healthy" personality type. Research findings from more recent work have repeatedly found no links between poor health outcomes and Type A behavior (Petticrew et al., 2012).

In addition, Big Five Personality Factors (BFPFs) have also been applied to the study of well-being and health outcomes (Strickhouser et al., 2017). The five central factors are conscientiousness, agreeableness, extraversion, neuroticism/emotional stability, and intellect/openness. For example, studies have found that higher conscientiousness and lower neuroticism were related to healthier behaviors, choices, and general health (Graham et al., 2018; Rochefort et al., 2018). Ratings of conscientiousness were collected from participants in Terman's longitudinal study to study a range of childhood personality traits. In this sample, conscientiousness provided good predictive instruction for health and longitudinal outcomes (Friedman et al., 1995). In addition, career success impacted longevity but was moderated by measures of conscientiousness and motivation from childhood (Friedman et al., 1995; Kern et al., 2009). The BFPF have also been applied to understanding the link between intellectual ability and personality. Gifted individuals rate higher on factors of openness and emotional stability than non-gifted individuals. Where these ratings overlapped (e.g., intelligence and conscientiousness), some interesting insights have been provided to "long-term survival likelihood of those who are in childhood high in intelligence and conscientiousness versus those who are low in intelligence and conscientiousness" (Deary et al., 2008, p. 73) and how this might look practically with educators, medical practitioners, or counselors.

EDUCATIONAL/COUNSELING IMPLICATIONS

Research dating back to the very earliest studies of gifted children concluded that they were not sickly, frail, and/or had poor sight. The findings from longitudinal studies both in the United States and the United Kingdom also found that children with high IQs experienced better health outcomes in mid-life and in old age. Systems-based conceptions of giftedness such as the Actiotope model (Ziegler et al., 2017) include access to health-promoting resources as a factor in talent development. If gifted children and those with advanced academic abilities do have health issues, these likely have little to do with their co-occurring academic abilities. Rather than ascribing health issues to intellect, psychological or physiological issues should be investigated as potential causal mechanisms.

In responding to these health issues, educators, parents, community organizations, and counselors can all actively participate and collaborate to support the children in prognosis, services, and treatment. There are a number of school-community frameworks that address these holistic issues facing students and families. Community stakeholders can collaborate with schools to address the academic, physical, emotional, and social health of students. These partnerships are particularly crucial for children and their families who lack access to resources in support of the child and/or family. These suggestions include establishing a leadership team representative of school and community members, understanding student and family need and ways in which they are currently addressed, leveraging high-quality community resources to address unmet student/family needs, identifying a point person at the school to coordinate these school-community partnerships and activities, offering professional development for all collaborative partners, and evaluating the partnership programs and services (Anderson & Emig, 2014; Mapp & Kuttner, 2013) This holistic approach has the best chance of facilitating healthy development.

REFERENCES

Anderson M. K. & Emig, C. (2014). Integrated student supports: A summary of the evidence base for policymakers. Bethesda, MD: Child Trends. Retrieved from http://www.childtrends.org/wp-content/uploads/2014/02/2014-05ISSWhitePaper3.pdf

Baudson, T. G. (2016). The mad genius stereotype: Still alive and well. *Frontiers in Psychology*, 7, 368. https://doi.org/10.3389/fpsyg.2016.00368

Benbow, C. P. (1986). Physiological correlates of extreme intellectual precocity. *Neuropsychologia, 24*(5), 719–725.

Bergold, S., Hastall, M. R., & Steinmayr, R. (2021). Do mass media shape stereotypes about intellectually gifted individuals? Two experiments on stigmatization effects from biased newspaper reports. *Gifted Child Quarterly*, *65*(1), 75–94. https://doi.org/10.1177/0016986220969393

Borland, J. H. (2004). *Issues and practices in the identification and education of gifted students from under-presented groups.* https://files.eric.ed.gov/fulltext/ED485164.pdf

Brown, M. I., Wai, J., & Chabris, C. F. (2021). Can you ever be too smart for your own good? Comparing linear and nonlinear effects of cognitive ability on life outcomes. *Perspectives on Psychological Science.* https://doi.org/10.1177/1745691620964122

Burt, C. (1962). Francis Galton and his contributions to psychology. *British Journal of Statistical Psychology*, *15*(1), 1–41. https://doi.org/10.1111/j.2044-8317.1962.tb00081.x

Cannon, W. B. (1929). Organization for physiological homeostasis. *Physiological Review*, *9*(3), 399–431.

Chapman, P. D. (1988). *Schools as sorters: Lewis M. Terman, applied psychology, and the intelligence testing movement, 1890–1930.* New York University Press.

Christman, S. D. (2012). Handedness. In V. S. Ramachandran (Ed.), *Encyclopedia of human behavior* (2nd ed.; pp. 290–296). Elsevier. https://doi.org/10.1016/B978-0-12-375000-6.00188-9

Deary, I. J., Batty, G. D., Pattie, A., & Gale, C. R. (2008). More Intelligent, More Dependable Children Live Longer. *Psychological Science*, *19*(9), 874–880. https://doi.org/10.1111/j.1467-9280.2008.02171.x

Deary, I. J., Thorpe, G., Wilson, V., Starr, J. M., & Whalley, L. J. (2003). Population sex differences in IQ at age 11: The Scottish Mental Survey 1932. *Intelligence*, *31*, 533–542. https://doi-org.proxy.library.vcu.edu/10.1016/S0160-2896(03)00053-9

Deary, I. J., Whiteman, M. C., Starr, J. M., Whalley, L. J., & Fox, H. C. (2004). The Impact of Childhood Intelligence on Later Life: Following Up the Scottish Mental Surveys of 1932 and 1947. *Journal of Personality and Social Psychology*, *86*(1), 130–147. https://doi.org/10.1037/0022-3514.86.1.130

Ehrman, L. & Perelle, I. B. (1983). *Laterality. Mensa Research Journal*, *16*, 3–31.

Finch, F. (April 2017). *Mathematics in popular culture: The good, the bad, and the bogus.* https://www.wiley.com/network/researchers/topical-food-for-thought/mathematics-in-popular-culture-the-good-the-bad-and-the-bogus

Freeman, F. N., & Carter, T. M. (1924). A new measure of the development of the carpal bones and its relation to physical and mental development. *Journal of Educational Psychology*, *15*(5), 257–270. https://doi.org/10.1037/h0071194

Friedman, H. S., Tucker, J. S., Schwartz, J. E., Martin, L. R., Tomlinson-Keasey, C., Wingard, D. L., & Criqui, M. H. (1995). Childhood conscientiousness and longevity: Health behaviors and cause of death. *Journal of Personality and Social Psychology*, *68*(4), 696–703. https://doi.org/10.1037/0022-3514.68.4.696

Galton, F. (1865). Hereditary character and talent. *Macmillan's Magazine*, *12*, 157–166. https://galton.org/essays/1860-1869/galton-1865-macmillan-hereditary-talent.html

Gillham, N. M. (2001). Sir Francis Galton and the birth of eugenics. *Annual Review of Genetics*, *35*, 83–101.

Goldstein, H. (2012). Francis Galton, measurement, psychometrics and social progress. *Assessment in Education: Principles, Policies & Practice*, *19*(2), 147–158.

Gomez-Pinilla, F. & Hillman, C. (2013). The influence of exercise on cognitive abilities. *Comprehensive Physiology*, *3*(1), 403–428. https://doi.org/10.1002/cphy.c110063

Graham, E. K., Bastarache, E. D., Milad, E., Turiano, N. A., Cotter, K. A., & Mroczek, D. K. (2018). Physical activity mediates the association between personality and biomarkers of inflammation. *SAGE Open Medicine*, *6*(9), 1–10. https://doi.org/10.1177/2050312118774990

Gross, M. U. M. (2006). Exceptionally gifted children: Long-term outcomes of academic acceleration and nonacceleration. *Journal for the Education of the Gifted*, 29(4), 404–429. https://doi.org/10.4219/jeg-2006-247

Hall, J. & Suutamm, C. (2020). Numbers and nerds: Exploring portrayals of mathematics and mathematicians in children's media. *International Electronic Journal of Mathematics Education*, 15(3), em0591. https://doi.org/10.29333/iejme/8260

Halpern, D. F., Havilland, M. G., & Killian, C. D. (1998). Handedness and sex differences in intelligence: Evidence from the medical admission test. *Brain and Cognition*, 38(1), 87–101. https://doi.org/10.1006/brcg.1998.1021

Hollingworth, L. S. (1926). *Gifted children: Their nature and nurture*. Macmillan.

Jenni, O. G., Chaouch, A., Caflisch, J., & Rousson, V. (2013). Infant motor milestones: Poor predictive value for outcome of healthy children. *Acta Paediatrica*, 102(4), e181–e184. https://doi.org/10.1111/apa.12129

Jolly, J. L. (2018). *A history of American gifted education*. Routledge.

Jolly, J. L. & Bruno, J. (2010). Historical perspectives: The public's fascination with prodigious youth. *Gifted Child Today*, 33(2), 61–65. https://doi.org/10.1177/107621751003300214

Karnes, F. A. & Lewis. J. (1995). Examining the media coverage of gifted education: Study tracks trends in major news reports of issues affecting gifted education. *Gifted Child Today*, 18, 28–30. https://doi.org/10.1177/107621759501800609

Karpinski, R. I., Kinase Kolb, A. M., Tetreault, N. A., & Borowski, T. B. (2018). High intelligence: A risk factor for psychological and physiological overexcitabilities. *Intelligence*, 66, 8–23. https://doi.org/10.1016/j.intell.2017.09.001

Kern, M. L. & Friedman, T. (2011). Personality and pathways of influence of physical health. *Social and Personality Compass*, 5(1), 76–87. https://doi.org/10.1111/j.1751-9004.2010.00331.x

Lubinski, D. (2016). From Terman to today: A century of findings on intellectual precocity. *Review of Educational Research*, 86(4), 900–944. https://doi.org/10.3102/0034654316675476

Lutostanski, S. (2018). Sports that work for gifted children. *Parenting for High Potential*, 7(1), 9–11.

Mannino, D. M., Homa, D. M., Akinbami, L. J., Moorman, J. E., & Gwynn, C. (2002). *Surveillance for Asthma – United States, 1980–1999*. Retrieved 3/13/2021 from https://www.cdc.gov/mmwr/preview/mmwrhtml/ss5101a1.htm

Mapp, K. L. & Kuttner, P. J. (2013). *Partners in education: A dual capacity-building framework for family-school partnerships*. SEDL.

Michel, G. F., Nelson, E. L., Babik, I., Campbell, J. M., & Marcinowski, E. C. (2013). Multiple trajectories in the developmental psychobiology of human handedness. *Advances in Child Development and Behavior*, 45, 227–260. https://doi.org/10.1016/B978-0-12-397946-9.00009-9

National Institute of Allergy and Infectious Disease (2017) *Autoimmune diseases*. Retrieved 8/25/2021 from https://www.niaid.nih.gov/diseases-conditions/autoimmune-diseases

Papadatou-Pastou, M. & Tomprou, D. (2015). Intelligence and handedness: Meta-analyses of studies on intellectually disabled, typically developing, and gifted individuals. *Neuroscience & Behavioral Reviews*, 56, 151–165. https://doi.org/10.1016/j.neubiorev.2015.06.017

Petticrew, M. P., Lee, K., & McKee, M. (2012). Type A behavior pattern and coronary heart disease: Philip Morris's "Crown Jewel", *American Journal of Public Health*, 102(11), 2018–2025. https://doi.org/10.2105/AJPH.2012.300816

Platts-Mills, T. A. E. (2015). The allergy epidemics: 1870–2010. *Journal of Allergy and Clinical Immunology*, 136(1), 3–313. https://doi.org/10.1016/j.jaci.2015.03.048

Rochefort, C., Hoerger, M., Turiano, N. A., & Duberstein, P. (2018). Big Five personality and health in adults with and without cancer. *Journal of Health Psychology*, 24(11), 1494–1504. https://doi.org/10.1177/1359105317753714

Strickhouser, J. E., Zell, E., & Krizan, Z. (2017). Does personality predict health and well-being? A metasynthesis. *Health Psychology*, *36*(8), 797–801. https://doi.org/10.1037/hea0000475

Tandon, P. S., Tovar, A., Jayasuriya, A. T., Welker, E., Schober, D. J., Copeland, K., Dev, D. A., Murriel, A. L., Amso, D., & Ward, D. S. (2016). The relationship between physical activity and diet and young children's cognitive development: A systematic review. *Preventive Medicine Reports*, *3*, 379–390. https://doi.org/10.1016/j.pmedr.2016.04.003

Tannenbaum, A. J. (1983). *Gifted children: Psychological and educational perspectives.* Macmillan.

Terman, L. M. (1925). *Genetic studies of genius: Vol 1. Mental and physical traits of a thousand gifted children.* Stanford University Press.

Terman, L. M. & Oden, M. H. (1947). *The gifted child grows up: Twenty-five years' follow-up for a superior group.* Stanford University Press.

Terman, L. M. & Oden, M. H. (1959). *Genetic studies of genius: Vol. 5. The gifted group at mid-life.* Stanford University Press.

Theophanous, C., Modjtahedi, B. S., Batech, M., Marlin, D. S., Luong, T. Q., & Fong, D. S. (2018). Myopia prevalence and risk factors in children. *Clinical Ophthalmology*, *12*, 1581–1587. https://doi.org/10.2147/OPTH.S164641

Vaivre-Douret, L. (2011). Developmental and cognitive characteristics of "high-level potentialities" (highly gifted) children. *International Journal of Pediatrics*. https://doi.org/10.1155/2011/420297

Vaivre-Douret, L., Lalanne, C., Charlemaine, C., Cabrol, D., Keita, G., Sebbane, O., Golse, B., & Falissard, B., (2010). Relationship between growth status at birth and motor and cognitive development in a French sample of gifted children. *Revue européenne de psychologie appliquée*, *60*, 1–9.

Vialle, W. J. (2007). Pink or Paris? Giftedness in popular culture. *Australasian Journal of Gifted Education*, *16*, 5–11.

Whalley L. J. & Deary I. J. (2001) Longitudinal cohort study of childhood IQ and survival up to age 76. *British Medical Journal*, *322*, 1–5. https://doi.org/10.1136/bmj.322.7290.819

Wilson, H. (April 2019). Twice-exceptionality in early childhood academically talented children using the ECLS-B [Conference presentation]. AERA 2019 Convention, Toronto, ON, Canada.

Whipple, G. M. (1924). *The twenty-third yearbook of the National Society for the Study of Education, Part I*. Public School Publishing.

Wraw, C., Deary, I. J., Gale, C. R., & Der, G. (2015). Intelligence in youth and health at age 50. *Intelligence*, *53*, 23–32. https://doi.org/10.1016/j.intell.2015.08.001

Wraw, C., Der, G., Gale, C., R., & Deary, I. J. (2018). Intelligence in youth and health behaviours in middle age. *Intelligence*, *69*, 71–86. https://doi.org/10.1016/j.intell.2018.04.005

Ziegler, A., Chandler, K. L., Vialle, W., & Stoeger, H. (2017). Exogenous and endogenous learning resources in the Actiotope model of giftedness and its significance for gifted education. *Journal for the Education of the Gifted*, *40*(4), 310–333. https://doi.org/10.1177/0162353217734376

CHAPTER 3

The psychology of learning

Modalities and their application to advanced academics

James Bishop and Julia Hujar

The main objective of education is the nurture and development of human potential. This potential is achieved, individually and collectively, through the process of learning. Although there are many theories on how people learn, the most effective are those that have been subject to rigorous research. In this chapter, we will review how three research-based theories and approaches to learning can be interpreted and applied to children with advanced academic potential. The three theories selected for this chapter include: (1) Behaviorism; (2) Social Cognitive Theory; and (3) Constructivism.

WHAT IS LEARNING?

Just what is learning? It is a question that is often taken for granted, but an important question that is foundational to our understanding of education. Surprisingly, there is little consensus in the educational field regarding a definitive definition of learning. Lachman (1997) defines learning as "the process by which a relatively stable modification in stimulus–response relations is developed as a consequence of functional environmental interaction via the senses." De Houwer and colleagues (2013) define learning as "changes in the behavior of an organism that are the result of regularities in the environment of that organism." Harel and Koichu (2010) describe learning as "a multi-dimensional and multi-phase phenomenon occurring when individuals attempt to solve what they view as a problem." These are just a few examples of the many competing definitions of learning.

For the purposes of this chapter, we will focus on a simple and functional definition of learning: learning is the process by which a person gains new insight, ability, or wisdom through practice or experience. Learning results from an exposure to stimuli, and how that exposure occurs can significantly impact the success of learning (Crawford & Snider, 2000). This view of learning as the interaction between stimulus and response began with the rise of Behaviorism as a dominant theory of psychology.

DOI: 10.4324/9781003025443-4

BEHAVIORISM

Behaviorism, as indicated by its name, focuses on the *behavior* of humans and animals. It takes a mechanistic view of organismic behavior, arguing that human and animal behavior is the result of reflexive responses to stimuli or driven by conditioned responses that are influenced by motivational operations and controlling stimuli. Initial work connecting environmental information to reflexes began with biologists, most famously Ivan Pavlov and his experiments with stimuli that led to salivation reflexes in dogs (Pavlov, 1928). Classical conditioning involves biological reflexes that are generally applicable to all humans. A different form of conditioning, operant conditioning, is more relevant to understanding individual differences in development.

Behaviorism as a methodological science originated with psychologists such as John B. Watson. Methodological behaviorism eschewed the internal workings of the mind and focused on the outward physical behaviors of subjects, as Watson believed that only motor behaviors could be objectively observed (Watson, 1994). In his book, *The Psychological Care of Infant and Child* (Watson, 1928/1972), Watson argued that the child's environment was predominantly responsible for the person they were to become, and that parents and teachers should take an analytical, not emotional, approach to rearing children. Watson was so certain of the developmental efficacy of his approach that he made the following statement in his 1958 book *Behaviorism*:

> Give me a dozen healthy infants, well-formed, and my own specified world to bring them up in and I'll guarantee to take any one at random and train him to become any type of specialist I might select – doctor, lawyer, artist, merchant-chief and, yes, even beggar-man and thief, regardless of his talents, penchants, tendencies, abilities, vocations, and race of his ancestors. I am going beyond my facts and I admit it, but so have the advocates of the contrary and they have been doing it for many thousands of years.
>
> (Watson, 1958)

B. F. Skinner expanded upon Watson's ideas, including rather than excluding cognition and emotions in the spectrum of observable behaviors. Taking psychologist Edward Thorndike's law of effect (which holds that behaviors are more likely to be repeated if the consequences are pleasant) as a principal component, Skinner's application of behaviorism to the activity of learning focused on shaping the learner's behavior through the use of repetition and reinforcement (Iversen, 1992). He referred to this process as operant conditioning. In operant conditioning, knowledge is fundamentally a collection of conditioned responses to environmental stimuli. The acquisition of a defined body of knowledge (conditioning) is achieved through a process of repetition and reinforcement.

Behavior can be changed through modifying the environment in several ways. If one is wanting to increase a behavior the intervention is called reinforcement and if one wants to decrease a behavior it is called punishment. You can change environments by either adding or subtracting stimuli. Adding and subtracting are described as "positive" and "negative" reinforcement and punishment. If you *add* something into the environment to *increase* a behavior it is called positive reinforcement and if you *subtract* something from the environment to *increase* a behavior it is negative reinforcement. The same with punishment, there is positive and negative depending on whether you *added* or *subtracted* something from the environment to *decrease* a behavior. Positive reinforcement is sometimes called reward because a favorable stimulus is given. Negative reinforcement in education can be seen when students do not have to take an exam if their semester grade is an A. The stress of taking an exam is removed from their environment in order to increase the behavior of studying to maintain an A average. Positive punishment would be assigning worksheets to be completed silently as a result of receiving a report that your students misbehaved for a substitute teacher. Negative punishment would be taking away a privilege, such as requiring students to sit according to homeroom during lunch rather than sitting with their friends from other classes, in order to decrease the behavior of dropping trash on the floor of the lunchroom.

FIELD NOTE 3.1

Erin Morris Miller

Parent and Psychology Professor

I allow a great deal of freedom for my children but there are some behaviors that must be punished. When my son was 4, he did not want his 1 year old sister to follow him. He would push her and run. I informed him that he could be alone in his own room, but if he pushed his sister he would have to go to time-out. He looked at me for a moment and then said, "I agree." He pushed her and then went to the time-out spot. Afterwards, time-out as a deterrent for anything did not work. Compliance was more of a punishment for him than being in time-out. I had to figure out something that was stronger than his own willpower. He loved Star Wars early readers and he could spell his name. I created a chart with four levels: (1) Luke Skywalker: (2) Obi-Wan Kenobi: (3) Darth Vader: and (4) Emperor Palpatine. Each was accompanied by a picture and then I made a picture of him with his name. If he misbehaved, I would tell him that I would have to move him off the Luke Skywalker onto a lower level. The thought of it bothered him enough to get him to be basically civil to his sister. You just need to find the right reward/punishment!

Applying behaviorism in advanced academics

While behaviorism and operant conditioning may not seem to be ideal ways to educate high-ability students, operant conditioning techniques are powerful ways to change behavior and apply to all people equally. The key is to consider what is specifically rewarding or aversive to a particular student. This may be similar or different for advanced learners as compared to typically developing students depending on the context. For example, all humans need to feel that their work is valued and appreciated, and children with high cognitive ability are not different in this regard. Praise can be expressed verbally or in writing, such as telling a student "You did a really good job, and I am proud of you!" or writing "Great job!" on a completed test. But take care that the work that you praise is actually challenging for the student. It can be confusing to be praised for products that require little effort. You want to reinforce the satisfaction that comes from hard work, not what the student may see as just rote work they completed, just to get it done.

It is understandable that sometimes for reasons of documentation or the meeting of curricular standards, the advanced learner must complete work that is not challenging or is a repetition of previously mastered content or skills. In this case, it may be more cognitively rewarding for the student to resist and engage in off-task behavior than complete the work. The intellectual stimulation of an argument or pursuing an esoteric tangent is much more enjoyable than boredom. In this case, negative reinforcement can be implemented. Negative reinforcement is when you remove an aversive stimulus in order to increase a behavior (remember: the negative means subtract.) Make an agreement that if the advanced student can quickly and cheerfully document their mastery, they can take part in a preferred activity, such as time on a tablet or computer, playing a game, or reading a book.

Tangible reinforcers can also be a good motivator for learning. One tool for enhancing extrinsic motivation is the token economy system. A token economy system is a system of rewards that can be earned for desirable performance. Rewards are generally categorized in terms of perceived value, with rewards having higher perceived value more difficult to achieve. Although a token economy often works well for the typically developing student, it can be counterproductive with advanced students. The rewards need to be difficult to achieve. One system that often falls apart is rewarding students for each book they read. An advanced and ravenous reader will collect an inordinate amount of tokens. One way to make a token economy work is to create a system where once a certain goal is met, the students must "level-up" to a more challenging task in order to get the next reward. Model your reinforcement schedule like a videogame – once you conquer the first "boss" each of the next are more and more challenging. This kind of reward system is a powerful way to promote learning and is one reason why videogames are able to command consistent engagement.

There are some challenges to the utilization of a behavioristic/operant conditioning approach in the education of high-ability youth. One challenge is that the motivation to learn is generally extrinsic for the learner. Grades are the key extrinsic reward given to students for hard work. All students will vary in how rewarding they find high grades and how punishing they find low grades. For many academically advanced students, grades are very rewarding and they will do anything in order to maintain a high GPA. But there are also equally cognitively advanced students for which grades are not particularly rewarding or are not more rewarding than the pain caused by not following their own interests and passions. Operant conditioning in the classroom is largely achieved through positive reinforcement, and grades alone may not be enough to motivate some high-ability youth.

SOCIAL COGNITIVE THEORY

Social cognitive theory is a theory of human development advanced by a psychologist Alfred Bandura. Like behaviorism, social cognitive theory stresses the importance of the environment in the development of knowledge and behavior. However, social cognitive theory emphasizes that behavior is learned from the environment through observing the modeled behavior of others. Bandura called this form of learning *observational learning* (Bandura, 1986). Models can be found in the learner's immediate environment or can be found through media sources. Learners observe these models and encode the models' behavior into their memory. The more similar the model is to the learner and/or the higher the model's status, the more likely the learner is to imitate the observed behavior.

Like operant conditioning, subsequent reinforcement or punishment helps determine whether the learner continues to imitate the behavior. In addition to their own reinforcement, the learner will also observe how others respond to the model's behavior and take cues from those observations. Through this process, the learner develops schema to organize knowledge and guide cognition and behavior. Unlike behaviorism, social cognitive theory stresses the agency of the learner, which occurs via the learner's control of their environment, another agent acting on their behalf, or a group of agents working toward achieving common interests.

According to Bandura (1977), the likelihood of observational learning depends on many factors, such as a student's developmental status, how they perceive the prestige and competence of the model, what consequences they see the model receive, how relevant the model's behaviors and consequences are to the student's own goals, and the student's personal sense of self-efficacy. Self-efficacy is the belief a person holds about their own ability to successfully perform a behavior. Self-efficacy may be developed in four ways: (1) personal experience of success, (2) social modeling (demonstrating the task to the learner), (3) improving physical and emotional states, and (4) verbal persuasion (providing encouragement to the learner (Bandura, 1977; Laranjo, 2016).

Applying social cognitive theories in advanced academics

There is a clear connection between social cognitive theory's emphasis on observational learning impacted by agency and self-efficacy and the natural inclination toward introspection and metacognition among advanced students. The importance

EYE FOR DIVERSITY 3.1 INTENTIONALITY AND VARIETY IN APPLICATION OF LEARNING THEORY

Dante D. Dixson

When applying Behaviorism, Social Cognitive Theory, and Constructivism to high-ability students from diverse backgrounds, it is important to intentionally keep their life experiences in mind and implement these theories in a variety of ways. Although it is easier to have the same reinforcers for an entire class or to provide a whole class an opportunity to observe the same model, students from diverse backgrounds may respond differently to these situations due to their different life experiences (as compared to the majority population). The more variety employed when implementing these learning theories with high-ability students (e.g., diverse reinforcements, models, and learning experiences), the higher the chances that all students will engage with the learning opportunity and respond as theorized.

of creating opportunities for high-ability learners to observe and model their behavior from those perceived as having similar or higher ability is emphasized by this theory of learning.

Social cognitive theory highlights the need for social and academic interaction between same (high) ability peers since individuals are more likely to model their behavior on those who they view as most similar to themselves. The best way to accomplish this is through homogeneous grouping of students with high cognitive ability. Homogeneous grouping can be done in a full-time or part-time setting and can be done within-classes or between-classes. Grouping together students with high cognitive ability has been shown to provide benefits to achievement without costs in academic self-concept (Preckel et al., 2019). A popular service delivery model at the elementary level is the pull-out model, which brings together high-ability students from across a grade level (or multiple grade levels) to one classroom where they receive enrichment, extension, and acceleration opportunities (Burney, 2008). This setting provides a space where students have a perception of similarity within the group and are therefore more likely to model their behavior on one another's. However, homogeneous grouping can also be done at the individual teacher level when creating seating arrangements or cooperative/collaborative learning groups; this type of grouping is called cluster grouping (Gentry, 2014).

At the middle and high school level, it is more likely that homogeneous groups are created when students are assigned to higher leveled courses (e.g., advanced mathematics), thereby creating whole classes of students of similar ability levels; it is still possible at this level for the teacher to create even more refined clusters of high-ability students within the class. If homogeneous grouping is not occurring during a students' normal academic time, it is also possible to seek opportunities outside of school that would provide the high-ability learner with time to interact with same-ability peers. This could be accomplished through summer programming or extracurricular activities with academic focuses (e.g., robotics, chess, etc.). But not all summer and extracurricular programs need to involve same-ability peers. Making connections among a diverse range of individuals and perspectives is associated with increased divergent thinking and creativity (Csermely, 2017). It is important that all students, including students with high ability, have opportunities to interact with both same ability and diverse peers.

Another important way for students with high cognitive ability to partici-pate in observational learning is through appropriately matched mentorships (Callahan & Dickinson, 2014). These relationships provide high-ability students the opportunity to model their behavior on exemplars of achievement or success. Mentoring has several different definitions and practical executions, which vary significantly from one another, and is appropriate for all students. Retrospective studies of eminent adults often identify the role of mentors in their development towards expertise (i.e., Paik et al., 2018; Prado & de Souza Fleith, 2020). Mentor-mentee relationships can vary with respect to the number of mentors, number of mentees, the status hierarchy of the relationship, and the degree of formality in the relationship (Grassinger et al., 2010). These varying structures often result in a mentorship that takes the form of one or more youths paired with one or more adults for the purpose of exploring a specific topic or development of a deeper understanding (e.g., career mentoring, subject mentoring, and athletic mentoring). Mentoring can also take the form of peer-to-peer mentoring for the purpose of developing specific skills. What is different for high-ability students is in matching the students with an equally high-ability mentor who can introduce them to advanced studies or careers.

Career mentoring between an adult professional and a student with high cognitive ability is likely the most popularly conceived of mentor-mentee rela-tionship. In this scenario, a student with high cognitive ability and an interest in pursuing a specific career path is paired with an adult who is successful in that field. This provides the cognitively advanced student with exposure to the field of work, a deeper understanding of processes related to that career, and skills that will benefit the student in their future pursuit of this career. Shadowing a professional throughout their workday is a good starting point, but to be most effective the mentorship should involve reflective conversations after multiple shadowing experiences.

Mentoring relationships between adults and children with high cognitive ability can also be related to particular skills rather than entire career fields. For example, a mentorship program could exist that pairs adults who have extensive backgrounds in mathematics with mathematically advanced students to complete enrichment activities such as computer programming or engineering tasks. It is important for the high-ability student to perceive the mentor as having a high cognitive ability as well as a similarity in interests in order for behavior modeling to have a strong effect on student learning (Grassinger et al., 2010).

Cross-age mentoring is a type of peer-to-peer mentoring that can benefit both young high-ability students as well as older high-ability students. This particular type of mentorship pairs a young (typically elementary aged) student with a mentor from an older grade (potentially upper middle or high school). Through the observation of the mentor, the mentee can model their behavior in a way that results in learning. This type of mentorship would be beneficial for a high-ability youth who is not achieving in accordance with their potential (Besnoy & McDaniel, 2016). The mentor, however, also receives the benefit of the development of their leadership skills and an understanding of the importance of their role as a model for younger students (Gonsoulin et al., 2006; Manning, 2005). Mentors and mentees could participate in a range of activities, such as doing homework or studying simultaneously, participation in community service activities, or even recreational activities (e.g., games, sports, etc.). Although specific programs exist to facilitate these mentorships, it is completely possible to arrange such a relationship on one's own if given the connections.

Informal peer-to-peer mentoring or relationships with students of the same ability level can also be extremely important in the development of skills related to perseverance in the face of challenges. Although research results are mixed on the topic, many have indicated that students with high cognitive ability who do not have experience with the importance of hard work to improve performance can show avoidant behavior or self-handicapping when challenged (Chan, 2012; Mofield & Parker Peters, 2018a, 2018b, 2019; Shih, 2011; Snyder et al., 2014). If the students have neither experienced and overcome a challenge nor been able to observe an intelligent individual who has faced a difficult task and overcome it, they may doubt their own abilities when faced with a challenge. However, it is possible to teach students to believe in the importance of hard work to develop one's abilities, so that when they encounter challenges, they respond in an adaptive way that allows them to grow rather than quit. Students can learn coping strategies when working with peers of similar cognitive ability on material that challenges them. Through observation of other high-ability students' behaviors as they persevere through challenges, the students around them can see the positive outcomes related to effort. A positive synergy can develop from the interaction of challenging work and supportive peers. The understanding that effort can lead to academic success is a core part of self-efficacy. Specifically, when a student with high cognitive ability encounters and surmounts a challenge, that student now believes themselves capable of completing that particular task or performing that skill, something which was previously not possible for them. Thus, it is important that cognitively advanced students are presented with curriculum and instruction that is challenging enough to require the same degree of effort being put forth by typically developing students. Ultimately, challenging work leads to the development of self-regulatory skills.

CONSTRUCTIVISM

Cognitive constructivism

French psychologist, Jean Piaget developed a theory of learning called cognitive constructivism. Piaget explained that learning is a result of an individual constructing meaning through their own reflection on the world they observe. Piaget theorized that the building block of understanding is the schema, or a mental model of what the world is like. The learner then reflects upon challenges to their understanding through assimilation or accommodation (Bond, 2012).

Assimilation occurs under two situations. One, when a learner is faced with an environment that does not challenge their current level of understanding and therefore the new information can be combined seamlessly with prior understanding. In the context of learning, this occurs when students are faced with content they have already mastered. The other is when the learner is not at an appropriate developmental stage to understand a concept and modifies the information to fit their current schema. When the learner is ready they can change their schema in some way based on new information that does not fit within their mental model; they accommodate or adapt their prior schema to fit. These processes occur through student's individual cognitive reflection, the result of which is learning (Bond, 2012).

For high-ability learners, this theory of learning reiterates the importance of exposure to advanced content. Students with high cognitive ability need to be presented with challenges so that they have the chance to adapt and accommodate new information into their previously held schema. Additionally, cognitive constructivism places importance on the individual learner engaging in reflection on their own world and schema. This emphasis on the individual is one of the most important differences between cognitive constructivism and social constructivism, which will be covered in the next section.

Applying cognitive constructivism in advanced academics

Through a cognitive constructivist lens, learning for students with high cognitive ability can be enhanced through self-directed or independent learning where they are given varying degrees of choice and freedom. There are several learning models that have been thoroughly explored in the advanced academics literature (Westberg & Leppien, 2018). A few examples are Treffinger's (1975) *Self-Directed Model*, Renzulli's (1976) *Enrichment Triad Model*, or Feldhusen and Kolloff's (1978) *Three Stage Model*. Although each has their differences, they share the importance of student choice and independent exploration. Each of these methods of structuring independent study aligns with the emphasis on individual construction of meaning that dominates cognitive constructivist learning theory.

Treffinger's (1975) self-directed learning model suggested four phases: (1) identification of goals and objectives: (2) assess entering behavior: (3) identify and implement instructional procedures: and (4) assessment of performance. Each of these phases requires the teacher to serve as a facilitator who presents students with choices. For example, a teacher may realize that one (or a few) of their students has high ability and interest in a particular unit. The teacher could then work with the student(s) to set independent learning goals, pre-assess understanding in order to guide activities, help the student structure their independent exploration, and create a culminating activity that allows the student to demonstrate their learning.

As the name implies, Feldhusen and Kolloff's (1978) Three-Stage Model contains three phases, which allow teachers to progressively increase the difficulty and independence of student thinking and learning. The first phase consists of activities designed to strengthen divergent and convergent thinking skills; the second phase expands to more creative thinking and problem-solving skills; and the third phase involves student-chosen independent learning. The activities completed in the final phase require students to take the lead and create some sort of end product that demonstrates the learning that occurred during the time spent independently exploring their chosen topic.

One of the most well-known enrichment models for advanced learners is Renzulli's (1976) Enrichment Triad Model. This model also consists of three sections: (1) general exploratory activities: (2) group training activities: and (3) individual projects. The final phase can be conducted in sequence with the other phases or separately. This section of the model requires teachers to facilitate the student's identification of a topic or problem of interest, guide acquisition of skills for authentic exploration of the topic or problem, and help the student determine an appropriate end product (Renzulli, 1977).

Social constructivism

Social constructivism has similarities to and differences from both social cognitive theory as well as cognitive constructivism. In contrast to social cognitive theory, social constructivism emphasizes the importance of interaction, particularly through verbal exchanges, over individual observation and reflection. Social constructivist theory focuses on construction of knowledge through interaction with more knowledgeable others rather than the individual construction of knowledge that characterizes cognitive constructivism. Social constructivism was developed by Soviet psychologist Lev Vygotsky, who argued that all cognitive functions have their root in social interactions and that knowledge is developed collaboratively within a community (Vygotsky, 1978).

Vygotsky identified two levels of development: (1) actual and (2) potential. Actual development is the degree of development already achieved by the learner, and potential development is the degree of development a learner may achieve in a social context with at least one "more knowledgeable other" guiding them. Vygotsky coined the phrase "zone of proximal development" (ZPD) to describe the area of potential knowledge where interactions promote cognitive development. Co-construction of knowledge occurs in this zone during interactions between the learner and at least one more knowledgeable other. Vygotsky also believed that language and culture played essential roles in the development of knowledge. The use of language, either spoken or written, allows interaction to occur in such a way that facilitates the creation of new ideas, solves problems, or develops understanding. Additionally, the nuanced understanding of culture and norms within a group allow communication to more effectively construct understanding.

Applying social constructivism in advanced academics

In contrast to the cognitive constructivist models that focused on individual exploration, social constructivist models focus on meaningful interactions. The best way to craft these interactions so that learning is enhanced is through structured collaborative learning experiences.

It is important to first understand the difference between cooperative and collaborative learning. Cooperative learning can be defined as a situation in which a heterogeneous group must work together to complete a task; often each group member has a specific role to play. The effects of cooperative learning for advanced students have been neutral, though some older studies have shown that gifted students do not prefer this learning setting since it frequently involves the most able student(s) tutoring the less able or completing the entire task on their own (Cera Guy et al., 2019; Matthews, 1992; Patrick et al., 2005). Patrick and colleagues (2005) explained that cooperative learning typically involves reproduction of knowledge, whereas collaborative learning involves both reproduction and production of knowledge. This additional step raises the level of thinking required for the group tasks. Collaborative learning, therefore, emphasizes a conceptual learning developed through dialogue, which directly aligns with the social constructivist learning theory. Additionally, although collaborative learning can be accomplished with heterogeneous groups, homogeneous grouping is still preferable for high-ability learners (Walker et al., 2011).

One example of a specific type of collaborative learning that has been demonstrated numerous times as an effective method of learning for students with high cognitive ability is the Problem-Based Learning framework (PBL; Gallagher & Gallagher, 2013). Stepien and Pyke (1997) adapted this PBL framework from its initial use in medical schools to one that can be used in K-12 settings. Their model includes five phases: (1) problem engagement, (2) inquiry and investigation, (3) problem definition, (4) problem resolution, and (5) problem debriefing. PBL requires teachers to serve as a coach, while the students are the primary stakeholders (Horak & Galluzzo, 2017). Although PBL can be conducted by students independently, the final phases are best suited for discussion that leads to the co-construction of knowledge. The most challenging part of implementing PBL is finding a truly ill-structured problem. This problem needs to be real and not have one singular, simple solution, but several multi-faceted complex and realistic solutions. See Hmelo-Silver (2004) for an in-depth description of the application of PBL.

FIELD NOTE 3.2

Kelly Hedrick, Ph.D.

Principal
Old Donation School
Edward E. Brickell Academy for Advanced Academics and Arts

When you examine the characteristics of gifted learners including: advanced levels of abstraction, early recognition of complex concepts and patterns, and the ability to analyze and synthesize beyond that of their same-aged peers, the design elements of curriculum and instruction are clear. At Old Donation School (ODS), teachers unpack the state and local standards to establish learning targets for each unit that is concept-based. Using discipline-based and thematic concepts (i.e., grade level themes), ODS teachers establish learning outcomes that provide a rich and dynamic foundation for learning.

With sophisticated concepts organizing the learning goals for every unit, teachers at ODS work collaboratively to identify the teaching and learning methods that align with the goals and the needs of students. For example, an examination of the scholarship associated with William and Mary curriculum reveals the use of models for thinking and for production, such as Paul's Reasoning Model and Literature Webs. Another example of a model that supports meeting the needs of gifted students is the use of Creative Problem Solving 2.0 (CPS). Here, students work in open-ended situations to solve real problems using the CPS model inclusive of the generating and the focusing tools. One final example of methods prevalent in gifted education is problem-based learning (PBL). Teachers at each grade level at ODS involve students in a unit organized using PBL. The goals are to solve an authentic problem applying thinking skills in advanced content using multiple and varied resources. The teachers at ODS utilize the experiences of Shelagh Gallagher as outlined in her work with gifted learners to ensure appropriate use of the methods that work best for this model with these children. To challenge and to engage gifted learners, the team at ODS understands curriculum and instruction methods must be derived from the literature in the field. It grounds our practice.

Another learning model that aligns well with social constructivist theory is Complex Instruction (Cohen & Lotan, 2014; Tomlinson, 2018). Although homogeneous grouping of high cognitive ability students is preferred, it is not always possible. The complex instruction framework provides ways for heterogeneous groups to work together in ways that are beneficial and result in the co-construction of knowledge for learners of varying abilities. This learning model is complex and multifaceted for both teachers and learners, therefore, only a brief overview will be provided (see Cohen & Lotan, 2014 for a full description). Similar to the importance of an ill-structured problem in PBL, complex instruction requires "group worthy tasks." These types of tasks are "organized around big ideas, ... call on multiple intellectual abilities, ... are open ended, ... are designed to be rich and complex, ... require both student interdependence and individual accountability, ... and provide clearly stated criteria for both process and product" (Tomlinson, 2018, p. 9). These group tasks must be ones that the high-ability learner could not accomplish on their own and that requires many different skill sets.

CONCLUSION

This chapter has provided an overview of behaviorism, social cognitive theory, and constructivism (both cognitive and social) as well as practical applications for each theory of learning to advanced academics. Although it may seem that some of these theories of learning have competing priorities, it is important to understand that each of these have their own value in certain situations.

Application of behaviorism to advanced academics can come in various forms. Principles of behaviorism are based on reinforcement and punishment. Verbal praise could be provided as a positive reinforcement for effort for persevering through challenging tasks, assuming the result is an increase in student effort. Care should be taken to ensure praise is not being provided for low-effort tasks since reinforcement aims to increase the target behavior. A negative reinforcer could be the removal of aversive stimuli (e.g., extra work) after demonstration of mastery.

In social cognitive learning theory, the process of learning occurs through observation of other high-ability peers or adults and reflection on these observations. Therefore, it is most appropriate that students of high cognitive ability are grouped homogeneously with other like-ability peers so that they have the opportunity to model their learning on others. Additionally, mentorships between high-ability youth and either adults or older high-ability youth would provide students with the opportunity to observe and reflect on those models, resulting in learning.

Constructivist learning theory dictates that knowledge is constructed, though cognitive constructivism emphasizes the individual construction of knowledge and social constructivism emphasizes group interaction for the co-creation of knowledge. Models of learning that would follow a cognitive constructivist theory would be the various ways of engaging high-ability students in self-directed learning or independent study. Social constructivist theory would be applied through the use of learning frameworks such as PBL or complex instruction; each requiring collaborative learning through discussion and research into ill-structured problems or group worthy tasks.

This chapter has focused on academic applications and implications. However, learning theory applies to all aspects of life. Gifted and other cognitively advanced students are not different from any other students in this respect. Operant conditioning and modeling affect non-academic behaviors; for example, teens are rewarded by peers for following trends and modeling their behavior after celebrities. Schema learning applies to social schemas and stereotype learning as well academic content. There is no evidence to suggest that cognitively advanced individuals differ in the processes of social learning. Also every child is unique. It is important to apply each of these theories in ways that best suit the needs of the particular high-ability students with which you are working. Although these theories and applications have all been thoroughly researched and the evidence supporting them has been documented with high-ability students, finding what works best for individual students with high cognitive ability may still be a process of trial and error. These theories and applications should serve as starting points for your exploration.

REFERENCES

Bandura, A. (1977). Self-efficacy: Toward a unifying theory of behavioral change. *Psychological Review*, 84(2), 191–215. https://doi.org/10.1037/0033-295x.84.2.191

Bandura, A. (1986). *Social foundations of thought and action: A social cognitive theory.* Prentice-Hall, Inc.

Bond, T. G. (2012) Piaget's learning theory. In Seel N.M. (Eds) *Encyclopedia of the Sciences of Learning*. Springer. https://doi.org/10.1007/978-1-4419-1428-6_39

Burney, V. H. (2008). Applications of social cognitive theory to gifted education. *Roeper Review*, 30(2), 130–139. https://doi.org/10.1080/02783190801955335

Besnoy, K. D. & McDaniel, S. C. (2016). Going up in dreams and esteem: Cross-age mentoring to promote leadership skills in high school-age gifted students. *Gifted Child Today*, 39(1), 18–30. https://doi.org/10.1177/1076217515613386

Callahan, C. M. & Dickinson, R. K. (2014). Mentors and mentorships. In J. A. Plucker and C. M. Callahan (Eds), *Critical issues and practices in gifted education* (2nd ed., pp. 413–426). Prufrock Press, Inc.

Cera Guy, J. N. M., Williams, J. M., & Shore, B. M. (2019). High- and otherwise-achieving students' expectations of classroom group work: An exploratory empirical study. *Roeper Review*, 41, 166–184. https://doi.org/10.1080/02783193.2019.1622166

Chan, D. W. (2012). Life satisfaction, happiness, and the growth mindset of healthy and unhealthy perfectionists among Hong Kong Chinese gifted students. *Roeper Review*, 34(4), 224–233. https://doi.org/10.1080/02783193.2012.715333

Cohen, E. & Lotan, R. (2014). *Designing groupwork: Strategies for the heterogeneous classroom* (3rd ed.). Teachers College Press.

Crawford, D. B. & Snider, V. E. (2000). Effective mathematics instruction the importance of curriculum. *Education and Treatment of Children*, 23(2), 122–142. https://www.jstor.org/stable/42940521

Csermely, P. (2017). The network concept of creativity and deep thinking: Applications to social opinion formation and talent support. *Gifted Child Quarterly*, 61(3), 194–201. https://doi.org/10.1177/0016986217701832

De Houwer, J., Barnes-Holmes, D., & Moors, A. (2013). What is learning? On the nature and merits of a functional definition of learning. *Psychonomic Bulletin & Review*, 20(4), 631–642. https://doi.org/10.3758/s13423-013-0386-3

Feldhusen, J. F. & Kolloff, M. B. (1978). A three-stage model for gifted education. *Gifted Child Today*, 4, 15–18. https://doi.org/10.1177/107621758801100104

Gallagher, S. A. & Gallagher, J. J. (2013). Using problem-based learning to explore unseen academic potential. *Interdisciplinary Journal of Problem-Based Learning*, 7(1), 111–131. https://doi.org/10.7771/1541-5015.1322

Gentry, M. (2014). Cluster grouping. In J. A. Plucker and C. M. Callahan (Eds), *Critical issues and practices in gifted education* (2nd ed., pp. 109–117). Prufrock Press, Inc.

Gonsoulin, W., Ward, R. E., & Figg, C. (2006). Learning by leading: Using best practices to develop leadership skills in at-risk and gifted populations. *Education*, 126, 690–701.

Grassinger, R., Porath, M. & Ziegler, A. (2010) Mentoring the gifted: a conceptual analysis, *High Ability Studies*, 21(1), 27–46, https://doi.org/10.1080/13598139.2010.488087

Harel, G. & Koichu, B. (2010). An operational definition of learning. *The Journal of Mathematical Behavior*, 29(3), 115–124. https://doi.org/10.1016/j.jmathb.2010.06.002

Hmelo-Silver, C. E. (2004). Problem-based learning: What and how do students learn? *Educational Psychology Review*, 16(3), 235–266. https://doi.org/1040-726X/04/0900-0235/0

Horak, A. K. & Galluzzo, G. R. (2017) Gifted middle school students' achievement and perceptions of science classroom quality during problem-based learning. *Journal of Advanced Academics*, 28(1), 28–50. https://doi.org/10.1177/1932202X16683424

Iversen, I. H. (1992). Skinner's early research: From reflexology to operant conditioning. *American Psychologist*, 47(11), 1318–1328. https://doi.org/10.1037/0003-066x.47.11.1318

Lachman, S. J. (1997). Learning is a process: Toward an improved definition of learning. *The Journal of Psychology*, 131(5), 477–480. https://doi.org/10.1080/00223989709603535

Laranjo, L. (2016). Social media and health behavior change. *Participatory Health Through Social Media*, 83–111. https://doi.org/10.1016/b978-0-12-809269-9.00006-2

Manning, S. (2005). Young leaders: Growing through mentoring. *Gifted Child Today*, 28, 14–20. https://doi.org/10.4219/gct-2005-163

Matthews, M. (1992). Gifted students talk about cooperative learning. *Educational Leadership*, 48–50. http://www.ascd.org/publications/educational-leadership/oct92/vol50/num02/Gifted-Students-Talk-About-Cooperative-Learning.aspx

Mofield, E. L. & Parker Peters, M. (2018b). Shifting the perfectionist mindset: Moving to mindful excellence. *Gifted Child Today*, 41(4), 177–185. https://doi.org/10.1177/1076217518786989

Mofield, E. L. & Parker Peters, M. (2018a). Mindset misconception? Comparing mindsets, perfectionism, and attitudes of achievement in gifted, advanced, and typical students. *Gifted Child Quarterly*, 62(4), 327–349. https://doi.org/10.1177/0016986218758440

Mofield, E. & Parker Peters, M. (2019). Understanding underachievement: Mindset, perfectionism, and achievement attitudes among gifted students. *Journal for the Education of the Gifted*, 42(2), 107–134. https://doi.org/10.1177/0162353219836737

Paik, S. J., Choe, S. M., Otto, W. J., & Rahman, Z. (2018). Learning about the lives and early experiences of notable Asian American women: Productive giftedness, childhood traits, and supportive conditions. *Journal for the Education of the Gifted*, 41(2), 160–192. https://doi.org/10.1177/0162353218763927

Pavlov, I. P. (1928). *Lectures on conditioned reflexes*. (Translated by W.H. Gantt) Allen and Unwin.

Patrick, H., Bangel, N. J., Jeon, K., & Townsend, M. A. R. (2005). Reconsidering the issue of cooperative learning with gifted students. *Journal for the Education of the Gifted*, 29, 90–108. https://doi.org/10.1177/016235320502900105

Prado, R. M. & de Souza Fleith, D. (2020). Talented women in Brazil: Trajectories and career challenges in contemporary society. *Psicologia Em Estudo*, 25, 1–14.

Preckel, F., Schmidt, I., Stumpf, E., Motschenbacher, M., Vogl, K., Scherrer, V., & Schneider, W. (2019). High-ability grouping: Benefits for gifted students' achievement development without costs in academic self-concept. *Child Development*, 90(4), 1185–1201. https://doi.org/10.1111/cdev.12996

Renzulli, J. S. (1976). The enrichment triad model: a guide for developing defensible programs for the gifted and talented. *Gifted Child Quarterly*, 20(3), 303–306. https://doi.org/10.1177/001698627602000327

Renzulli, J. S. (1977). The enrichment triad model: A plan for developing defensible programs for the gifted and talented. *Gifted Child Quarterly*, 21(2), 227–233. https://doi.org/10.1177/001698627702100216

Shih, S. (2011). Perfectionism, implicit theories of intelligence, and Taiwanese eighth-grade students' academic engagement. *The Journal of Educational Research*, 104(2), 131–142. https://www.jstor.org/stable/10.2307/26505672

Snyder, K. E., Malin, J. L., Dent, A. L., & Linnenbrink-Garcia, L. (2014). The message matters: The role of implicit beliefs about giftedness and failure experiences in academic self-handicapping. *Journal of Educational Psychology*, 106(1), 230–241. https://doi.org/10.1037/a0034553

Stepien, W. J. & Pyke, S. (1997). Designing problem-based learning units. *Journal for the Education of the Gifted*, 20, 380–400. https://doi.org/10.1177/016235329702000404

Tomlinson, C. A. (2018). Complex instruction: A model for reaching up- and out. *Gifted Child Today*, 41(1), 7–12. https://doi.org/10.1177/1076217517735355.

Treffinger, D. J. (1975). Teaching for self-directed learning: A priority for the gifted and talented. *Gifted Child Quarterly*, 19, 46–59. https://doi.org/10.1177/001698627501900109

Vygotsky, Lev (1978). *Mind in Society*. Harvard University Press.

Walker, C. L., Shore, B. M., & French, L. R. (2011). A theoretical context for examining students' preference across ability levels for learning alone or in groups. *High Ability Studies*, 22(1), 119–141. https://doi.org/10.1080/13598139.2011.576082

Watson, J. B. (1928/1972). *Psychological care of infant and child*. Arno Press.

Watson, J. B. (1958). *Behaviorism*. University of Chicago Press.

Watson, J. B. (1994). Psychology as the behaviorist views it. *Psychological Review*, 101(2), 248–253. https://doi.org/10.1037/0033-295X.101.2.248

Westberg, K. L. & Leppien, J. H. (2018). Student independent investigations for authentic learning. *Gifted Child Today*, 41(1), 13–18. https://doi.org/10.1177/1076217517735354

The role of superior attention and memory abilities in the lives of cognitively advanced individuals

Erin M. Miller

An exceptional ability to remember relevant information and procedures, in comparison to typically developing children, is one of the main reasons that children are identified to receive advanced academic instruction in school. Memory is key to academic success and most people find the topic of memory to be fascinating. Why do we remember what we do? Why do we forget? What is happening in our heads that makes this all happen? Throughout the chapter a key concept is the changes that take place in the cerebral cortex as a result of experiences. One of the most interesting things about the human brain is that it has evolved to continually adapt to the environment. The brain changes in its structure and function in response to experiences. Cognitive psychologists call this neuroplasticity. For example, researchers asked a group of people to learn to juggle. The areas of their brains devoted to manual dexterity and hand-eye coordination became denser. The areas went back to their previous density when the individuals stopped practicing. This is the way of the brain. Any change in behavior or ability will always be reflected in the density, function, or connections in the brain. Memory is no different although our knowledge of the exact processes are still incomplete. However, we do have a basic idea of how memory works, and the discussion begins with differences in attention.

ATTENTION

Before any information can become part of memory one must be aware of it. No one can fully process every bit of information coming from the environment; there simply is too much and our resources would be overwhelmed. Our brains have evolved to be selective and choose only that information which is most relevant. As a result, we only process either what we choose to focus upon, or what captures our

DOI: 10.4324/9781003025443-5

attention because it might be important (Broadbent, 1958). Selective attention is like a spotlight or zoom lens that gives focus to one part of the stage at a time (Muller et al., 2003; Posner, 1980). Attention then shifts to another area, and then another. Many people are relatively good at shifting attention, even to the extent that they think they are multi-tasking, or paying attention to several things simultaneously, when in fact, they are just shifting repeatedly from one task to the next. Tasks that are new and challenging require greater effort and attention. After multiple instances of engagement and practice, a task requires fewer cognitive resources. Over time tasks that at first were challenging, such as driving a car, become automatic and do not require as much conscious effort or direct attention.

Intellectually, gifted children are usually exceptional in their ability to direct their attention, sustain it, and shift their focus to important details (Shi et al., 2013). Often it may seem that gifted children are not paying attention at all. This is a common but often erroneous observation shared by parents and teachers in magazines and blogs (e.g., Alloway, 2020; Bainbridge, 2020). But attention depends on context. The brain is stingy with its energy use. People do not use the energy necessary to pay attention unless they must do so to accomplish an engaging task (Lindsay, 2020). In a laboratory setting, working on progressively more difficult challenges to attention, most gifted individuals excel (Duan & Shi, 2014; Zhang et al., 2016). Many gifted children have learned from experience that they do not need to direct all their attention to their teachers or parents in order to learn the content and skills of their grade level. It is a similar situation to observing a top professional athlete, who might not seem fast when they are just walking down the hall. But once on the pitch/field, they are quick and nimble. The attention and memory skills of most gifted children are fast and nimble *when required*. The phrase "pay attention" is quite descriptive. Attention is a limited quantity that we must use or *pay* to be able to process information (Lindsay, 2020). The role of context with regard to attention is recognized within the task commitment element of the three-ring conception of giftedness (Renzulli, 1978; 2016) and also is one factor in the Actiotope Model of Giftedness (Ziegler & Phillipson, 2012). Cognitively advanced children seem to have a larger total capacity for attention, in addition to being able to recognize and rapidly shift their focus to the most important or most relevant aspect of their learning environment.

Despite their observable differences in capacity and efficiency, there is no evidence that attention works differently in cognitively advanced children. Attention is limited, such that even the most adept individuals reach their limit at some point. No one can focus on more than one thing simultaneously, but normal attention allows us to shift our spotlights so quickly that it may seem that we can. Further, among gifted children, there are also individual differences, and as with any general trend, there are always exceptions. One major exception is students who show advanced cognitive abilities and have additionally a diagnosis of an attention deficit disorder. It is not common to have these two exceptionalities, but it is possible and is not just a matter of misdiagnosis or misunderstanding of reactions to boredom (Antshel et al., 2007; Gomez et al., 2019). This small population of students possesses two independent characteristics:

(1) insufficient attentional focus and (2) superior ability in one or more cognitive areas (Mullet & Rinn, 2015). These areas interact, and this interaction can make it difficult to diagnose these individuals correctly, a topic that is given more explanation in the mental health chapter. When working with children who show both deficits of attention and exceptional academic abilities, it is important to focus on their strengths and develop those abilities (Baum et al., 2014). Of course, the interaction between attention and other cognitive abilities is not limited to students with challenges. While clearly important, attention is just the first step in memory. The next step is working memory.

WORKING MEMORY

As soon as one pays attention to something the brain can start initial processing of the stimuli for immediate use. The brain temporarily holds the information visually and auditorily and we begin repeating or revisualizing it to begin committing it to memory (Dosher, 2003). Scientists have differing theories about the exact components, structures, and processes in this step of memory. Some see working memory as a separate ability, while others view it as one component of an overall memory system (Baddeley et al., 2009; Davachi et al., 2004). Regardless of how the different parts of the memory system are labeled, its components include a visual component that involves mental images, an auditory component that involves the interpretation of sound, and mechanisms that integrate these aspects together. The working memory holds relevant information and begins to process it in the face of distraction and while also considering other information.

Working memory is limited in capacity. An easy way to think about this is to visualize trying to remember a phone number. A phone number has ten digits. We repeat these digits until we can either write them down or enter the numbers into our own phone. If someone interrupts this process we might not be successful in recording the number. The numbers in working memory are easily replaced with new information as attention shifts and new content takes the place of the old. Unless it is continuously refreshed, information is held in working memory for less than a minute. Many psychologists think that working memory relies on a temporary chemical change in the brain to hold information (Constantinidis & Klingberg, 2016). The brain is always changing in response to the environment. At first, there are temporary chemical changes and then the structure of the brain can change to record a more permanent memory (Langille & Brown, 2018).

It is common to hear that working memory has a capacity of five to nine "chunks" of information. However, the true state of working memory is more complicated and its capacity at any one time is affected by competing information in the environment, the type of information being processed, the emotions and moods of the individual, and the perceived importance of the information (Drew & Vogel, 2009; Garrison & Schmeichel, 2018). Environmental distractions and stressful emotional states can decrease capacity, while heightened interest/arousal and ease of linking to previously gained knowledge can increase it. There are also individual differences in working memory capacity that appear to be innate.

Intellectually, gifted children tend to have superior working memory ability (Alloway & Elsworth, 2012; Dark & Benbow, 1991; Pesenti et al., 2001). They can hold and process more information than the average child. This may be due to greater capacity, greater efficiency of processing, better strategy use, or a combination of factors (Zhang et al., 2017). A superior ability to maintain the information and avoid distraction, for example, would represent greater efficiency of processing. This advantage, and the advantage of greater capacity, extend, in turn, to all other aspects of memory. A child, who can process more information to start with, can access more information and use it in later steps. The source of these differences is not fully clear, but they likely are due to both genetic and environmental (learned) influences.

The good thing about the learned component (i.e., strategy use) is that it suggests everyone can improve their working memory with practice and training. One way to do this is to organize the information into small chunks rather than attempting to recall it as individual parts. For example, the chain of letters, XCATBINWEB, is hard to remember, but X, CAT, BIN, WEB is much easier. Another way is to practice visualizing information in ways that allow multiple approaches to manipulating knowledge, which is something that many experienced teachers naturally do (e.g., Morin, 2020). The application of multiple ways of processing information is also important for moving information from working memory to the next step: long-term memory.

FIELD NOTE 4.1

Michele, parent and college professor

My daughter had a difficult fourth grade year. She came home crying from frustration and boredom. She craved intellectual challenge and a sense that things mattered and could be fair. I was pleased when her test scores came at the end of the year and I found that she had placed at the 99th percentile in both intelligence and achievement. This qualified her to be tested for placement in the district's gifted classroom the next year! However, again she was declined admission, this time based on a memory subscore on which she had scored at the 60th percentile. The psychologist was annoyed at how the test was being interpreted and told us to bring our daughter back to retake the memory portion of the test. This time she used a computer version of the test that kids often found more interesting. My daughter knew this memory test was keeping her from the program she desperately wanted to get into. She scored at the 99th percentile. We successfully appealed the decision and she was admitted to the program. As we sat in the appeal meeting, one member of the board asked how it was possible that our daughter could score at the 60th percentile one week and 99th the next. I thought to myself, "Have you ever met a gifted child?" When motivated, they rise to the occasion.

LONG-TERM MEMORY

Long-term memory is the organization and storage of memories for later retrieval. Any one "memory" is not a singular thing but rather a distributed collection of pieces. Each part of the memory is stored in the area of the cerebral cortex that processes that aspect (Zola & Squire, 2000). For example, visual information is stored in the occipital lobe in the back of the cerebral cortex. Auditory information is stored in the temporal lobe on the sides of the cortices. Every element has its specific location. Memory is formed from the pattern of connections among these different elements, and each memory has a unique network of connections (Rissman & Wagner, 2012). Initially, when a memory forms the change to the brain is temporary, but over time the change becomes permanent and the memory becomes more stable. The brain is perpetually changing with the inclusion of new experiences and ideas (Guerra-Carrillo et al., 2014). New memories can be formed throughout one's life.

Long-term memory includes three interacting types. These are semantic memories, episodic memories, and procedural/implicit memories (Squire, 1986, 1993). Semantic memories are facts and general knowledge. This is the type of knowledge that is gained through education. Episodic memories are autobiographical, meaning memories of one's own life story. Most people have a better memory for the events of their own lives than for semantic memories (Tulving, 2002). Procedural memories involve learned skills and actions. Riding a bike, driving a car, or playing musical instruments, video games, or sports uses procedural memory. Implicit memories are related to the classical and operant conditioning discussed in the Learning chapter in this volume. These often become automatic over time. This means that you do not have to expend energy trying to remember consciously the steps of the task.

When you want to recall a memory, the different connections are activated and the information is sent to the frontal lobe and constructed into a memory (Feldman & Shastri, 2003; Henke, 2010). What generally falls under "forgetting" can happen for several different reasons. The authors of scholarly reviews such as Sadeh et al. (2014) and Wixted (2004) present several reasons for failures of memory. It is possible that the brain never created the connections to form the memory. It is possible that the network was created, but some of the connections subsequently have become weak and no longer work well. It is also possible that the network triggers some connections that are not relevant, in which case the memory is not accurate. Several of these could be happening at the same time. For example, when you forget where you are parked it is possible that you both were not paying attention in the first place and that there is interference from memories of where you usually park when at that location.

Most people can more easily remember things that are important to them and capture the core ideas. But human memory is not like a video that one can call up and replay. Every time a memory is recalled the brain re-constructs it from its constituent elements, each of which may change over time. As a result, memories are very susceptible to suggestion and distortion (Loftus, 2001). Usually these inaccuracies are minor, but it is not always easy to know which memories are accurate and which are in error. The fact that memories are stored according to how they are processed is why many teachers believe in learning styles, despite the fact that learning styles is a neuromyth. For nearly all learners, retention and recall will be better if there are many different links created through processing the information in several different ways (auditorily, visually, and kinesthetically). There is no need to try to match students to a style: just teach using as many different modalities as appropriate for the materials.

MEMORY AND GIFTED ABILITY

Individuals with exceptional cognitive ability usually excel at long-term memory by definition. Parents and teachers often remark upon the volume of knowledge demonstrated by gifted children and how easy it seems to be for them to learn new information (Inman & Breedlove, 2018). This includes both semantic and episodic knowledge. Procedural memory is independent of semantic and episodic (Squire, 1993). Intellectually gifted children may or may not also be experts at learning new procedural skills. To understand gifted children's memory ability, one needs to understand the normal process for creating and retrieving a memory.

Among the best ways to create a strong memory is to use elaborative encoding (Craik & Lockhart, 1972). This simply means trying to make as many connections among the different aspects of the memory as possible. This can be done by involving multiple senses: sight, sound, touch, etc. One should also use the most sophisticated thinking that is relevant to the task. This includes asking questions about the information, linking the new knowledge to previously stored information, making connections to one's own life, and organizing the information into hierarchies. This results in the Web connecting the parts of the memory having many different connections spread across the entire brain. Activation of one part will result in activation of the rest of the network. As a result, it is easier to remember the information and the memory itself contains a richer set of elements.

The ability to create rich memory networks falls along a continuum. Children identified as gifted or high achieving tend to create rich networks of memory with increased connections and interactions across both sides of their brain (Desco et al., 2011; Geake, 2008; Jin et al., 2007). They generally are able to access their networks with greater speed and efficiency. They select the most important aspects to link together and ignore superfluous details. When retrieving information, they can make connections to other related ideas and knowledge. A helpful metaphor is to imagine the brain as a house. The frontal lobe is a combined kitchen and home office. The kitchen has your recipes and instructions. New recipes can be created there (i.e., memories are assembled and re-assembled each time you remember something). This is also where packages are delivered. This is where new information is first processed. There are different rooms where information is stored. There is a room with big windows where everything visual is stored. A room with an awesome speaker system is where sound-related information is stored. There is an exercise area where muscle and movement related information is stored. There is a specific room for everything. To make something (retrieve a memory) you must zip around and gather all the parts from all the rooms and put it together on your kitchen table and make sense of it. The challenge is to find the right parts and avoid the wrong parts. Next, imagine that things that should go together are connected by paths. These are the paths you have created throughout your life. For some people, the paths are clear and easy. There are even multiple paths to the same information.

Children with advanced cognitive ability likely have a more efficient set-up to their houses. The paths are many and travel around them is rapid. Paths are well maintained. Storage is well organized. There are even little side paths that allow for new combinations of items. The typically developing child's house has all the same rooms, but the paths are not as clearly drawn. Some things are misplaced. Many things no longer have clear paths to reach them. Sometimes packages are delivered but don't make it into the kitchen workspace. Often when they go to gather the "ingredients" for the recipe they grab some wrong things. And the recipe doesn't work out. These kinds of problems also happen for the cognitively advanced child, but not as often. The typically developing child can work hard and create good paths. But it takes much more effort. There are some techniques that anyone can use to improve their memory. For example, the "mind palace" used by Sherlock Holmes in the BBC television series is based on a memory technique used by ancient Greek orators called the method of loci.

But why do gifted children have these great mind houses? Like all aspects of human development, the answer is an interaction between biological and environmental factors. It is likely that there are natural biological differences in mental capacity and speed (Haier et al., 1988; Haier & Jung, 2008). There also seems to be greater or more efficient use of memory strategies in children identified as gifted or talented (Coyle et al., 1998; Zhang et al., 2017). This might be natural or it might be learned, but is likely both. Cognitively advanced children do seem to have superior metacognition as compared to other children (Oppong et al., 2018) meaning they have more insight into their thinking. However, this does not make them better peer tutors (Little, 2018). Superior brain capacity and speed is the core difference between typically developing students and cognitively advanced students. But *why* they have superior abilities is complex and remains incompletely understood.

A key aspect to understanding people in general is that we tend to repeat actions that work and to cease repeating actions that do not work out. An initial difference in ability is compounded over time because success leads to more enjoyment of the task. Let's say a particular child finds it is easy to make connections to her existing knowledge. So, because this is helpful, she keeps making connections. As a result, she gets better and better at making connections. It is unlikely that cognitively advanced children form their memories differently than typically developing children do. But they do seem to create their memories more effectively. Sternberg (2001) suggested that the memory skills and patterns of gifted children are more similar to those of experts who have worked hard to master their field of knowledge, than they are to those of typically developing children.

FIELD NOTE 4.2

Carolyn, parent and teacher

My children are both talented academically, but they differ greatly in their tolerance for sensory input and their ability to filter out distractions. My daughter struggles more when there are too many things drawing her attention. My son seems able to completely block out anything and anyone. Yet they both can marshal their cognitive abilities to be successful in the classroom. They are so different, but both manage to achieve!

One of the ways I helped my children improve their working memory was through games. Not just games that explicitly train memory such as ... Memory. But any game that requires students to scan the environment and keep up with what all the other players are doing. This ranges from simple card games, to fast-action games such as Spot-It (McRobbie, 2018), to long-term strategy games in which one has to try to figure out others' strategies by what they play or discard. For this to be most effective, the skill level among the players needs to be similar so that everyone is challenged.

Few children, even those who are exceptional, are perfect in their memory. When gifted children forget, it is for the same reasons that everyone forgets. Maybe they were not paying enough attention in the first place and never processed the information. Maybe they got distracted. Perhaps the connections were not strong enough, or they have faded over time from disuse. Like everyone, fatigue and stress affect how strong a memory will be. No one is at their best when tired. And like everyone, gifted children can work to improve their memory by learning new strategies. When the academic challenge becomes high enough, at some point even children identified as gifted will need to employ memory strategies to help them retain information. Teachers and parents can help all children learn specific strategies, such as chunking, to help them recall new information more efficiently.

IMPLICATIONS AND APPLICATIONS

The average person remembers information because it is perceived to be of importance or because they have made a particular effort to study and retain that information. This is not necessarily the case with highly able children. They just seem to remember things. This ability to remember things especially well when others would not can be misunderstood, particularly during discussion or often, arguments. Parents and teachers may wonder why something was so important that a gifted child remembers it years later. In fact it probably wasn't more important than other things. But memory doesn't make judgements. It just does what is designed to do, which is recalling information and experiences. It is normal.

That said, exceptional children's superior memory is a double-edged sword. For school and work, having a strong semantic memory ability is great. It allows individuals to excel in school and to make connections that can lead to impressive new ideas. It gives these children the freedom to apply some of their energy elsewhere, rather than having to devote all of it to learning new information. A superior episodic memory can also be great. It is useful to be able to hold on to so many details from the past. But it can be a cause of stress. For most people memories of sad or embarrassing events fade over time. Some cognitively children can recall all the details and feelings as if it just happened. This can make it seem as if they are more emotional or dramatic than children whose memory is more typical. But experiencing emotion is normal when something happens that is, in fact, emotional.

For parents and counselors, simply understanding how a child is different from average, while still quite normal, is helpful. Children with high cognitive ability require guidance in understanding how their memory is both different from and similar to the typically developing child's memory. Sometimes exceptional children's memory abilities can be a source of stress, particularly when others express surprise or confusion regarding the child's abilities. Children may turn to their parents or teachers to help them explain to others what is going on. It is not a super-power, but it sometimes can seem so to others and it often feels that way to the child. Additionally, because their memory usually is so dependable, it can be particularly distressing to the gifted child when it fails them. But like everyone, they have the right to sometimes be wrong. Their memories are not immune to all the possible errors that happen to everyone else. It is important that children understand this. There will be times of challenge, and if they already are comfortable with their own strengths and limitations, then the child will be better able to overcome those challenges.

GOING FORWARD

Although scientists have learned a tremendous amount about attention and memory over the last 100 years, our understanding is still quite limited. New measurement techniques such as those used in the imaging of neural structure and functioning have answered some questions, but so many more questions remain. One of the biggest of these is whether cognitive ability can be attributed to a single overarching factor, a hierarchy of interacting systems, or whether these abilities emerge from separate independent systems. Even though subtests of specific abilities (i.e., digit span, matrix reasoning, vocabulary, and similarities) tend to be positively correlated, which suggests a single overarching factor, it is *possible* for independent abilities to be positively correlated if they all interact with each other (Kovacs & Conway,

2016; Savi et al., 2019). Much more work needs to be completed to answer these questions. Among individuals who demonstrate exceptional academic performance there is a wide variety of cognitive profiles with some having more consistency in their cognitive abilities while others have a more jagged profiles, even if all subtests are above average (Lohman et al., 2008; Rowe et al., 2014).

Researchers are also learning more about the effect of brain plasticity on learning. We already know that gifted students are particularly able in their attention and memory abilities. These children are identified based on these abilities. Current research in neuroscience cannot tell whether the neural differences are due to biological development, experiences, or the interaction between biology and experience. It is difficult to tease these differences apart. But the existence of differences is inevitable. The question that researchers are trying to answer is not *whether* there are differences, but *how* and *where*. Understanding the how and where is the goal for the future.

REFERENCES

Alloway, T. P. (2020, March 22). *Gifted or ADHD? Psychology Today.* https://www.psychologytoday.com/us/blog/keep-it-in-mind/202003/gifted-or-adhd.

Alloway, T. P. & Elsworth, M. (2012). An investigation of cognitive skills and behavior in high ability students. *Learning and Individual Differences, 22,* 891–895. https://doi.org/10.1016/j.lindif.2012.02.001

Antshel, K. M., Faraone, S. V., Stallone, K., Nave, A., Kaufmann, F. A., Doyle, A., Fried, R., Seidman, L., & Biederman, J. (2007). Is attention deficit hyperactivity disorder a valid diagnosis in the presence of high IQ? Results from the MGH Longitudinal Family Studies of ADHD. *Journal of Child Psychology and Psychiatry, 48,* 687–694. https://doi.org/10.1111/j.1469-7610.2007.01735.x.

Baddeley, A. D., Eysenck, M. W., & Anderson, M. C. (2009). *Memory.* Psychology Press.

Bainbridge, C. (2020, November 25). *Why gifted children often have issues with focus.* https://www.verywellfamily.com/inattentiveness-of-gifted-children-1449317.

Baum, S. M., Schader, R. M., & Hébert, T. P. (2014). Through a different lens. *Gifted Child Quarterly, 58*(4), 311–327. https://doi.org/10.1177/0016986214547632

Broadbent, D. E. (1958). *Perception and communication.* Oxford University Press.

Constantinidis, C. & Klingberg, T. (2016). The neuroscience of working memory and training. *Nature Reviews Neuroscience, 17,* 438–449. https://doi.org/10.1038/nrn.2016.43

Coyle, T. R., Read, L. E., Gaultney, J. F., & Bjorklund, D. F. (1998). Giftedness and variability in strategic processing on a multitrial memory task: Evidence for stability in gifted cognition. *Learning and Individual Differences, 10*(4), 273–290. https://doi-org.proxy.library.vcu.edu/10.1016/S1041-6080(99)80123-X

Craik, F. I. M., & Lockhart, R. S. (1972). Levels of processing: A framework for memory research. *Journal of Verbal Learning and Verbal behavior, 11,* 671–684. https://doi.org/10.1016/S0022-5371(72)80001-X

Dark, V. J. & Benbow, C. P. (1991). Differential enhancement of working memory with mathematical versus verbal precocity. *Journal of Educational Psychology, 83,* 48. https://doi.org/10.1037/0022-0663.83.1.48

Davachi, L., Romanski, L. M., Chafee, M. V., & Goldman-Rakic, P. S. (2004). Domain specificity in cognitive systems. In M. S. Gazzaniga (Ed.), *The cognitive neurosciences* (pp. 665–678). MIT Press.

Desco, M., Navas-Sanches F. J., Sanches-González J., Reig, S., Robles O., Franco C., et al. (2011). Mathematically gifted adolescents use more extensive and more bilateral areas of the fronto-parietal network than controls during executive functioning and fluid reasoning tasks. *Neuroimage, 57*, 281–292. https://doi.org/10.1016/j.neuroimage.2011.03.063

Dosher, B. (2003). Working memory. In *Encyclopedia of Cognitive Science* (Vol. 4, pp. 569–577). Nature Publishing Group.

Drew, T. & Vogel, E. K. (2009). Working memory: Capacity limitations. *Encyclopedia of Neuroscience,* 523–531. https://doi.org/10.1016/b978-008045046-9.00428-9

Duan, X. & Shi, J. (2014). Attentional switching in intellectually gifted and average children: Effects on performance and ERP. *Psychological Reports, 114*, 597–607. https://doi.org/10.2466/04.10.PR0.114k21w8

Feldman, J. A. & Shastri, L. (2003). Connectionism. In L. Nadel (Ed.), *Encyclopedia of cognitive science* (Vol. 1, pp. 680–687). Nature Publishing Group.

Garrison, K. E. & Schmeichel, B. J. (2018). Effects of emotional content on working memory capacity. *Cognition and Emotion, 33*(2), 370–377. https://doi.org/10.1080/02699931.2018.1438989

Geake, J. G. (2008). High abilities at fluid analogizing: A cognitive neuroscience construct of giftedness. *Roeper Review, 30*(3), 187–195. https://doi.org/10.1080/02783190802201796

Gomez, R., Stavropoulos, V., Vance, A., & Griffiths, M. D. (2019). Gifted children with ADHD: How are they different from non-gifted children with ADHD? *International Journal of Mental Health and Addiction, 18*(6), 1467–1481. https://doi.org/10.1007/s11469-019-00125-x

Guerra-Carrillo, B., Mackey, A. P., & Bunge, S. A. (2014). Resting-State fMRI: A window into human brain plasticity. *The Neuroscientist, 20*(5), 522–533. https://doi.org/10.1177/1073858414524442

Inman, T. F & Breedlove, L. (2018). *Gifted 101*. National Association for Gifted Children. https://www.nagc.org/sites/default/files/Publication%20PHP/NAGC-TIP%20Sheets-Gifted%20101.pdf

Haier, R. J. & Jung, R. E. (2008). Brain imaging studies of intelligence and creativity: What is the picture for education? *Roeper Review, 30*(3), 171–180. https://doi.org/10.1080/02783190802199347

Haier, R. J., Siegel, B. V., Nuechterlein, K. H., Hazlett, E., Wu, J., Paek, J., Browning, H., & Buchsbaum, M. S. (1988). Cortical glucose metabolic rate correlates of abstract reasoning and attention studied with positron emission tomography. *Intelligence, 12*, 199–217. https://doi.org/10.1016/0160-2896(88)90016-5

Henke, K. (2010). A model for memory systems based on processing models rather than consciousness. *Nature Reviews Neuroscience, 11*, 523–532. https://doi.org/10.1038/nrn2850

Jin, S-H., Kim, S. Y., Park, K. H., & Lee, K.-J. (2007). Differences in EEG between gifted and average students: Neural complexity and functional cluster analysis. *International Journal of Neuroscience, 117*(8), 1167–1184. https://doi.org/10.1080/00207450600934655

Kovacs, K. & Conway, A. R. (2016). Process overlap theory: A unified account of the general factor of intelligence. *Psychological Inquiry, 27*(3), 151–177. https://doi.org/10.1080/1047840x.2016.1153946

Langille, J. J. & Brown, R. E. (2018). The Synaptic Theory of Memory: A historical survey and reconciliation of recent opposition. *Frontiers in Systems Neuroscience, 12*. https://doi.org/10.3389/fnsys.2018.00052

Lindsay, G. W. (2020) Attention in psychology, neuroscience, and machine learning. *Frontiers in Computational Neuroscience, 14*. https://doi.org/10.3389/fncom.2020.00029

Little, C. (2018, August 6). *Op-ed: Rethink Peer Tutoring by Gifted Learners*. UConn Today. https://today.uconn.edu/2018/08/op-ed-rethink-peer-tutoring-gifted-learners/

Loftus, E. F. (2001). Imagining the past. *The Psychologist, 14*(11), 584–587.

Lohman, D. F., Gambrell, J., & Lakin, J. (2008). The commonality of extreme discrepancies in the ability profiles of academically gifted students. *Psychology Science, 50*(2), 269–282.

McRobbie, L. R. (2018, December 12). *The Mind-Bending Math Behind Spot It!, the Beloved Family Card Game.* Smithsonian.com. https://www.smithsonianmag.com/science-nature/math-card-game-spot-it-180970873/.

Morin, A. (2020, December 1). *8 Working Memory Boosters.* Understood. https://www.understood.org/en/school-learning/learning-at-home/homework-study-skills/8-working-memory-boosters.

Muller N. G., Bartelt, O. A., Donner, T. H., Villringer, A., & Brandt, S. A. (2003) A physiological correlate of the "Zoom Lens" of visual attention. *Journal of Neuroscience, 23,* 3561–3565. https://doi.org/10.1523/JNEUROSCI.23-09-03561.2003

Mullet, D. R. & Rinn, A. N. (2015) Giftedness and ADHD: Identification, misdiagnosis, and dual diagnosis. *Roeper Review, 37*(4), 195–207. https://doi.org/10.1080/02783193.2015.1077910

Oppong, E., Shore, B. M., & Muis, K. R. (2018). Clarifying the connections among giftedness, metacognition, self-regulation, and self-regulated learning: Implications for theory and practice. *Gifted Child Quarterly, 63*(2), 102–119. https://doi.org/10.1177/0016986218814008

Pesenti, M., Zago, L., Crivello, F., Mellet, E., Samson, D., Duroux, B., et al. (2001). Mental calculation in a prodigy is sustained by right prefrontal and medial temporal areas. *Nature Neuroscience, 4,* 103–107. https://doi.org/10.1038/82831

Posner, M. I. (1980) Orienting of attention. *Quarterly Journal of Experimental Psychology, 32,* 3–25. https://doi.org/10.1080/00335558008248231

Renzulli, J. S. (1978). What makes giftedness? Reexamining a definition. *Phi Delta Kappan, 60,* 180–184, 261.

Renzulli, J. S. (2016). The three-ring conception of giftedness: A developmental model for promoting creative productivity. In S. M. Reis (Ed.), *Reflections on gifted education: Critical works by Joseph S. Renzulli and colleagues* (pp. 55–90). Prufrock Press, Inc.

Rissman, J. & Wagner, A. D. (2012). Distributed representation in memory: Insights from functional brain imaging. *Annual Review of Psychology, 63*(1), 101–128. https://doi.org/10.1146/annurev-psych-120710-100344

Rowe, E. W., Dandridge, J., Pawlush, A., Thompson, D. F., & Ferrier, D. E. (2014). Exploratory and confirmatory factor analyses of the WISC-IV with gifted students. *School Psychology Quarterly, 29*(4), 536–552. https://doi.org/10.1037/spq0000009

Sadeh, T., Ozubko, J. D., Winocur, G., & Moscovitch, M. (2014). How we forget may depend on how we remember. *Trends in Cognitive Sciences, 18*(1), 26–36. https://doi.org/10.1016/j.tics.2013.10.008

Savi, A. O., Marsman, M., van der Maas, H., & Maris, G. (2019). The wiring of intelligence. *Perspectives on Psychological Science, 14*(6), 1034–1061. https://doi.org/10.1177/1745691619866447

Shi, J., Tao, T., Chen, W., Cheng, L., Wang, L., & Zhang, X. (2013). Sustained attention in intellectually gifted children assessed using a continuous performance test. *PLoS ONE, 8*(2). https://doi.org/10.1371/journal.pone.0057417

Squire, L. R. (1986). Mechanisms of memory. *Science, 232*(4578), 1612–1619. https://doi.org/10.1126/science.3086978

Squire, L. R. (1993). The organization of declarative and nondeclarative memory. In T. Ono, L. R. Squire, M. E. Raichle, D. I. Perrett, & M. Fukuda (Eds.), *Brain mechanisms of perception and memory: From neuron to behavior* (pp. 219–227). Oxford University Press.

Sternberg, R. J. (2001). Giftedness as developing expertise: A theory of the interface between high abilities and achieved excellence. *High Ability Studies*, *12*, 159–179. https://doi.org/10.1080/13598130120084311

Tulving, E. (2002). Episodic memory: From mind to brain. *Annual Review of Psychology*, *53*(1), 1–25. https://doi.org/10.1146/annurev.psych.53.100901.135114

Wixted, J. T. (2004). The psychology and neuroscience of forgetting. *Annual Review of Psychology*, *55*, 235–269. doi:10.1146/annurev.psych.55.090902.141555

Zhang, H., Zhang, X., He, Y., & Shi, J. (2016). Inattentional blindness in 9- to 10-year-old intellectually gifted children. *Gifted Child Quarterly*, *60*(4), 287–295. https://doi.org/10.1177/0016986216657158

Zhang, H., Zhang, X., He, Y., & Shi, J. (2017). Clustering strategy in intellectually gifted children: Assessment using a collaborative recall task. *Gifted Child Quarterly*, *61*(2), 133–142. https://doi.org/10.1177/0016986216687825

Ziegler, A. & Phillipson, S. N. (2012). Towards a systemic theory of gifted education. *High Ability Studies*, *23*(1), 3–30. https://doi.org/10.1080/13598139.2012.679085

Zola, S. M. & Squire, L. R. (2000). The medial temporal lobe and the hippocampus. In E. Tulving & F. I. M. Craik (Eds.), *The Oxford handbook of memory* (pp. 485–500). Oxford University Press.

CHAPTER 5

Language development and education of advanced learners and precocious readers

Mary Slade

Many traditionally identified gifted learners possess advanced language ability and develop language skills early (Hoh, 2005). Traits reflective of advanced language skills and early development are often evident as early as the age of two. Language performance appears advanced, often comparable to that of children one or two years older. It is believed that early language development of gifted learners is closely connected to their generally advanced learning ability (Hayes et al., 1998). There is a correlation between early onset of speech and subsequently early reading (Gross, 1999). In fact, many children who will later be identified for gifted programming enter school already knowing how to read. Research conducted early in the study of gifted education, led by early twentieth century psychologists Louis Terman and Leta Stetter Hollingworth, indicated that gifted children often learn how to read with little or no assistance (Gross, 1999).

Cognitively advanced learners often have more sophisticated language abilities in comparison with typically developing children of the same age and demonstrate language development milestones earlier than their peers. The language development process for academically advanced children resembles that of other children yet the pace is often accelerated (Hoh, 2005). Precocious readers exhibit movement through the earliest stages of language development so rapidly that needs arise requiring specific attention from parents and school personnel (Jackson & Roller, 1993). A study of identified gifted learners recorded a history of early reading, reading at advanced levels, advanced processing in reading, advanced language skills, and in some cases, reading abilities appear to be self-taught (Reis et al., 2004).

The early development of speech and reading are typical indicators of high cognitive ability. The advanced and fluent command of language and the love of wordplay characterize many cognitively advanced children (Gross, 1999). A subset

DOI: 10.4324/9781003025443-6

of these learners, gifted readers, excels at reading, and engaging with text (Mason & Au, 1990). Gifted readers read voraciously, perform well above their grade levels, and possess advanced vocabularies (Reis, 2009). They use words easily, accurately, and creatively in new and innovative contexts and speak in semantically complex and syntactically complicated sentences (Bonds & Bonds, 1983). Advanced vocabulary and early reading comprehension are indicators of high intelligence in verbal areas (Gottfried et al., 1994). In addition to accelerated reading and language skills, verbally advanced learners may possess high aptitude in other areas of literacy, including creative writing, literary analysis, oral communication, linguistic and vocabulary development, and critical or creative reading (VanTassel-Baska & Stambaugh, 2005).

Given their abilities, the general education curriculum alone is insufficient in supporting learning gains and continuous progress in literacy education for learners with advanced academic needs (Levande, 1999). The central emphasis of literacy instruction in early grades consists of fluency development in order to build comprehension skills. This type of focus is not consistent with the independent gifted learner's need for challenge, as the students may already be independent readers and possess grade-level comprehension skills. Thus, the general curriculum is not challenging for the advanced reader (Little, 2001). Therefore, literacy education for advanced students must be aligned with the specific language development needs of these learners (Levande, 1999). First, verbally advanced learners need increasingly difficult vocabulary and concepts. Second, these students must be allowed to pursue sophisticated interests and passions through literacy curriculum and instruction. Third, a need exists for literacy instruction to be taught at a rate appropriate to the advanced pace of learning. For example, most advanced learners require less drill and practice than their same-age peers (Rogers, 2002). Finally, all students must have regular access to interact with appropriate texts in order to make continuous progress in reading (National Reading Panel, 2000; Reis et al., 2004; Reis & Boeve, 2009). Specifically, advanced learners require access to reading content above their current grade level as well as texts with complexity (Reis et al., 2005). Unfortunately, without appropriate differentiation of curriculum and programming for learners who are advanced readers, literacy education is often stymied by grade-level curricula that fail to provide intellectual challenge requisite for the development of full potential (Reis et al., 2004).

An essential component of advanced academics is matching the learning experience to the diverse needs of all learners, including those who are verbally gifted. An important part of the differentiation process is understanding how various populations of students vary from expected developmental theories. Additionally, knowledge of how all students learn is critical in making adjustments in literacy education. Thus, parents, counselors, and educators who understand all learning and language development theories are best equipped to differentiate literacy education for advanced learners.

The emphasis of this chapter is understanding the nature of language development in verbally advanced children based on theoretical frameworks. Both learning and language development theories will be explored in terms of understanding the impact on understanding and supporting learners who require advanced academic services. In addition, best practices for the support and enrichment of language development in cognitively able children based on language and related theoretical frameworks.

THE IMPACT OF LEARNING AND LANGUAGE THEORIES ON LANGUAGE DEVELOPMENT

Historically, gifted education has been rooted in the theoretical foundations of both psychology and education (Phelps, 2015). An example of the prevailing relationship between psychological and educational theories when applied to gifted education is the reliance on intelligence tests and traits of advanced cognitive ability as exhibited in the classroom for the identification of gifted learners. Since the initial conception of the field of gifted education, the intertwining of psychological theory and constructs has been applied to educational practice. Theoretical frameworks are necessary given that the absence of theory in educational practices in the field can lead to inconsistent, unsustainable, unrelated practices that result in ineffective services (Renzulli, 2012). However, theoretical frameworks alone are not sufficient for guiding the development of effective advanced academic programming. In order to enhance the utility of transforming theory to practice, there must be alignment between the psychological foundations and theory-guided educational services provided to students. Further, the application of theoretical constructs to advanced or gifted learners must be a logical extension of their psychological and educational underpinnings (Renzulli, 2012).

Theoretical frameworks explain how cognitive, emotional, environmental, and experiential influences impact students. Learning theory describes the process of how students receive, process, retain, and retrieve knowledge and skill sets. Additionally, theories explain the relationship between teacher and learner. When applied to the classroom, learning theories influence the curriculum, instruction, assessment, and the learning environment. Thus, learning theories dictate educational practice, policy, and related professional learning.

There are four major learning theories that impact education today. Specifically, behaviorism, constructivism, cognitive, and humanist theories provide infrastructure for understanding, developing, implementing, and evaluating educational practice. Although constructivism is closely aligned with cognitive theory, it is significantly different in ways that warrant a separate discussion. No other theory adequately explains all aspects of teaching and learning; rather, each has specific implications for practice and policy. Collectively, various theories have advantages for application to advanced learners and literacy education. For example, today *behaviorism* largely serves to provide procedures for classroom management. On the other hand, cognitivism explains and guides the process of teaching and learning. Rather than focusing on behavior, cognitivism strives to explain how the brain works during the process of learning. *Constructivism* theory purports that learners make meaning from their environment, but more importantly, dictates that learning is student-centered and is optimized by engagement with peers. The notion that learning evolves from self-actualization versus prescribed learning outcomes is the crux of *humanism*. In addition to the application of traditional learning theories to language development, two specialized theories of language development exist. The nativist approach reflects the completely innate and natural evolution of language. In opposition, Halliday's Theory of Language Functions (Halliday, 1993) articulates how development reflects specific needs that arise as the learner interacts with the environment. An understanding of learning and language development theories helps teachers think and act deliberately with the goal of serving students in mind. Educators can focus on different approaches to teaching to augment student learning. The use of various theories supports diverse student needs and pathways to learning.

Learning and language theories' applications impact all learners and advanced learners in particular. In gifted education, it is imperative that curricular and instructional adaptations are steeped in theoretical frameworks versus implemented without coordination and intent. Learning theories help plan educational interventions, including literacy education (Burney, 2008).

Behaviorism learning theory

Behavioral learning theorists such as B. F. Skinner defined learning as permanent change resulting from the effects of a stimulus or experience. The translation of theory to educational practice suggests that students learn from adults through the processes of imitation, association, and conditioning. It follows that in a behavioral approach to education, instructional practice includes the use of sustained positive reinforcement to increase the frequency of desired responses (Morrow, 2020).

Implications for language development in general learner populations

When applied to language development for all children, behaviorism suggests that instruction must contain meaningful interactions with the environment. Parents and teachers model language and children learn through imitation. Initially, language is modeled by caregivers, family, and educators with whom very young children interact every day. Learning is further supported by positive reinforcement of children's imitation of oral language. Thus, language development is facilitated by adults through interactions designed to extend meaning.

In schools, behaviorism is used to manage children's behavior both socially and academically. Typically, children with classroom management concerns and low academic performance are targeted for behavioral interventions. Relative to language development, behavioral pedagogies such as direct instruction are used to build language when deficits exist. Applied behavioral analysis is used to limit maladaptive behavior and build socially acceptable conduct. In today's classroom more student-centered strategies are used for whole group instruction versus direct instruction and similar didactic pedagogies.

Implications for language development for cognitively advanced learner populations

The explicit application of behaviorism to language development and literacy education in advanced learners has more limited utility than it does with their typically developing peers. Initial speech and language acquisition seem to be more independent, requiring little or no direct assistance from others (Gross, 1999) which would suggest that imitation and positive reinforcement are not constructs that align directly with the needs of gifted learners. Further, given that many advanced learners demonstrate accelerated language development, explicit direct instruction is usually not warranted. Thus, behaviorism has less applicability to advanced learners as a pedagogical option.

The behavioral constructs of imitation and positive reinforcement, however, can be applied to all learners as means for supporting continuous progress and advanced language development. First, behavioral learning theory would suggest the importance of same-ability peer instructional grouping to language development. With early onset language development and advanced use of language evident in young gifted learners, it follows that they will not increase or expand their language acquisition from interactions with most same-age, typically developing peers. However, when placed with similar-ability peers for group studies, cognitively advanced learners are more likely to imitate one another's advanced language skills and vocabulary (Lin, 2018). Same-ability peers do not typically harbor resentment over each other's advanced intelligence and are more likely to positively reinforce one another during collaborative learning activities. A recent study of reading and vocabulary development in gifted learners found positive learning outcomes when learning occurs amongst same-ability peers with greater language development (Lin, 2018).

Cognitivism learning theory

Cognitivism is a learning theory that focuses on thought or what happens in the brain that leads to behavior. There are two primary approaches to the cognitive theory of learning that apply to language development and associated educational practice. First, information processing states that rather than responding to stimuli as behaviorism proclaims, children process the information they receive from interactions with the environment. Second, Piaget's theory illustrates how children's cognition develops across four distinct stages and presents several cognitive constructs that explain how children learn. A third cognitivist theory, constructivism, is significantly different from the first two approaches given the emphasis on socio-cultural influences, hence, it is discussed separately.

Information processing learning theory asserts that not unlike a computer, children learn by attending, decoding, storing, and retrieving information. According to cognitive theory, faster processing speed can influence language development directly by allowing operations to be performed more rapidly, indirectly, and by increasing the functional capacity of working memory. Similarly, memory is vital for accruing all forms of knowledge, including language. Persistent attention to stimuli leads to enhanced language acquisition. The rate and quality of information processing is related to the success of literacy education.

Learning is impacted by the learner's level of language development (Feldman, 1982). Cognitive stage development theory explains how maturation transpires across four stages as conceived by Jean Piaget. Cognitive development theory addresses the learner's ability to understand abstract and complex concepts in stages. Individual differences in knowing are explained by different rates of development (Gross, 1999).

In addition to stage theory, Piagetian theory explains several cognitive constructs that demonstrate how children learn. Specifically, Piaget states that children learn new knowledge through assimilation and accommodation of existing schemas. Schemas are organized sets of related ideas that form the knowledge acquired. The creation of schemas symbolize that children are active participants in their own learning, changing, and reorganizing their own knowledge (McCarrick & Xiaoming, 2007). The development and subsequent access to schemas is critical to memory and retrieval which reflect learning.

Implications for language development for general learner populations

The study of cognitivism and its application to language development primarily encompasses two different approaches: (1) information processing and (2) developmental stage theories. Both approaches to cognitive theory have implications for understanding and supporting language development through literacy education for all children.

Processing speed often accounts for performance differences on a wide variety of cognitive tasks in childhood. For example, low processing speed limits language acquisition by interfering with building up lexical and grammatical representations essential for language development. Further, auditory processing problems have been known to be associated with language impairments (Rose et al., 2009). Processing speed correlates with differences in levels of intelligence (Steiner & Carr, 2003). There is evidence that higher processing speeds leads to larger quantities of knowledge acquisition.

It is important to remember that the learner is very much an active participant in the learning process. Language development relies on cognition and social interactions (McCarrick & Xiaoming, 2007). In particular, three important relationships exist between language development and each of the following: (1) social interactions; (2) lexical phonology; and (3) general cognitive processes (Rose et al., 2009). Specifically, language develops as a result of children's interactions with adults, phonological and lexical coding, and information processing.

Multiple aspects of cognitive theory apply to understanding and supporting language development in all children. Piaget's stage theory of cognitive development reflects children's readiness to practice phonological and morphological processes necessary for word building at each stage of cognitive maturation. Essentially, expected cognitive behaviors are assigned to broad age ranges that help to predict how and when children think both quantitatively and qualitatively. Piaget emphasized the sequence of changing intellectual abilities across ages. Generally, most pedagogies that require authentic experiences and engagement that involves exploration or play are consistent with Piagetian assumptions (McCarrick & Xiaoming, 2007).

In addition to developmental stage theories, Piagetian constructs describe the learning process in all children. Equilibrium explains the process of acquiring new language. When children are introduced to words they don't already know, their schemas become imbalanced. In order to find equilibrium, two simultaneous processes occur: (1) assimilation and (2) accommodation. As a result, new language structures are acquired.

Implications for language development for cognitively advanced learner populations

The relationship between advanced cognition and language development is strong (Hoh, 2005), which contributes to early reading and language skills acquisition for gifted learners. Gifted learners differ from their same-age peers in the quality and amount of knowledge possessed (Steiner & Carr, 2003). Further, these students rely less on social interactions and demonstrate greater independence in language development when compared to the general population (Gross, 1999).

Research (Steiner & Carr, 2003) in cognition has demonstrated a positive relationship between information processing speeds and intelligence. Metacognition is correlated with high performance in highly intelligent students. These learners have knowledge bases equal to those of older students (Gross, 1999; Steiner & Carr, 2003). These attentional skills in a social context can lead to larger receptive and productive vocabularies (Rose et al., 2009).

When applied specifically to gifted education, the equilibration theory explains how the child makes sense of the environment. Through four universal stages, Piaget explains how children explore the world. Although Piagetian theory applies to the general population, unique implications exist for the gifted learner population. Consensus exists that there is a faster or different movement through the stages by gifted learners (Cohen & Kim, 1999). While they do not typically enter a higher stage of development earlier, the quality or breadth of ability within each stage is evident (Cohen & Kim, 1999). Additionally, Piaget's equilibration theory explains some aspects of intellectual giftedness. For example, challenge brings disequilibrium requiring restoring the balance. This is done through assimilation and accommodation (Cohen & Kim, 1999).

Individual differences of intellectual ability and language development are attributed to varying rates of development. The rate of development equates to the movement through Piaget's stages of cognition. Gifted learners move through Piaget's stages of cognitive development (Hoh, 2005) faster than non-gifted peers. Further, the gifted learner demonstrates a greater breadth of ability within a given stage.

Gifted learners tend to possess schemas that are larger and more enriched than those of their non-gifted peers. Given their advanced ability, interests, and quest for the unknown gifted learners' schemas are more networked and greater numbers of sub-structures (Vaivre-Douret, 2011). Their increased background knowledge reflects more complex schemas. Gifted learners' schemas focus more on concepts than just actions like their non-gifted peers. Related pedagogies include concept-mapping.

Constructivism learning theory

Constructivism is a socio-cultural theory that explains the dynamics of the relationship between the child and environment in learning. Constructivists see the learner as an architect of knowledge. Learning is shaped by the existing knowledge or schemas that students possess. One of the most influential constructivist learning theorists, Lev Vygotsky, writes about optimal learning with his theory of the Zone of Proximal Development (Vygotsky, 1978). An essential belief held by Vygotsky is that learning is collaborative, especially, with peers with greater competence (a more knowledgeable other), and that social interaction is crucial to development. Thus, Vygotsky provides two impactful concepts related to learning, the More Knowledgeable Other and the Zone of Proximal Development. Additionally, in a classroom based on constructivist theory, the environment is student-centered, and the teacher acts as facilitator.

Implications for language development for the general learner population

Vygotsky's (1986) theories on instruction and learning emphasize social interaction and language experiences between adults and children, as well as peer engagement. Interactions between teacher and learner provide opportunities for mastering tasks that cannot be completed independently. This is an example of both the Zone of Proximal Development and the More Knowledgeable Other concepts being applied to support all learners' progression to advanced developmental levels.

The concept of the Zone of Proximal Development reflects the belief that learners' developmental level of skill development can be raised through instruction (Vygotsky, 1978). When applying the concept of the Zone of Proximal Development to language development, the immediate implication is determining the level of rigor needed in order for learners to make continuous progress. For example, a reader must encounter new concepts and language in order to learn (Reis & Boeve, 2009). Zone of Proximal Development concept reflects a range of levels of rigor appropriate for diverse learners. Thus, some learners gain more from an instructional set than others if the same level of difficulty or rigor is employed (Vygotsky, 1986). Csikszentmihalyi (1990) explains the differential zones that promote achievement as Flow or the area between boredom and frustration. Flow is dependent upon both ability and experience.

When provided stimuli, the child reacts physically or mentally to understand it. Through assimilating or accommodating the stimuli into existing structures, equilibrium is restored. The incompatibility with existing structures and related gaps initiates disequilibrium which gives rise to developing new understandings. Thus, assimilating and organization are the key to continuous learning through cognitive growth (Cohen & Kim, 1999). Self-selection based on advanced aptitude and interests can lead to greater opportunities for equilibration (Cohen & Kim, 1999). The role of the teacher in this process is to create scaffolding by the more-experienced other on behalf of the learner.

Learning occurs as children acquire new concepts or schemas. All types of mental functions are acquired through social relationships. For example, learning requires children to interact with others who provide feedback or help them to complete a task that cannot be done independently. The Zone of Proximal Development refers to the point whereby children can complete some of a task independently but needs support or scaffolding to complete it. Proximal development ends when the child can work independently.

Language is developed through interactions with the environment. Learners utilize problem-solving in order to assimilate [integrating knowledge into existing schemas] and accommodate [modifying schemas for integrating new knowledge] new knowledge into existing schemas. Learning occurs when children interact with the teacher and peers in a social setting while interacting with the environment. Language develops through their actions and sensory experiences with the environment. Making errors is an important part of learning how language works. Children learn by playing with language themselves and with others (Morrow, 2020).

Teachers provide the language children need to solve problems. Children learn by internalizing the language and actions of others into their own world. To promote language development, adults must interact with children in order to encourage, motivate and support them. Positive interactions encourage practice which further develops language. Vygotsky's theories on language acquisition emphasize interaction of language and thought. Therefore, collaborative learning activities whereby peers engage with one another aligns with Vygotsky's approach to learning (McCarrick & Xiaoming, 2007).

EYE FOR DIVERSITY 5.1 THE VERBAL DOMAIN DOES NOT JUST MEAN ENGLISH

Dante D. Dixson

Advanced verbal ability typically presents as an early, or advanced, development of speech, reading, or vocabulary skills. However, advanced verbal ability is not English language specific, and the typical presentation depends on the learner having had some degree of exposure to books, vocabulary, or speech feedback to develop. As a result, advanced verbal ability in students from diverse backgrounds (e.g., English language learners and students from low-income backgrounds) may present differently than students in the majority as they may not be able to display their advanced verbal abilities in English or via traditional activities (e.g., reading advanced texts or using an advanced vocabulary). They may not be able to exhibit their verbal ability via traditional activities because they may have had less access to the tools and opportunities that encourage the typical presentation (e.g., books and high-quality verbal interactions). Thus, a more holistic assessment of verbal abilities, taking into account the learner's exposure and learning opportunities within the verbal ability domain, might be most appropriate for students from diverse backgrounds.

Implications for language development in cognitively advanced learner populations

When applying Vygotsky's Zone of Proximal Development to gifted learners, a significant assertion exists that a substantial level of challenge is required for them to work with guided practice until independence is sustained. The purpose of differentiated education for the advanced learner is to create learning experiences that provide a "supported struggle" which must exist in all learning much like that available in models of enrichment in gifted education (Reis & Boeve, 2009). An illustration of this construct being applied to reading asserts that the optimal text is above grade level and requires enough effort that the occasional assistance will be required before independence is reached (Reis & Boeve, 2009). Therefore, grade-level curricula are not always appropriately challenging for advanced learners and above-grade level materials are necessary.

One instructional practice that aligns with constructivism and the needs of advanced learners involves collaborative learning with same-ability peers. Vygotsky believed that learners should work with peers who possess more experience versus working independently (McCarrick & Xiaoming, 2007). When applied to advanced learners, the notion that peers should possess the same or greater experience with the task at hand not only dispels the myth that the advanced learner "will get it on their own" but also demonstrates how to create a context for an appropriate Zone of Proximal Development.

Curriculum based on predicted developmental stages and ignores developmental differences. We should prescribe learning tasks based on curriculum and not the children.

FIELD NOTE 5.1

A young gifted learner went to the library for the weekly lesson with her class. After concluding a lesson on illustrations in Newberry winning children's books, the media specialist allowed the students to select two books for weekly independent reading. Knowing that not all students would choose appropriately challenging books, the specialist pulled grade-level reading material on carts for her students during class visits. The young student stood in front of the cart and then went to a shelf in the library and selected a book that is the third volume in a science-fiction series. The specialist told the student to put the book back on the shelf as it reflected a reading level appropriate for older students. After the young student went home and told her parents about the library experience, her father called the assistant principal who explained that most educators do not have training in gifted education and are not aware that they often read at least two grade levels above their grade. As a result, the principal planned a professional learning event to better explain the characteristics and needs of advanced readers.

Humanism learning theory

Humanism is related to constructivism but uniquely focuses on the idea of self-actualization singularly. The process of self-actualization equates to having all of one's needs met which purports to support optimum and fully realized capacity for learning. The application to education in general is in guiding the creation and maintenance of classroom environments that help students move toward self-actualization. Generally, a conducive learning environment would fulfill all of a learner's needs, including emotional, physical, safety, and sustenance needs. In other words, when students feel that they belong, are supported, feel safe and have plenty of food their needs are being addressed (Morrow, 2020).

Implications for language development in general populations

Essentially, humanism theory applied to language development implies that the whole child is involved in the learning process, including socio-emotional, physical, and cognitive needs being addressed. In order for all learners to develop language skills, self-actualization should be met. The educator's willingness to address all of the learner's needs will optimize literacy education.

The role of the educator is to be sure that in addition to the learner's intellectual needs, the affective needs are addressed. For example, a focus on positive growth, as opposed to deficit approaches to learning are emphasized. A nurturing approach to learning and creation of an environment is paramount to the humanistic learning environment. Further, the teacher serves in the role of facilitator who guides and supports student-focused learning. In regard to literacy education, humanistic principles manifest in terms of the learner's individual choice and responsibility. For example, educators must be mindful of the learner's choice of texts for reading as well as an alignment of instructional activities to interests and passions to optimize learning in a self-actualized environment.

Implications for language development in cognitively advanced learner populations

Humanism is a viable approach to literacy education for advanced learners given some of their unique developmental traits. For example, in applying a humanistic approach to supporting language development and teaching literacy for advanced learners, self-actualization is positively impacted by the learner's strong sense of self-regulation. Evidence of more advanced self-regulation skills in gifted learners in comparison to non-gifted learners exist (Reis, 2004). In addition, a strong locus of control in advanced learners is consistent with humanism given that taking control of one's learning supports self-actualization. In general, these learners are supported in a humanistic environment when their unique differences are respected and understood by all.

Humanistic classroom environments support advanced learners' needs for differentiated education, including adapting and modifying general education literacy programs of study. For example, humanistic classrooms support all learners' individual choice and responsibility. Given the early, advanced, and passionate interests of learners with exceptional cognitive ability, humanistic approaches to literacy education are aligned with differentiated learning needs. Subsequently the use of inquiry-based reading strategies (Thompson, 2002), a recommended instructional practice for advanced readers, is enhanced when learners are immersed in their passions through specific texts during reading instruction. Another characteristic of humanistic teaching and learning that is consistent with good practice in differentiation in gifted education, involves self-evaluation by the learner. An example of self-evaluation in literacy education includes self-monitoring of reading comprehension strategies or skills. Finally, in a humanistic classroom the teacher acts as facilitator, a desired role in gifted education as targeted learners require less direct instruction and more student-centered learning experiences.

Humanism aligns with respect to finding and serving all types of learners. High cognitive ability exists in all populations, including those who are culturally diverse and those impacted by poverty. Thus, a humanistic approach to gifted education recognizes that cognitive ability and advanced language development is impacted by the lack of access to the resources that help gifted learners realize their advanced language aptitude. Equity issues result in a lack of experiences and resources that create gaps in necessary learning success strategies. Therefore, appropriately differentiated literacy programs must support both strengths and gaps in learning. A focus on self-actualization and support for the whole child aligns with the needs of special populations of gifted learners.

FIELD NOTE 5.2

A teacher working primarily with gifted learners impacted significantly by poverty at a Title I school developed a study skills/effective learning strategies program that reflected both giftedness and gaps in learning created by inequities or a lack of access to necessary learning resources and materials. The program reflected the teaching of deficit skills in a gifted education approach. In essence the teacher integrated study and learning strategies into regular literacy instruction. However, instead of using excessive amounts of direct instruction or drill and practice, the teacher taught the new skills at advanced levels with less practice in a student-centered approach.

Nativist theory of language development

The Nativist theory of language development asserts that children make meaning from the world innately. Language development is a genetically hard-wired process whereby children learn how to make meaning naturally. Thus, language development is a naturally occurring experience that progresses automatically as children interact with their environments.

Perhaps the most recognizable and influential linguist and nativist is Noam Chomsky. This nativist theorist described a set of rules of language that innately exist among all children known as universal grammar (Morrow, 2020). He believed that the rules for acquiring and using language are built into our genetic code and occur naturally as students begin to interact with the environment initiating needs for language. Chomsky has experienced both critics and proponents of this nativist theory and the concept of universal grammar in particular.

When linguistic and educational theories align, beyond an explanation of language development exist implications for teaching and learning. However, given the emphasis on the natural origination of language and innate rules of language acquisition held by the nativist theory, there are few logical implications for teaching and learning. Thus, the utility in this language development theory lies exclusively in explaining initial first language development versus intervention, support, and nurturing of linguistic maturation in the K-12 environment.

Halliday's theory of language functions

Language helps children make meaning of the world. Halliday's theory of language development shows the process whereby children learn how to make meaning across predictable stages. Language is learned when it is relevant and functional. Children's language increases according to their need to use it, their interests, and the meaning it holds for them (Morrow, 2020). Thus, Halliday's developmental theory reflects the functions of language.

In addition to stage theory, Halliday asserted that language acquisition is a byproduct of interactions between adults and children. Language acquisition occurs through exploration and invention within predictable periods of development that dictate the structure of language and its conventions. The application of Halliday's theory of linguistic development has been more effectively replaced by the impact of the theories of Vygotsky and Piaget given similar assumptions about language development.

SUPPORTING LANGUAGE DEVELOPMENT IN ACADEMICALLY ADVANCED CHILDREN

It's important to see a child's advanced ability neither as a benefit nor an obstacle; instead, accepting and nurturing advanced academic ability is imperative. It follows that early and advanced language similarly is neither a cause for celebration nor concern. Instead, it is essential that the adults in young children's lives understand, support, and advocate for continuous progress in language development. Therefore, it is critical that families and educators communicate about early language development and reading skills in order to initiate appropriate assessment and curriculum differentiation (Jackson & Roller, 1993). Consequently, understanding and applying best practices for language development in advanced learners are warranted.

Studies of general education classrooms demonstrate that learners who have been identified as having advanced academic ability aren't receiving appropriately differentiated or challenging literacy education (Reis et al., 2004; Westberg et al., 1993), proving that advocacy and action on their behalf is warranted. Taking no action on behalf of the advanced language development of these learners is failing them as grade-level literacy programs can be punitive (Levande, 1999). Enriching education for the advanced learner prevents a "more of the same" approach to literacy education and support. In fact, simply placing students in high-level reading groups does not address their unique literacy needs (Catron & Wingenbach, 2001) due to the lack of challenge provided by learning materials and activities (Levande, 1999). As much as one-half of literacy curriculum prescribed for grade-level children is not sufficiently challenging for advanced learners (Reis et al., 2011).

There are four primary components to consider when accounting for the variance between advanced and typically developing learners. First is speech development, which refers to the emergence and evolution of oral language in an acceptable communicative format. Second, reading development includes fluency and comprehension, but is atypical in advanced learners. Third, advanced learners exhibit early onset and qualitatively different vocabulary development as compared to their typically developing peers. Finally, the early use and complexity of sentence structure is evident in most advanced learners' language development. Each component of language development is discussed below in reference to strategies for supporting and sustaining advanced development for these learners.

Speech

The early onset of speech is typical for children who are later identified for gifted education programming, with initial emergence beginning approximately two months prior to that of their same-age peers (Gross, 1999). Similarly, a gap in speech performance between gifted and typically developing peers exists for initial speech. In fact, this gap is even greater when comparing typically developing peers to highly or verbally intelligent learners (Gross, 1999). Another developmental difference that advanced learners exhibit in comparison to their typically developing peers is the gap in the development of receptive and expressive language skills. For all children, receptive language develops faster than expressive language, and the gap is wider amongst the skills in advanced learners (Brewer, 2016). Essentially, this means that these learners understand language more readily and easily than they can express themselves. Further, the continued speech development of cognitively advanced children is characterized by moving through stages earlier and more rapidly. Specifically, children of similar age but varying abilities demonstrate different fluency of words and complexity as exemplified by varying lengths of word phrasing.

In addition to understanding the unique aspects of speech as part of overall language development in advanced learners, advocacy and action must follow in order for children to reach their full potential. First and foremost, caregivers and educators can support and nurture early language development and advanced reading ability by encouraging children's enthusiasm for learning and language. Second, adults can interact with children around their passions and intense interests that characterize exceptional cognitive ability. This is perhaps the best time for the adults in a child's life to initiate and sustain conversation to enhance and expand speech (Brewer, 2016). Third, as educators work with advanced learners, they can use pedagogy that supports continued advanced speech development, such as Socratic seminars to encourage student-to-student and student-to-teacher oral language.

FIELD NOTE 5.3

In a four-year old classroom, a gifted English Language Learner was among eight children selected after an initial screening for gifted education services starting in Kindergarten. The students participated in a mini lesson led by the gifted education teacher while the classroom teacher observed their participation according to a checklist of gifted behavior. The teacher discussed how picture books tell a story through pictures. Students were introduced to the concepts of main character, theme, and the beginning-middle-end concept of storytelling. The students were given watercolors, brushes, and paper. They were asked to create a picture that told their story of who they are. The gifted education teacher reminded them that the picture should "tell" a beginning, middle, and ending to their story. One boy drew a picture of a car driving into a horizon at sunset. When a translator asked the boy about his title, he said, "My Life Here." When asked to tell the story contained in his drawing to a translator, the boy said that he was the car driving into the horizon as fast as he can. He said that the sky (horizon) was blank because he didn't know where he was going but he could be anything he wanted since moving to the United States. When asked to describe the ending of the story, he replied, "We will see, we will see."

Reading

A study of regular classroom literacy education justifies the need to differentiate reading curricula for advanced learners (Reis et al., 2004). Specifically, these readers require opportunities to engage in critical reading analysis with similar-ability peers, participate in advanced vocabulary development, and experience sustained advanced reading opportunities. Cognitively advanced learners require a reorganization of the literacy curriculum as such that it allows for enhanced reading instruction through enrichment and challenge that fosters continuous progress (Smith, 2009). A clear distinction exists between presenting readers access to advanced level reading materials and opportunities to engage with advanced reading curricula (Wood, 2008).

When general education classrooms consistently target instruction for the needs of typically developing or below-average learners, advanced readers become those who read well below their advanced reading ability as a result of no differentiated instruction occurring (Reis et al., 2004). However, when advanced readers receive minimal levels of appropriately differentiated instruction, student development of literacy skills emerges as lacking and motivational concerns surface (Slade & Burnham, 2020). Sustained periods without appropriate levels of differentiation in the reading curriculum can lead to lapses in reading development (Wood, 2008). In addition to providing challenging texts and higher-level critical reading strategies, advanced learners need to be taught through challenging literacy curricula (Slade & Burnham, 2020).

Best practices in differentiated literacy education to address these learners' advanced language development include the consideration of appropriate instructional grouping, critical discussion of appropriately challenging reading content, and the selection of texts at the appropriate level of challenge. For example, one of the most strategic instructional strategies appropriate for advanced learners involves the creation of intellectual peer-groups in order to conduct complex book discussions. Book selection should close the gap between student aptitude and basic curricula, as well as include a diversity of genres (Slade & Burnham, 2020). Approaches may include those outlined by the Great Books Foundation or Socratic method (Slade & Burnham, 2020). Once the appropriate grouping and selection of text transpires, emphasis on critical discussion of the content is warranted.

With early onset and advanced development of readings skills, "the emphasis should be on reading to learn and not learning to read" (Catron & Wingbach, 2001, p. 140). Given early reading and vocabulary development, the focus of reading instruction should not be on decoding but higher-level comprehension with emphasis on creative, critical, and inquiry thinking skills. Regardless of the discussion format, it is imperative that advanced readers be provided time to delve deeper through quality content through engagement using higher level thinking skills (Kenney, 2013). Similarly, inquiry reading is recommended (Catron & Wingbach, 2001). When focused on non-fiction texts, advanced learners can use inquiry strategies to research their areas of interest and passions. With fictional texts, inquiry reading techniques can lead to a deeper and more analytical examination of literature.

The choice of appropriate reading content is relative to students' advanced literacy development when applied to advanced learners. Because of their accelerated reading levels, the Lexile level should be 1–2 years above grade level for younger children and 3–4 years above for older students (VanTassel-Baska, 2017). In addition to a higher reading level, text selection should include advanced language and vocabulary. In order to address the advanced affective needs of exceptional learners, the text content should be developmentally appropriate in addition to being intellectually challenging (Cramond, 2004).

FIELD NOTE 5.4

An entire fourth-grade classroom consisted of above average to gifted readers. Students read a novel, Number the Stars. While the grade-level teacher worked with eight students in a discussion group focusing a lesson on the symbolism of the star in the novel about prison camps in Nazi-occupied Germany, the gifted education teacher organized and observed three student-led Socratic seminars. Based on the results of a pre-assessment that the two teachers collaboratively developed and analyzed, students were assigned to a reading discussion group. Prior to beginning their discussion, the gifted students read a copy of an authentic letter written by a child their age while confined in a similar prisoner camp. The teacher explained the concept of historical accuracy in fiction as well. Then, the gifted teacher asked students to prepare questions for the seminar using question stems she provided. After all student-developed questions were discussed, the student leaders posed one or two open-ended questions focused on the writing of the novel from the author's perspective the gifted education teacher had written. When a parent inquired as to why her student was placed in one group versus the other, the classroom teacher explained that the student was assigned the level of critical reading they needed based on an assessment of their understanding of the novel's vocabulary, use of figurative language such as symbolism, and historical accuracy. Therefore, the activity was based on current student needs.

Vocabulary

While advanced intellect is associated with earlier and qualitatively different language development, concurrently, vocabulary and language development are closely correlated (Lin, 2018). Advanced vocabulary can consist of either the number or type of words used. Strong vocabulary is absolutely essential for reading comprehension. At an early age, gifted learners possess an expansive vocabulary (Reis, 2009). Although these learners typically display strong word knowledge or aptitude, the acquisition of new vocabulary remains a priority in literacy education (Slade & Burnham, 2020). It is the precocious cognitive ability along with the onset of fluent and complex speech that leads to an interest in word play at a young age (Gross, 1999).

Vocabulary studies is preferred to reliance on word building through independent reading alone because the learner is likely focused on the comprehension of text versus word study. Implementing explicit vocabulary building strategies after intensive reading (Lin, 2018) via group work is recommended practice. Reading non-fiction can help build vocabulary within specific disciplines (Slade & Burnham, 2020). When it comes to learning vocabulary through reading, the application of Vygotsky's constructivist approach to building vocabulary, one would argue that collaborative group work as learning occurs through communication occurring within a group of peers (Lin, 2018). In the case of application to advanced learners, the group should be comprised of same-ability peers to allow for "knowledgeable others" to engage with one another; otherwise, the zone of proximal development may not be achieved for advanced learners in a heterogenous grouping format.

There are several recommended approaches to the provision of differentiated programs of vocabulary studies. First, cognitively advanced learners can study the most common words appearing in great works of literature (Thompson, 2002). Second, etymology and the study of Greek and Latin roots provides an appropriately differentiated approach to vocabulary studies for exceptional learners (Slade & Burnham, 2020). Third, Michael Thompson's (2002) work in direct vocabulary instruction using the study of Latin and Greek word origination offers examples of differentiated curricular approaches that align with the advanced literacy abilities of advanced learners. Finally, students can study the words of specific disciplines, such as science (Job & Coleman, 2016). Therefore, a comprehensive and strong differentiated literacy program for exceptional learners contains vocabulary development, analogies, etymology, and an understanding of semantics, linguistics, and language history (VanTassel-Baska, 1998).

One final instructional strategy has gained popularity in addressing the advanced vocabulary development of exceptional learners. Research has shown the effectiveness of using graphic organizers for vocabulary instruction (McKenzie, 2014). Once previously used with older students, Kindergarten teachers are employing the strategy with all students. One of the most substantial vocabulary-based graphic organizers is the Frayer model (VanTassel-Baska, 1998; VanTassel-Baska & Stambaugh, 2005).

FIELD NOTE 5.5

In a large, urban school district, gifted students are identified in the second grade based on intelligence and achievement tests. One of the third-grade gifted learners was asked to read the grade-level chapter book assigned to every student in the classroom as part of the literacy curriculum. Each learner was told to read a grade-level text independently. While reading the book, each learner was expected to identify at least ten previously unknown words as a vocabulary study assignment. After reading the book, the gifted learner asks his mother whether or not it was permissible to tell the teacher a lie. The mother, one of two parents who are teachers, said that lying was never a good choice, and in particular, he should not lie to his teacher. When queried about why he was considering a lie, the young boy said that he went to the teacher and told her that he had read the book but did not find any new words. The teacher responded that this wasn't possible for a third-grade student and instructed him to read it again. He didn't want to read the book again and wanted to just find ten words that seemed hard for his friend and then his word study assignment would be complete.

It helps to organize essential information about a word to enhance learning by guiding higher-level word study. With gifted learners in particular, the Frayer Model has been used to study discipline – specific vocabulary.

Sentence structure

Consistent with other aspects of language development, the exceptional learner demonstrates the early emergence and advanced performance in sentence structure as compared to typically developing peers. Typically, children begin forming word phrases comprised of two or three words by age two. However, at the same age, cognitively advanced children often speak in much fuller sentences. Other examples of sophisticated sentence structure in oral language include the use of time markers (such as now, later, first, etc.), more complex vocabulary, and more complete sentences. Some gifted three-year old children can carry on full conversations with adults at this point (Bainbridge, 2020). Highly gifted or verbally gifted children will form more complex sentences even earlier than their moderately gifted counterparts.

Typical language development involves sounds initially, then words, and finally the formation of sentences (Bainbridge, 2020). The behaviors that constitute creating sentences through oral language include putting words in the correct order and understanding and following the rules of sentence structure or early grammatical correctness. Only the nativist theory suggests that the rules or structure of language are innate and aren't taught. On the other hand, behaviorist theory would suggest that these skills emerge from sequences of imitation and positive reinforcement while cognitive theory would explain the development of sentence structure skills over time in stages; and socio-cultural theory would support enhanced sentence structure skills due to engagement with one's environment.

Understanding syntactic structure is a critical part of an appropriately differentiated literacy program of study (VanTassel-Baska, 1998). In order to support the continuous progression of early onset or use of advanced sentence structure by a cognitively advanced child, adults can take certain actions while avoiding others. In order to achieve Vygotsky's Zone of Proximal Learning, young children need opportunities to engage in oral language with others with more experience. Further, the socio-cultural theory asserts that young children require opportunity to engage with stimuli in the environment with others in order to build meaningful and purposeful sentences in an attempt to communicate orally. Therefore, adults can initiate conversation around people, places, and things in the child's environment. Giving children opportunities to converse with one another around play and shared experiences. Further, Piaget's stages of cognitive development guide caregivers and educators in predicting milestones at various times with an understanding of how to enrich and expand children's development within designated phases. An example of supportive activities include reading aloud or shared readings, playing word games, providing opportunities for play and learning with same-ability peers, and asking higher-level questions to extend conversations while encouraging elaboration of ideas.

In addition to knowing what they should do, the adults in highly able children's lives should avoid certain practices as well. For example, parents should sidestep the tendency to talk in fragmented sentence structures or "baby talk" when children are very young. When children struggle with less advanced expressive oral language and become frustrated, parents should avoid speaking on their behalf because this may shorten the length and complexity of the sentences they create. Finally, teachers should not always serve as the facilitator of discussions of what these learners are reading, but rather, encourage student-to-student engagement.

SUMMARY

Many cognitively advanced learners possess an exceptional aptitude for language, display sophisticated language development and exhibit language skills early. When compared to other students of the same age, these learners speak earlier than other children, possess rich vocabulary, display advanced comprehension skills, and learn to read early. Despite these and other typically advanced language traits, established learning theories do inform their literacy education through differentiated curricula and instruction. Although language development in advanced learners is atypical of same-age and typical peers in terms of timing, existing learning and language theories do address the unique nuances and pathways that they experience. Thus existing theoretical frameworks that define learning and language development in all children are applicable to cognitive advanced learners as well; however, the type of impact is different for the two populations of children. The application of learning and language theories to education can support student growth by guiding instructional practices, choice of pedagogy, and services related to literacy education.

Theoretical frameworks and related constructs impact educational practice, including curriculum, instruction, and assessment. Implications for advocacy and related action in support of language development in advanced learners should be shared with family members, caregivers, and educators alike. Without the necessary differentiation of the school's literacy curriculum, these learners' advanced verbal ability may be unactualized. Best practices in literacy education for advanced learners should address the early emergence and development of language that address differentiated development of speech, reading, vocabulary, and sentence structure.

Generally, differentiated literacy programming for advanced learners should be led by several guiding principles. First, advanced cognitive and language development are correlated. Second, imitation and positive reinforcement help students to develop significant speech and vocabulary capacities. Third, educators and caregivers should engage these learners meaningfully with the environment in order to support movement through language development stages. Fourth, advanced learners' language development is facilitated when learning involves interaction with a more knowledgeable other or same-ability peer. Fifth, advanced learners require access to differentiated reading, vocabulary, and oral language instruction that necessitates facilitation by a more knowledgeable other, followed by independence of learning. Sixth, word study that includes analogies, semantics, linguistics, etymology, and the history of language is essential to differentiated vocabulary development for advanced learners. Seventh, these learners' complex and elaborate development of sentence structure is critical to oral and written communication. Finally, these guiding principles must be sustained over time in order for consistent and continuous progress is made in language development for these exceptional learners.

Although most literacy programs meet the language development needs of many typically developing learners, without differentiation these programs are not supportive and perhaps are even punitive for advanced learners. Existing curriculum, choice of pedagogies and instructional activities must be evaluated and subsequently differentiated for the early emergence and development of language for advanced learners. Learning and language development theories must be applied to educational practice and child rearing by families and caregivers in order for cognitively advanced learners to reach their full potential in the area of exceptional verbal ability.

REFERENCES

Bainbridge, S. (2020). *Gifted children and language development.* Very Well Family. https://www.verywellfamily.com/gifted-children-and-language-development-1449117?print

Bonds, C. W. & Bonds, T. T. (1983). Teacher, is there a gifted reader in first grade? *Roeper Review, 5*(3), 4–6. https://doi.org/10.1080/02783198309552690

Brewer, A. (2016). *Exploring speech and language skills: A parent perspective.* Honors Research Project. The Honors College, University of Akron: Akron, OH.

Burney, V. (2008). Applications of the social cognitive theory to gifted education. *Roeper Review, 30*(2), 130–139. https://doi.org/10.1080/02783190801955335

Catron, R. M. & Wingenbach, N. (2001). Developing the potential of the gifted reader. *Theory Into Practice, 25*(2), 134–140. https://doi.org/10.1080/00405848609543213

Cohen, L. M. & Kim, Y. M. (1999). Piaget's equilibration theory and the young gifted child: A balancing act. *Roeper Review, 21*(3), 201–206. https://doi.org/10.1080/02783199909553962

Cramond, B. (2004). Reading instruction for the gifted. *Illinois Reading Council Journal, 32*(4), 31–36.

Csikszentmihalyi, M. (1990). *Flow: The psychology of optimal experience.* Harper Collins.

Feldman, D. H. (1982). A developmental framework for research with gifted children. In D. H. Feldman (Ed.), *Developmental approaches to giftedness and creativity: New directions for child development.* Jossey-Bass.

Gottfried, A. W., Gottfried, A. E., Bathurst, K., & Guerin, D. W. (1994). *Gifted IQ: Early developmental aspects. The Fullerton Longitudinal Study.* Plenum Press.

Gross, M. (1999). Small poppies: Highly gifted children in the early years. *Roeper Review, 21*(3), 207–214. https://doi.org/10.1080/02783199909553963

Halliday, M. A. K. (1993). Towards a language-based theory of learning. *Linguistics in Education, 5*(2), 93–116. https://doi.org/10.1016/0898-5898(93)90026-7

Hayes, P., Norris J., & Flaitz, J. (1998). Evidence of language problems in underachieving gifted adolescents: Implications for assessment. *Secondary Gifted Education, 9*(4), 179–194. https://doi.org/10.1044/0161-1461.2903.158

Hoh, P. S. (2005). The linguistic advantage of the intellectually gifted child: An empirical study of spontaneous speech. *Roeper Review*, 27(3), 178–185. https://doi.org/10.1080/02783190509554313

Jackson, N. & Roller, C. (1993). *Reading with young children.* The National Research Center for the Gifted and Talented.

Job, J., & Coleman, M. R. (2016). The importance of reading in earnest: Non-fiction for young children. *Gifted Child Today*, 39(3), 154–163. https://doi.org/10.1177/1076217516644635

Kenney, J. (2013). Fostering critical thinking skills: Strategies for use with intermediate gifted readers. *Illinois Reading Council Journal*, 41(2), 28–39.

Levande, D. (1999). Gifted readers and reading instruction. *CAG Communicator*, 30(1), 41–42.

Lin, S. F. (2018). The effect of group work on English vocabulary learning. *Journal of Education and Learning*, 7(4), 163–178. https://eric.ed.gov/?id=EJ1179662

Mason, J. & Au, K. (1990). *Reading instruction for today.* Harper Collins.

McKenzie, E. (2014). Vocabulary development using visual displays. *Dimensions of Early Childhood*, 42(2), 12–17.

McCarrick, K. & Xiaoming. (2007). Buried treasure: The impact of computer use on young children's social, cognitive language development and motivation. *AACE Journal*, 15(1), 153–179.

Morrow, L. M. (2020). *Literacy development in the early years: Helping children read and write* (9th edition). Pearson.

National Reading Panel (2000). *Teaching children to read: An evidence-based assessment of the scientific research literature on reading and its implications for reading instruction.* National Institute of Child Health and Human Development.

Phelps, C. (2015). Energizing conceptual foundations in gifted education through transdisciplinarity. *International Journal of Creativity and Talent Development*, 3(2), 59–63.

Reis, S. M. (2004). Self-regulated learning and academically talented students. *Parenting for High Potential*, National Association for Gifted Children. Retrieved from https://www.davidsongifted.org/search-database/entry/a10460

Reis, S. M., Gubbins, E. J., Briggs, C. Schreiber, F., Richards, S., Jacobs, J., Eckert, R., & Renzulli, J. S. (2004). Reading instruction for talented readers: Few opportunities for continuous progress. *Gifted Child Quarterly*, 48(4), 315–338. https://doi.org/10.1177/001698620404800406

Reis, S. M., Eckert, R., Jacobs, J., Coyne, M., Richards, S., Briggs, C.J., Gubbins, E., & Muller, L. (2005). *The schoolwide enrichment model-Reading framework.* The National Research Center for the Gifted and Talented, University of Connecticut.

Reis, S. M. (2009). *Research-based practices for talented readers.* Research into Practice Reading. https://assets.pearsonschool.com/asset_mgr/current/201216/ReaMonTalentedRdrsReis.pdf

Reis, S. M. & Boeve, H. (2009). How academically gifted elementary, urban students respond to challenge in an enriched differentiated reading program. *Journal for the Education of the Gifted*, 33(2), 203–240. https://doi.org/10.1177/016235320903300204

Reis, S. M., McCoach, D. B., Little, C. A., Muller, L. M., & Kaniskan, R. B. (2011). The effects of differentiated instruction and enrichment pedagogy on reading achievement in five elementary schools. *American Educational Research Journal*, 48(2), 462–501. https://doi.org/10.3102/0002831210382891

Renzulli, J. S. (2012). Reexamining the role of gifted education and talent development for the 21st century: A four-part theoretical approach. *Gifted Child Quarterly*, 56(3), 150–159. https://doi.org/10.1177/0016986212444901

Rogers, K. (2002). *Re-Forming gifted education: How parents and teachers can match the program to the child.* Gifted Unlimited Press.

Rose, S. A., Feldman, J. F., & Jankowski, J. J. (2009). A cognitive approach to the development of early language. *Child Development, 80*(1), 134–150.

Slade, M. & Burnham, T. (2020). Best practices in professional learning practices in literacy education for gifted and talented students. In *Best practices in professional learning and teacher preparation* (Volume 3). Weber, C. L. & Novak, A. M., Editors. The National Association for Gifted Children.

Smith, S. R. (2009). A dynamic ecological framework for differentiating primary curriculum. *Gifted and Talented International, 24*(2), 9–20. https://doi.org/10.1080/15332276.2009.11673526

Steiner, H. H., & Carr, M. (2003). Cognitive development in gifted children: Toward a more precise understanding of emerging differences in intelligence. *Educational Psychology Review, 15*(3), 215–246. https://doi.org/10.1023/A:1024636317011

Thompson, M. (2002). Vocabulary and grammar: Critical content for critical thinking. *Journal of Secondary Gifted Education, 13*(2), 60–66. https://doi.org/10.4219/jsge-2002-367

Vaivre-Douret, L. (2011). Developmental and cognitive characteristics of high-level potentialities (highly gifted) children. *International Journal of Pediatrics, 2011*, 14. https://doi.org/10.1155/2011/420297

VanTassel-Baska, J. (1998). *Excellence in educating gifted and talented learners* (3rd ed.). Love.

VanTassel-Baska, J. (2017). Curriculum issues: The importance of selecting literature for gifted learners. *Gifted Child Today, 40*(3), 183–184. https://doi.org/101177/1076217517713783

VanTassel-Baska, J. & Stambaugh, T. (2005). *Comprehensive curriculum for gifted learners* (3rd ed.). Pearson.

Vygotsky L. S. (1978). *Mind in society.* Harvard University Press.

Vygotsky, L. (1986). *Thought and language.* MIT Press.

Westberg, K., Archambault, F., Dobyns, S., & Slavin, T. (1993). *The classroom practices observation study. Journal for the Education of the Gifted, 16*(2), 103–119. https://doi.org/10.1177/016235329301600204

Wood, P. F. (2008). Reading instruction with gifted and talented readers: A series of unfortunate events or a sequence of auspicious results. *Gifted Child Today, 31*(3), 16–25. https://doi.org/10.4219/gct-2008-783

CHAPTER **6**

Problem-solving characteristics in gifted and advanced learners

Camelia Birlean, Emma Margaret Birlean,
and Bruce M. Shore

Cognitively advanced learners approach and solve problems using processes that are similar to those used by all problem solvers, but in some respects unique and fascinating. Some differences are related to the nature of the problems, others to the capabilities comprising giftedness. Some differences are more social. We summarize below how cognitively advanced learners find, create, and solve problems; the nature of their skills; and their preferences, highlighting the voice of one such problem solver.

WHAT IS PROBLEM SOLVING?

All problems share the common features of having a beginning or initial state and an end called a goal state. All the possible paths from the beginning to the end are called the problem space. Most narrowly, problem-solving occurs in a well-defined problem space such as doing practice examples from school lessons. These often have a known "right answer" (sometimes printed in the back of textbooks), relative clarity in what information is needed to solve the problem, and only a few paths from the beginning to the end. They commonly require just minutes to solve, usually individually by each pupil. Advanced learners often find these kinds of problems to be repetitive and uninteresting, especially after the first few. They do them quickly and accurately.

At another extreme are the world's great challenges: health, poverty, peace, equity, water, food, education, climate, racism, and more. These ill-defined problems have no clear end state to indicate when they are solved, there is uncertainty regarding what information is needed to address the problem, and the problem space includes possibly infinite paths. When given an opportunity, young people have played critical roles in addressing these, too.

DOI: 10.4324/9781003025443-7

In between these extremes, there is a wide range of school and home tasks that provide practice and invoke organizational and social skills, creativity, and finding the next topic to explore. Teachers and parents sometimes suggest topics, as in science, history, or other knowledge fairs, or students can choose or invent the questions. Sometimes even the experts do not know the answers to questions learners ask. These are learning experiences that build inquisitive dispositions, content knowledge, and methodological skills that can be combined and extended to bigger theoretical and practical challenges in the future. A problem is an opportunity to connect interests and motivation to knowledge about the material and how to understand it, and to ask important and challenging questions. These activities can extend over days, weeks, and months. Sometimes they can be tackled alone, but other times collaboration is an advantage, and sometimes group work is essential.

Problem solving mostly refers to school tasks that engage learners in complex thinking and that require a pause to think through the challenge before plunging in to begin providing an answer. Problems can arise from any source: the learner's own imagination, music lessons, sports, drama clubs, puzzle books, or elsewhere. Especially, valuable are learning experiences that involve tasks carefully selected to require the learner to go beyond what they already know, or can achieve alone without any help from peers, family, teachers, and other sources.

WHAT DO WE MEAN BY GIFTED?

We use the word gifted, but are not fixated on a single meaning. Many school districts define giftedness in terms of high IQ. IQ tests are collections of rather brief verbal, mathematical, or visual problems in which a higher score is obtained by quickly and accurately producing the one correct answer. Being accurate is more important than being quick, although excessive dawdling or daydreaming is counterproductive. Creativity is another aspect of giftedness, one that is expressed in seeing more than one solution to a question and coming up with original or unique questions or answers. An educationally useful way to understand giftedness is that it involves thinking and developing like an expert. Expertise differs across subjects: Chemists make new discoveries differently from historians. Nevertheless, most experts share some characteristics. They are passionate about their interests, plan before they act, self-evaluate, and are open to new evidence to update their knowledge.

In gifted or advanced learners, there is another important side to problem solving that happens more often than with many other children: problem finding. Advanced learners more often identify complex or big questions they are curious about, even though all children are curious. Even though all children ask questions, children identified as advanced learners typically ask more questions (surely, we have been hounded by why? how? and other questions we do not know the answers to!). One of our favorite stories is about the physics Nobel Laureate, Isidore Rabi. A magazine interviewer asked how he became a scientist (Schulman, 1993). He replied, most parents asked what their children learned in school that day. His mom asked what good questions he asked!

HOW ADVANCED LEARNERS SOLVE PROBLEMS – WHAT IS UNIQUE?

Let's begin with 12-year-old Emma's recollection, in her own words, of her science-fair project a year earlier. We'll then pick out some of the main points.

> Science fair is an important annual initiative at my school. Students work alone or with a peer on open-ended investigations, usually with countless solutions and driven by the student's interest. Reflecting back on my process, I see five major steps emerging.
>
> The first step was brainstorming. Unlike the majority of my peers, I prefer to work alone, and this proved itself as an asset during my brainstorming process. Numerous ideas went through my mind as potential topics for my science-fair project and I did not need to compromise on one idea that usually is approved in a democratic way by the majority, which oftentimes does not suit my needs. This time, I could allow myself to drift to different fields of science and explore, soon to find out that brainstorming requires not only reflection but also a great deal of research and learning in order to figure out the question one wants to pose. I specifically looked for examples and articles that would fit in with my ideas. I had three main ideas: (a) the design of a blood-pressure bracelet device connected to 911, which I decided to leave for a future science fair because of its complexity; (b) the exploration of an environmentally friendly alternative to the salt used to defrost streets during winter, which damages our fresh water streams and its fauna, not to mention our pets' paws and even our shoes, and finally (c) the investigation of a project on critical thinking that proved itself worthy and led me to receiving a bronze medal. It must have been early September when mom placed an article on my nightstand, as she usually does, that caught my attention. It was written by psychologist Daniel Willingham who shared about a classic experiment conducted in the 80s, in which university students were asked to solve a problem. They were asked if and how a malignant tumor could be treated with a particular type of ray that causes major collateral damage to the healthy tissue. Very few participants were able to solve the problem in the allotted 20 minutes. Prior to the problem-solving activity, the same group of students read a story describing a military situation similar to the medical problem. Instead of rays attacking a tumor, rebels were this time attacking a dictator hiding out in a fortress. The military story described the solution, but despite reading it moments before trying to solve the medical problem, participants did not see the analogy: Disperse the forces to avoid collateral damage and have forces converge at the point of attack. Simply mentioning that the story can help solve the medical problem boosted solution rates to nearly 100%. Using the analogy was not hard; the problem was thinking

to use it in the first place. Willingham made the point that university students fail to use generic thinking skills in their everyday life and questioned whether students are wasting their time learning these skills. This article was my Eureka! I wanted to learn if the same result holds true when the experiment is given to high school students, like me. So, my science-fair study looked at whether general critical thinking strategy transfers from a subject to another and to real world problems in general. If it does not transfer then I would agree with Dr. Willingham, in that learning about these skills in disconnect from discipline would be a waste of time for students and their teachers.

The second step was planning. It was important for me to get all my elements ready for my final project and organize them well. First, I read some research papers with similar experiments as the one I described above. The readings helped me develop the methods of investigation and helped me decide on the problems, I will give to the participants in my study. I hoped to get about 20–30 participants. Science fair was in February, and I had finished my planning stage in late December to early January.

The studies I read showed there is not yet a strategy proven effective to teaching generic thinking skills but there is a good understanding of how to teach more specific critical thinking skills. Willingham (2019) proposed a four-step plan that really talked to me and to the teachers who were curious about my science-fair project.

1. Identify what is meant by critical thinking in the specific domain.
2. Identify the content domain that students need to learn.
3. Teach the specific skills and knowledge explicitly and then have students practice them.
4. In order for skills to stick with students forever, or at least for a long time, the skills must be practiced in different ways over and over for a minimum of three to five years.

The third vital step was the actual experimentation process. Participants were expected to read two scenarios and solve two situational problems adapted from Gick and Holyoak (1980, 1983). The first was a science scenario and the problem required participants to apply a specific thinking strategy in order to solve it. For the science scenario, I wrote a paragraph explaining Newton's third law of motion (for every action there is an equal and opposite reaction) using the rocket-propulsion example. The problem that follows this explanation shows an astronaut who, while repairing the shuttle, starts drifting away with his toolbelt. The participants were asked to solve the problem by using their knowledge of Newton's third law of motion to bring the astronaut back to the shuttle safe and sound.

The second scenario was generic, and the problem connected to it required participants to apply a general thinking strategy. Both the scenario and the problems were inspired by Willingham's article, in which rebels trying to take over a well-protected fortress were led by a highly skilled general whose successful tactic was to surround the fortress and attack it from every angle at the same time. The problem required participants to pretend that they needed to cure a tumor using a type of chemical ray that could kill a tumor, but if used at high intensity could harm the healthy tissue. However, if used at low intensity, the ray had no effect on the tissue or the tumor.

Using critical thinking, participants were expected to find the similarities between the examples and exercises and solve the problems. If participants failed to solve the tumor problem, they were prompted to use the analogy (the tactic applied by the general). Participants were asked to record their time from start to end of the activity.

The fourth step was making sense of data and writing up my results. Unfortunately, from the 20 consent forms that I shared with potential participants that fit my criteria (12 to 14 years of age, strong in science) only five returned their completed tasks by deadline, so I have to work with a limited amount of data. In my analysis, I created a table and compared participants' solutions to the two problems with the solutions offered by experts in Willingham's article, while also considering whether my participants required any prompting along the way.

The results of this study, in agreement to research I read, show that general critical-thinking strategy is not an effective teaching and learning tool. My results made it clear that students are better off mastering lots of specific skills within a subject domain as opposed to learning a small amount of general skills (applicable across domains).

The fifth step in my process was the reflection process. When I look back, I realize how important planning of data collection is in the research process. This was the major setback in my study, and I thought it would be an easy step. I was only able to gather data from five participants, all excellent students. I learned that I should have planned out my experimentation process well in advance and should have allotted it more time.

The science fair was an excellent experience and helped me learn a lot about critical thinking and the problem-solving process by engaging in the actual process. What a better way to learn about content than by experiencing it firsthand? This project is an excellent first reference for what to do and not to do in my next science fair.

PROBLEM SOLVING IN EMMA'S SCIENCE-FAIR EXPERIENCE

Not every cognitively advanced student engages all of these or other processes simultaneously, but there are key processes we can observe. When faced with a new question or problem, nearly all learners do some of these to some degree.

Processes observable before beginning

Larger and more interconnected knowledge base

Typically, as a result of dialog and reading, and attending to their surroundings, advanced learners have a larger store of relevant prior knowledge and are better at retrieving it when needed. That knowledge is sometimes rather esoteric! Critically, this knowledge is interconnected – one idea leads meaningfully to another. New ideas are not just accumulated separately. They are rapidly integrated into the existing knowledge base through activities that form, alter, or strengthen links with knowledge already present. Cognitively advanced learners make more effective and efficient use (application) of what they already know and know how to do than others. They can illustrate this by drawing a concept or knowledge map in which each idea is placed on a sheet of paper, then drawing lines between knowledge points to show which ideas are connected to each other. Advanced learners make more such connections, connecting also to meaningful events and experience in their lives, and give better explanations of each connection. All learners can create knowledge maps. However, when making a concept map for a new problem, typically developing learners focus mainly on replicating information presented in the problem, whereas cognitively advanced learners include additional relevant information they know.

Support

Advanced learners typically receive supportive attention from adults, especially in early stages of learning, but later they prefer to figure out puzzling problems on their own rather than accepting direct assistance. Mothers of high-IQ preschoolers have been shown to give general prompts when assisting their children to do a puzzle (What do you think we should put here?) rather than specific hints (Where is the other green piece?). They also did not suggest what to draw, but asked what they would like to draw. Of course, the causes and effects are intertwined; parents are good at setting suitable levels of challenge for their children, but this poses a reminder to encourage autonomy as much and as soon as possible, while still sharing interesting articles, websites, and other experiences.

Lack of support is the most frequently cited reason students give when they cheat on a science-fair project (Shore et al., 2008), for example: copying data, taking an idea from a project book, and presenting it as their own, or copying work seen elsewhere. Having sufficient time, materials, help, and knowledge are critical. When professional scientists have cheated (remember "cold fusion"?), they give similar excuses! Instead of rushing in with a coil of wire and a screwdriver, we can ask if any help would be welcome, and what it would be – even just discussing their plans – and express appreciation of the thinking and work in progress.

Motivation and social context

Interest is the key to motivation, and advanced learners often have more, more varied, and sometimes weirder interests than other children. When a problem intersects interests, the learner's experience and intrinsic motivation are enhanced. The most positively recalled school experiences are those that offered opportunities to build on interests.

All students need clear and concise instructions for assignments, but advanced learners are more comfortable when they can exercise some influence over how the assignment is framed. This applies to the task itself, and also to the social context. Emma wanted to work alone on her science-fair project specifically because she wanted to pursue her own ideas. Advanced learners shun group work when they anticipate that some collaborating students will not "pull their weight," i.e., invest effort and time to do their best work. This is called the "free rider" effect (Orbell & Dawes, 1981). Parents of advanced learners also sometimes are hesitant about group work because they, too, care about fairness, and also because they realize that group rather than individual work on these kinds of projects could dilute their competitive advantage for scholarships and further education. For group work to be effective teachers need to give clear, well-understood, group-work directions to students, and stay engaged themselves. The contributions of each child, and not just the group overall, should be suitably reviewed. This requires ongoing teacher monitoring of major group-project work; it is reasonable to be wary of group assignments that are never seen by the teacher prior to completion, and in which the individual contributions of all participants are not known. That said, children identified as gifted or advanced learners do not always want to work alone on problem solving; they should be given some say in whom they work with, when, and on what kinds of problems.

Advanced learners sometimes behave in a group in ways that make others uncomfortable. They are more likely to tolerate and even enjoy friendly intellectual competition or sparring; they value both sides standing their ground in disagreements (Barfurth & Shore, 2008; Chichekian & Shore, 2017). Advanced students benefit from talking about how others respond to them, and the need to encourage every member of a group to participate – some other children initially might be shy to speak up, but will do so if someone else in the group stands up for them and reminds others to listen. This is a valuable skill for all children, but cognitively advanced learners may understand and articulate these relationships sooner.

Novelty

Welcoming novelty is characteristic of creativity and giftedness. Novelty takes many forms beyond being new or original. Problems need not be totally new, just new to the learner, or a new twist on an old problem. The military strategy Emma cited was used by General George Washington when his bedraggled army fired cannon down three streets toward the center of Trenton, New Jersey, with nary a casualty in its own ranks, defeating the professional Hessian mercenaries.

Advanced learners more often welcome the challenge of complexity. When we asked advanced learners how to improve a computer game, they suggested making it more complex and adding more difficult levels. They complicate tasks to amuse themselves. Other learners instead asked for more "bells and whistles" (Maniatis et al., 1998).

Advanced learners differ from average peers in their strategy development and preferences, and their use of these on novel problems, yet they use the same toolbox of strategies (Birlean & Shore, 2018). For example, expert mathematicians express aesthetic appreciation for mathematical beauty or elegance in problem solving (defined as simplicity and originality), but this is not especially apparent among mathematically advanced youth. Rather, it is a learned competence, nurtured within the professional community of mathematicians beyond high school. Prior to this level, all students focus on finding solutions.

Processes observable at the outset of solving a problem

Defining the problem

Defining the problem is step one in "self-regulated learning," a goal-focused approach to learning that takes into account the context, the learner's beliefs about her or his abilities and learning preferences, planning, and self-evaluation (Oppong et al., 2019). Effective learners carefully determine the nature of the task that faces them. Is it a new kind of problem or does it fit a known pattern? What do I know that is relevant? What do I know about how to solve it? Students identified as cognitively advanced typically excel at these processes, but do not exclusively own them.

Successful learners more extensively contextualize the problem, read and think widely about it, and brainstorm. When given several problems with instructions to categorize or group them, more able learners, unprompted, group them in terms of "deep" qualities such as underlying subject matter and effective solution strategies (Pelletier & Shore, 2003). They sometimes create subgroups. Less capable learners group problems on "surface" characteristics, for example, word-based versus numerical problems. All students can group problems, and all students group more when prompted to do so.

Proficient problem solvers initially better discern the problem to solve and set subgoals as they move toward the final solution. Perhaps you remember science or mathematics problems in which not all the information is given directly. Some measurement units needed to be converted, or some given information needed to be manipulated first, then combined with the rest; that illustrates a subgoal. When we taught both high and average performers to draw concept maps with the given information, the maps revealed the subclusters and all students improved their subsequent performance on multi-step problems (Austin & Shore, 1994).

Advanced and creative learners sometimes adapt, redefine, or personalize an assigned problem. So do others, but not as often or without a prompt or permission. To a greater degree, advanced learners enjoy finding or creating their own problems. They more readily set priorities and articulate goals, then focus on a specific question. They also more often see or represent a problem in different ways, with different solution paths. People who cannot understand a problem will not find and use suitable strategies, nor can they explain what they are doing and why, so ultimately they become unmotivated.

Planning

Emma spent months planning but only one month actually executing her project. Advanced learners more spontaneously and systematically generate appropriate solution sequences, rather than considering just one step at a time. All students know how to plan, but making a great plan is a sign of high ability. Outlining a story, sketching a sculpture or room decor, and specifying research steps, all exemplify planning. Successful learners spend relatively more time planning compared to actually executing a problem, in comparison to other learners.

Cognitively advanced learners do the actual solving of a problem more quickly than others, especially with one-step (e.g., plug in the numbers), trivial, or familiar tasks, mainly because of their fine-tuned procedural knowledge (automaticity developed through deliberate practice). They also spend relatively more time in the planning stage on nontrivial problems.

Processes observable especially during the actual problem solving

Commitment

The most impactful problem-solving experiences take place over extended periods of time, from hours to months. Perseverance and curiosity help. Even when difficulties arise, such as participants dropping out, they persist.

Many characteristics that distinguish learners with giftedness are learned. "Flow" (Csikszentmihalyi, 1990) or "being in the groove" is a feeling we experience when deeply immersed into the task at hand; we lose track of time, and do not hear the bell or the call to supper. All students experience flow from time to time, especially in their favorite subject. Regardless of the classroom teaching methods, high-achieving students experience more flow, but the most is reported by high-achieving students in inquiry-based classrooms. Students in these settings learn commitment or perseverance.

Monitoring progress on the task

Cognitively advanced learners think many steps ahead – forward thinking – when solving a problem. This is the same mental process that helps chess players anticipate early that a game is unwinnable. Emma asked herself if she could do all the steps of her project in the available time. Advanced learners more often and more effectively monitor their solution pathway and, if necessary, select another. They do not always wait until the end to find out if they got the "right answer." Genuine, important problems do not always have right answers. Rather, they have the best possible answer at that time.

Another way we can see superior problem solvers use a common strategy more effectively is called breaking a response set. Often several examples in a row require a particular approach, but then an example is given that requires shifting mental gears. Advanced learners typically analyze each problem, selecting the most appropriate strategy from their larger repertoire. They are less likely to be tricked by the shift.

Psychologists studying this sometimes then insert a new example that can be solved the old way as well; high ability learners more often spot it and switch strategies before they must. A famous example involves combining water jars to get a certain total volume. Five examples in a row could need three jars, but the sixth can be done with three or just two, and the seventh only with two. Almost everyone "gets it" eventually; individuals with exceptional IQs do so more spontaneously (Dover & Shore, 1991). However, if they fail to spot the initial pattern change, they can actually make more errors when the shift is needed (Shore et al., 1994); the reason why is not clear – two possibilities might be that they underestimated the difficulty of the task and rushed, or that they were redefining the task in their own minds (as observed by Getzels & Csikszentmihalyi, 1976, in successful young artists) but skirting the point of the originally-given task. Sometimes a reminder is helpful to take your time and focus on the task, not just finishing the task as quickly as possible (which does help with IQ scores).

Gathering evidence

Cognitively advanced learners typically are superior at organizing and analyzing data. They make more detailed tables, graphs, and charts. They make evidence-based decisions, and can be critical of the quality of the evidence. They are more tolerant of ambiguity, incomplete answers, and the need to try again from a different angle.

They are also more able to distinguish relevant and irrelevant information in a complex problem-solving task. This can happen as data occur, or in the planning stage. Do you recall school or puzzle-book problems that contained extra, irrelevant information? Gifted and academically able learners better sift that out.

Thinking adaptively and flexibly

Response-set breaking fits here, but here we want to emphasize solving a problem more than one way. A grade 10 mathematics teacher divided a high-performing class into three teams and asked one group to prove Pythagoras's square-on-the-hypotenuse theorem in right-angled triangles (= the sum of the squares on the other two sides) from Euclidean geometry using algebra; group 2 had to use trigonometry; and group 3 had to use functions. The class did it and shared their solutions. Average-ability students asked to solve mathematical problems in more than one way find the task to be difficult, time-consuming, and to require inordinate patience.

Despite superior strategic abilities, advanced learners acquiring and implementing freshly learned strategies are equally likely to be hindered in their problem solving, but they more quickly move out of this phase. When a solution appears to fail, they are more likely to choose another valid strategy and remain focused, rather than to give up or guess wildly. Typical learners more often resort to trial-and-error or guessing – they do not have or create a Plan B.

Processes observable after problem solving

Reflection on outcomes

When more able students complete a task, they more thoroughly reflect on the solution and the solution processes. They worry less about incomplete or ambiguous results. Reflection is the final step of self-regulated learning, and it can be learned to some degree by all students. Emma ended her description with what she learned about allowing more time for effective data collection, but also affirmed her results were consistent with the research that inspired her.

Discipline-based thinking

For decades, a number of critical-thinking programs have been marketed to schools and parents. However, the best way to build effective thinking and problem-solving skills in general is with problems that are real either in life or within specific subjects. Emma wrote, "students are better off mastering lots of specific skills within a subject domain as opposed to learning a small amount of general skills." Problem-solving first should be deliberately practiced in meaningful contexts, then the similarities and differences between contexts should be examined explicitly. Not only the thinking skills themselves need to be taught and practiced; transferring them among situations at school, home, work, or the community also must be modeled and practiced.

When the situations and contexts are similar, most students can apply known strategies in new problems ("near transfer"). When jumping across different contexts, such as from military to medicine ("far transfer"), more capable students make the connections more spontaneously and more quickly. It is specifically these processes that make advanced learners advanced. And because many of these also involve skills learned through deliberate practice, one can learn to be smarter.

CONCLUSION

Our children sometimes surprise us. Advanced children might do so more frequently. Building on interactions with their friends and family, teacher, the curriculum, and the other resources they encounter, they more effectively and spontaneously use widely available intellectual, creative, and social tools to enhance their ability to find, re-interpret, invent, and solve problems at school and elsewhere. In addition to Izzie Rabi's inspiration – What good question did you ask at school today? – we can encourage and enhance children's problem-solving skills by listening and watching for the processes described above, and asking for explanations and examples from advanced learners as they share their problem-solving experiences with us. Here is another example from Emma:

> This example required some quick thinking on my part to solve a problem in real life. I was vacationing with my family and in order to take advantage of the

beautiful sun, we decided to serve our lunch on the terrace. My seating, however, was not ideal as the sun was glaring straight into my eyes to the point that I started to tear up, even though I was wearing sunglasses. The menus arrived, and because of the pandemic measures, the menus were printed for single use on paper sheets. I took one look at the menu, chose my meal and knew immediately what to do next. I placed the paper on my head and secured it with my sunglasses. Although I looked indisputably strange, the sun was no longer burning my eyes, my face and the top of my head, and I could eat peacefully. Shortly after, other guests on the terrace used my trick to avoid the glaring sun.

Although this may seem like a silly solution to a small problem, I believe this was an excellent solution, given the resources at hand, that allowed my family members and me to eat peacefully and prevented them from listening to my complaints.

Problem solving is not all serious. People of all ages engage in games of skill, puzzles, and hobbies. Problem-solving ranges from obligation to playfulness and sometimes combines the two. Nevertheless, learners – advanced or not – differ in their openness to adventure and comfort with being different; social and emotional issues definitely need to be taken into account, even when focusing on the cognitive side. To become better at problem solving, we need to watch for and encourage opportunities for the processes we have described while engaging in deliberate practice in the context of topics of interest. Let's put that menu around our sunglasses!

REFERENCES

Austin, L. B., & Shore, B. M. (1994). The use of concept mapping as an instructional strategy in college-level physics. *Scientia Paedagogica Experimentalis – International Journal of Experimental Research in Education*, 31(2), 249–264. Retrieved from https://www.researchgate.net/publication/299299710_The_use_of_concept_mapping_as_an_instructional_strategy_in_college-level_physics/link/56f45d5d08ae81582bf0a384/download

Barfurth, M. A., & Shore, B. M. (2008). White water during inquiry learning: Understanding the place of disagreements in the process of collaboration. In B. M. Shore, M. W. Aulls, & M. A. B. Delcourt (Eds.), *Inquiry in education (vol. II): Overcoming barriers to successful implementation* (pp. 149–164). Erlbaum (Routledge).

Birlean, C., & Shore, B. M. (2018). Cognitive development of giftedness and talents: From theory to practice. In J. L. Roberts, T. F. Inman, & J. H. Robins (Eds.), *Introduction to gifted education* (pp. 95–118). Prufrock Press.

Chichekian, T., & Shore, B. M. (2017). Hold firm: Gifted learners value standing one's ground in disagreements with a friend. *Journal for the Education of the Gifted*, 40(2), 152–167. https://doi.org/10.1177/0162353217701020

Csikszentmihalyi, M. (1990). *Flow: The psychology of optimal experience*. Harper & Row.

Dover, A. C., & Shore, B. M. (1991). Giftedness and flexibility on a mathematical set-breaking task. *Gifted Child Quarterly*, 35(2), 99–105. https://doi.org/10.1177/001698629103500209

Getzels, J. W., & Csikszentmihalyi, M. (1976). *The creative vision: A longitudinal study of problem finding in art*. Wiley.

Gick, M. L., & Holyoak, K. J. (1980). Analogical problem solving. *Cognitive Psychology, 12*(3), 306–355. https://doi.org/10.1016/0010-0285(80)90013-4

Gick, M. L., & Holyoak, K. J. (1983). Schema induction and analogical transfer. *Cognitive Psychology, 15*(1), 1–38. https://doi.org/10.1016/0010-0285(83)90002-6

Maniatis, E., Cartwright, G. F., & Shore, B. M. (1998). Giftedness and complexity in a self-directed computer-based task. *Gifted and Talented International, 13*(2), 83–89. https://scholars.unh.edu/dissertation/127

Oppong, E., Shore, B. M., & Muis, K. R. (2019). Clarifying the connections among giftedness, metacognition, self-regulation, and self-regulated learning: Implications for theory and practice. *Gifted Child Quarterly, 63*(2), 102–119. https://doi.org/10.1177/0016986218814008

Orbell, J., & Dawes, R. (1981). Social dilemmas. In G. M. Stephenson & J. H. Davis (Eds.), *Progress in applied social psychology* (Vol. 1, pp. 37–65). Wiley.

Pelletier, S., & Shore, B. M. (2003). The gifted learner, the novice, and the expert: Sharpening emerging views of giftedness. In D. C. Ambrose, L. Cohen, & A. J. Tannenbaum (Eds.), *Creative intelligence: Toward theoretic integration* (pp. 237–281). Hampton Press.

Schulman, M. (1993). Great minds start with questions: Practical ways to enhance your child's natural ability to think and create. *Parents [Magazine], 68*(9), 99–102. (*As they grow/7 to 10 section.*) Retrieved from http://proquest.umi.com/pqdlink?index=45&sid=1&srch mode=3&vinst=PROD&fmt=6&startpage=1&clientid=10843&vname=PQD&RQT=30 9&did=5001740&scaling=FULL&ts=1293572316&vtype=PQD&aid=1&rqt=309&TS =1293572432&clientId=10843

Shore, B. M., Delcourt, M. A. B., Syer, C. A., & Schapiro, M. (2008). The phantom of the science fair. In B. M. Shore, M. W. Aulls, & M. A. B. Delcourt (Eds.), *Inquiry in education (vol. II): Overcoming barriers to successful implementation* (pp. 83–118). Erlbaum (Routledge).

Shore, B. M., Koller, M. B., & Dover, A. C. (1994). More from the water jars: Revisiting a cognitive task on which some gifted children's performance is exceeded. *Gifted Child Quarterly, 38*(4), 179–183. https://doi.org/10.1177/001698629403800405

Willingham, D. T. (2019). How to teach critical thinking. *Education: Future Frontiers* (Occasional Paper Series). Retrieved from https://apo.org.au/sites/default/files/resource-files/2019-06/apo-nid244676.pdf

Other Relevant Reading

Arikan, E. E., & Ünal, H. (2015). Investigation of problem-solving and problem-posing abilities of seventh-grade students. *Educational Science: Theory and Practice, 15*(5), 1403–1415. https://doi.org/10.12738/eap\tp.2015.5.2678

Bransford, J. D., & Stein, B. S. (1993). *The IDEAL problem solver*. Freeman.

Bruner, J. S. (1960). *The process of education*. Vintage.

Cankoy, O., & Darbaz, S. (2010). Effect of a problem posing based problem solving instruction on understanding problem. *Hacettepe Üniversitesi Eğitim Fakültesi Dergisi [Hacettepe University Journal of Education], 38*, 11–24. Retrieved from http://citeseerx.ist.psu.edu/viewdoc/download?doi=10.1.1.457.4670&rep=rep1&type=pdf

Carr, M., Alexander, J., & Schwanenflugel, P. (1996). Where gifted children do and do not excel on metacognitive tasks. *Roeper Review, 18*(3), 212–207. https://doi.org/10.1080/02783199609553740

Cera Guy, J. N. M. T., Williams, J. M., & Shore, B. M. (2019). High- and otherwise-achieving students' expectations of classroom group work: An exploratory empirical study. *Roeper Review, 41*(3), 166–184. https://doi.org/10.1080/02783193.2019.1622166

Coleman, E., & Shore, B. M. (1991). Problem-solving processes of high and average performers in physics. *Journal for the Education of the Gifted, 14*(4), 366–379. https://doi.org/10.1177/016235329101400403

Davidson, J. E., & Sternberg, R. J. (1984). The role of insight in intellectual giftedness. *Gifted Child Quarterly, 28*(2), 58–64. https://doi.org/10.1177/001698628402800203

Ericsson, K. A., Roring, R. W., & Nandagopal, K. (2007). Giftedness and evidence for reproducibly superior performance: An account based on the expert performance framework. *High Ability Studies, 18*(1), 3–56. https://doi.org/10.1080/13598130701350593

Gaultney, J. F. (1998). Utilization deficiencies among children with learning disabilities. *Learning and Individual Differences, 10*(1), 13–28. https://doi.org/10.1016/S1041-6080(99)80140-X

Gorodetsky, M., & Kavir, R. (2003). What can we learn from how gifted/average pupils describe their processes of problem solving? *Learning and Instruction, 13*(3), 305–325. https://doi.org/10.1016/S0959-4752(02)00005-1

Grundmeier, T. A. (2003). *The effects of providing mathematical problem-posing experiences for K-8 pre-service teachers: Investigating teachers' beliefs and characteristics of posed problems.* Unpublished doctoral dissertation, University of New Hampshire, Durham. Retrieved from https://core.ac.uk/download/pdf/215514709.pdf

Mann, E. L. (2006). Creativity: The essence of mathematics. *Journal for the Education of the Gifted, 30*(2), 236–260. https://doi.org/10.4219/jeg-2006-264

Matsko, V., & Thomas, J. (2014). The problem is the solution: Creating original problems in gifted mathematics classes. *Journal for the Education of the Gifted, 37*(2), 153–170. https://doi.org/10.1177/0162353214529043

Polya, G. (1957). *How to solve it?* (2nd ed.). Princeton University Press.

Renzulli, J. S. (2005). The three-ring conception of giftedness: A developmental model for promoting creative productivity. In R. J. Sternberg & J. E. Davidson (Eds.), *Conceptions of giftedness* (pp. 246–279). Cambridge University Press.

Robinson, N. M. (2000). Giftedness in very young children: How seriously should it be taken? In R. C. Friedman & B. M. Shore (Eds.), *Talents unfolding: Cognition and development* (pp. 7–26). American Psychological Association.

Shore, B. M., Aulls, M. W., Tabatabai, D., & Kaur Magon, J. (2020). *I is for inquiry: An ABC of inquiry instruction for elementary teachers and schools.* Prufrock Press.

Sriraman, B. (2003). Mathematical giftedness, problem solving, and the ability to formulate generalizations: The problem-solving experiences of four gifted students. *Journal of Secondary Gifted Education, 14*(3), 151–165. https://doi.org/10.4219/jsge-2003-425

Steiner, H. H. (2006). A microgenetic analysis of strategic variability in gifted and average ability children. *Gifted Child Quarterly, 50*(1), 62–74. https://doi.org/10.1177/001698620605000107

Sternberg, R. J., & Davidson, J. E. (1983). Insight in the gifted. *Educational Psychologist, 18*(1), 51–57. https://doi.org/10.1080/00461528309529261

Stott, A., & Hobden, P. A. (2016). Effective learning: A case student of the learning strategies used by a gifted high achiever in learning science. *Gifted Child Quarterly, 60*(1), 63–74. https://doi.org/10.1177/0016986215611961

Tarshis, E., & Shore, B. M. (1991). Differences in perspective taking between high and above average IQ preschool children. *European Journal for High Ability [now High Ability Studies], 2*(2), 201–211. https://doi.org/10.1080/0937445910020209

Threlfall, J., & Hargreaves, M. (2008). The problem-solving methods of mathematically gifted and older average-attaining students. *High Ability Studies, 19*(1), 83–98. https://doi.org/10.1080/13598130801990967

Tjoe, H. (2015). Giftedness and aesthetics: Perspectives of expert mathematicians and mathematically gifted students. *Gifted Child Quarterly, 59*(3), 165–176. https://doi.org/10.1177/0016986215583872

Willingham, D. T. (2020). Ask the cognitive scientist: How can educators teach critical thinking? *American Educator*, n.p. Retrieved from https://www.aft.org/ae/fall2020/willingham

CHAPTER 7

Motivation and achievement in gifted and advanced learners

Hope Elisabeth Wilson

Conceptualizations of motivation in psychology are rich and nuanced, with a plethora of theories, frameworks, and research from which to draw understanding. Rather than get lost in the depths and complexities of this broad topic, I have divided this chapter into two parts. In the first part, I introduce some key concepts from several of the fundamental theories of motivation and highlight their applicability to high ability children. Then I will address the educational and counseling implications of these theories, focusing on two conditions often associated with high ability children: perfectionism and underachievement.

MODELS OF MOTIVATION AND THE HIGH ABILITY CHILD

In this section, brief explanations of key concepts of motivation theories are accompanied by applications and connections specifically to high ability children. While research empirically studying the motivation of high-ability or gifted individuals is limited, I rely on theoretical and conceptual pieces written in peer-reviewed journals when this work is available. However, for some concepts, I have had to make my own extrapolations and explorations of the topic.

Intrinsic and extrinsic motivation

With the first theory of learning in psychology, behaviorism, psychologists, such as Pavlov and Skinner were able to teach behaviors through conditioning with external stimuli, such as rewards or punishments (Spielman et al., 2020). Skinner trained pigeons to perform tasks, including playing the piano and ping pong, using a series of rewards (bird seed), via positive reinforcement of desired behaviors (positive and negative reinforcement are discussed in more detail in Chapter 3: Learning). In this case, the bird seed functions as the external stimuli and playing

DOI: 10.4324/9781003025443-8

ping pong is the conditioned response. This conditioning, and the subsequent learning theory of behaviorism, led to our most fundamental understanding about motivation – the distinction between extrinsic (external) and intrinsic (internal) motivation (Spielman et al., 2020). Extrinsic motivation is associated with the Behaviorist school of thought, in which human behavior is motivated by the external environment including systems of reinforcements and punishments, much like Skinner's pigeons. Behaviorism is still used in contemporary settings in the form of Applied Behavior Analysis, and is also an integral part of cognitive-behavioral therapy approaches used to treat issues including anxiety and addiction treatment.

Intrinsic motivation, on the other hand, relies on more complex understandings of the human condition, taking into account the internal mechanisms and drives of individuals. More complex learning theories, such as Social Cognitive Theory developed by Albert Bandura, focused on ideas, such as modeling and vicarious learning (Spielman et al., 2020). A simple example of these learning theories is that a child can learn not to touch a hot stove by seeing someone else get burned, or even by having a parent tell them not to do so, rather than having to experience that external consequence firsthand. Examination of these internal learning processes led to greater understandings of the internal processes of motivation, i.e., intrinsic motivation. The processes of intrinsic motivation include components such as *self-efficacy*, or the desire to maintain or enhance a feeling of self-worth, and *interest* or sense of independence and choice. Thus, intrinsic motivation can explain why people, and children, in particular, engage in tasks that may not have an obvious external reward or punishment system.

Introductory psychology texts often present extrinsic and intrinsic motivations as discrete entities; however, the relationship between them is much more complex and interconnected. For example, most of us are motivated toward a chosen career for both intrinsic and extrinsic reasons. I may be passionate and love my job, but not many of us would show up every day if we did not receive a paycheck at the end of the week as well. Additionally, behaviors that start off as extrinsically motivated can become intrinsically motivated over time. For example, I may have begun to attend an aerobics class because my best friend asked me to go and I enjoyed spending time with her. However, as time went on, I found aerobics to be intrinsically motivating as exercising becomes part of my identity. Thus, the clear distinction between these two constructs quickly becomes muddled; see Figure 7.1.

There is no evidence to suggest that high ability children and typically developing children have different responses to extrinsic and intrinsic motivations. However, there is substantial individual variation at all levels of ability in terms of the relative motivation provided by any given specific reinforcement. For example, Lily may do practically anything for the opportunity to be "line leader" in the classroom, while Bella may not care one way or another about where in line she is to walk to the cafeteria.

High ability children may have different interests, and thus respond to different reinforcements, than their age-level peers. Specifically, high-ability and high-achieving

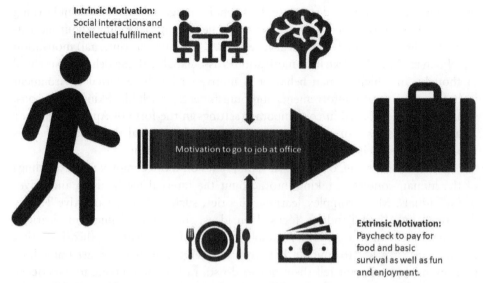

FIGURE 7.1 Illustration of Extrinsic and Intrinsic Motivation

children tend to have higher levels of academic intrinsic motivation; that is, they are more internally motivated by school-related tasks than their typically-developing peers are (Gottfried & Gottfried, 2004). Additionally, high-ability students who also have high levels of achievement demonstrate greater school-related intrinsic motivation and more favorable attitudes toward school and teachers on the *School Attitude Assessment Survey-Revised*, in comparison with high-ability students with lower levels of achievement (McCoach & Siegle, 2003).

This stronger internal motivation for school-related tasks may decrease the need for teachers and parents to provide extrinsic rewards for academic tasks for some advanced learners (see Sidebar); however, intrinsic motivation is an individual trait and group generalizations mask the variations between children. While many high-ability students may have high levels of intrinsic motivation toward academics, teachers and parents still should cultivate this intrinsic motivation through techniques discussed in the remainder of the chapter. Additionally, many underachieving high-ability students do not develop intrinsic motivation for school-related tasks (McCoach & Siegle, 2003) and therefore will need different types of interventions, as discussed in the underachievement section of this chapter.

Drive reduction theory

In a manner similar to the dichotomy of intrinsic and extrinsic motivation, Drive Reduction Theory frames motivation as the desire to satiate an innate physiological or psychological need (primary) and conditioned response (secondary; Hull, 1952; Spielman et al., 2020). These aspects of motivation, labeled drives, were hypothesized to explain the motivations for human behaviors. Primary drives reflect the

FIELD NOTE 7.1

Karen Rambo-Hernandez

Parent, Teacher, and Professor

I know as a teacher we're not supposed to have favorites, but sometimes kids wiggle into our hearts and leave a permanent mark behind. Michael is one of those. In his grade-level classes, Michael was a bit of a behavior problem. But he was brilliant. While I wasn't a teacher for his grade level, I had him as a student because he was accelerated two years in mathematics, and I also coached him on the math competition team. Now, I also want you to know, I am really good at mathematics. One afternoon, we were working on some competition problems- I worked alongside my students while they solved problems. We were solving a particularly gnarly one... and Michael finished first... before I did. His eyes got really big! He had beat me to the solution!

He marks this as his turning point. As a classroom teacher, I was amazed at what my students could accomplish. Every school has students that are underchallenged-kids who are sitting in classroom relearning material that they've already mastered. We can find these kids (relatively easily!) if we use local norms to identify the top students in every building for more advanced curriculum. A huge benefit of using local norms is those who are identified for additional services aren't a homogeneous group- they are not the kids who have had access to opportunities who come from families of means- these kids look a whole lot more like a cross section of kids in the United States. All kids deserve to be challenged... to be given rigorous, relevant curriculum. With Michael, he was accelerated in mathematics by two years. And he wasn't a discipline problem in my class. In my class, he wasn't wasting his time relearning something he already knew. What if we didn't instruct kids simply based on their birthday but based on their academic need? In education, one size certainly does not fit all.

struggle to survive, such as hunger or thirst. Secondary drives, on the other hand, are acquired and socially determined. For example, as a graduate student, I attended many optional lectures and seminars with the promise of free pizza, fulfilling my primary drive of hunger. However, I hoped that my professors and advisors believed that my motivation was to fulfill a secondary drive of intellectual curiosity, a drive that was certainly socially constructed and reinforced throughout my studies and the environment at the university.

The amount of drive (motivation) is proportional to the intensity of the stimulus (the deliciousness of the pizza) and the conditioned response (how fast I get to the seminar). Thus, Drive Reduction Theory is useful in framing motivation as the causes of behaviors, but it also can help explain the intensity of the drive (as the

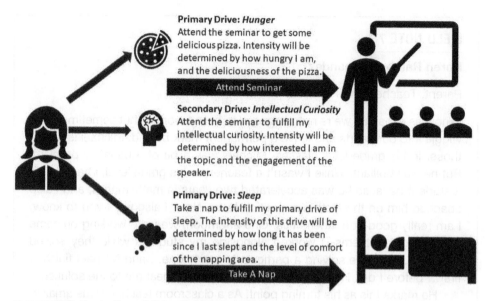

Primary Drive: *Hunger*
Attend the seminar to get some delicious pizza. Intensity will be determined by how hungry I am, and the deliciousness of the pizza.

Attend Seminar

Secondary Drive: *Intellectual Curiosity*
Attend the seminar to fulfill my intellectual curiosity. Intensity will be determined by how interested I am in the topic and the engagement of the speaker.

Primary Drive: *Sleep*
Take a nap to fulfill my primary drive of sleep. The intensity of this drive will be determined by how long it has been since I last slept and the level of comfort of the napping area.

Take A Nap

FIGURE 7.2 Illustration of Drive Reduction Theory

result of factors such as the likelihood the behavior produces the response, the time between the behavior and the response, and the amount of conditioning). The relative intensity of the drive can explain why a student chooses one activity over another. If my primary desire for sleep is stronger than the immediate need for food, I might choose to take a nap in the library rather than attend the seminar; see Figure 7.2.

Although Drive Reduction Theory largely has been replaced by more comprehensive models, such as Self-Determination Theory or Goal Orientation Theory in current thinking about motivation, it still can offer a useful framework for understanding behaviors exhibited in classrooms and at home. For example, a child who is disrupting class might be acting from a drive for attention and personal connections, or from a drive for intellectual stimulation in class. This type of analysis of behavior is closely associated with techniques commonly used in schools, particularly in special educational settings, such as Applied Behavioral Analysis (ABA). In ABA, the therapist looks for the antecedent (cause, preceding events), the target behavior (what we would like to change), and the consequences (effects of the behaviors; Madden et al., 2013). For example, if the target behavior is interrupting classwork time, the antecedent might be being assigned a workbook page of math facts and the consequences might be talking to the teacher and going to the principal's office. In this case, the student might have a drive for intellectual and social engagement. The math workbook page might not be providing intellectual and social engagement for the student; at the same time, by allowing the child out of the situation and giving them attention, they are fulfilling those drives through the disruptive behavior.

For high ability children, there is some evidence that ABA may be an effective intervention for underachievement (Ritchotte et al., 2015), and theoretically this approach could be used to modify a variety of behaviors in the classroom or home.

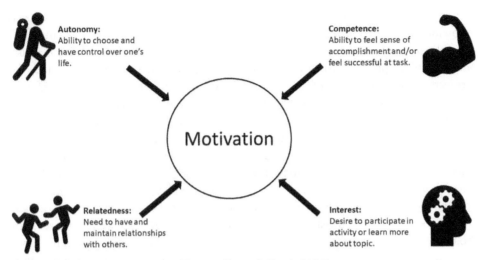

FIGURE 7.3 Self-Determination Theory (Ryan & Deci, 2000)

However, with the high capacity gifted children have to reason and make meaning of their own behaviors, I would encourage families and teachers to pursue therapeutic options that allow the child a more active role in changing and analyzing their own behaviors. For example, with the support of a therapist, family, and/or teacher, a high ability child might be able to identify the antecedents and consequences of their own behaviors, and find alternative (and more productive) ways to satisfy their internal drives.

Self-determination theory

Self-Determination Theory focuses on the importance of intrinsic motivation, rather than on the extrinsic drives that compel people to actions. In this model of motivation, people are best motivated to complete a task if they have autonomy in the task, if they are interested in the task, if it provides opportunities to connect to others, and if they feel competent to complete the task (see Figure 7.3; Ryan & Deci, 2000). Thus, engaging and relevant tasks become the primary driver of motivation in the Self-Determination Theory.

For educators and parents, Self-Determination Theory has implications for the design of lessons and activities for both high-ability and typically developing students. Primarily, when activities can be designed with student connectedness, autonomy (e.g., choice), and satisfaction in mind, students are more likely to be engaged with the task. This can have longer-lasting results than relying on extrinsic rewards, such as candy, pizza parties, or other reward or token systems, to convince learners to complete assignments and classroom tasks. An approach based upon these intrinsic motivators is particularly advised for parents of high-ability students to increase these learners' academic motivation (Garn et al., 2010).

Families and teachers can increase motivation by increasing autonomy, via allowing children to have choices in their activities and school work. This might be scaffolded simply at first, such as choosing the order in which to complete tasks, and gradually progress toward greater independence such as selecting topics for projects or a course of study in college. According to Self-Determination Theory, child-led decision-making increases motivation for children to engage in tasks. High ability children have greater levels of reasoning abilities and may be ready for greater autonomy at earlier ages, with appropriate scaffolding from families and teachers.

Similarly, motivation can be increased by providing greater opportunities for social connectedness. Children may seek this out on their own when this need is not met, such as by chatting during class or becoming the class clown. However, teachers and families can harness this motivation through the use of social interactions in classwork, e.g., think-pair-shares, Socratic Seminars, group projects, and discussion boards. In the case of high-ability learners, the desire for connectedness might extend to include a desire to connect with peers of similar intellectual ability, in addition to their age-peers. When engaging with academic content, high-ability students often are more motivated when they can interact with like-minded peers. Group projects can become de-motivating for high-ability learners when they become responsible for doing the lion's share of the work or when other group members leave all of the intellectual heavy-lifting to them.

Finally, children are intrinsically motivated to engage in a task when they have self-efficacy, or in other words, when they feel competent to complete the task and confident that they will experience success. Teachers and families can foster self-efficacy in children by providing opportunities in which students can experience success in tasks and by scaffolding lengthy tasks into manageable, smaller goals. For example, if a child is unmotivated and unsuccessful in writing a five paragraph essay, the teacher might start with having the student experience success in writing an outline of the essay, or by first writing just the introductory paragraph.

While high ability children may be more likely to experience success in tasks, this can be counter-intuitive, as they may internalize only an extremely high level of performance to indicate success, leading to perfectionism. This maladaptive expression of perfectionism may cause low self-efficacy, even if the child's actual level of performance is still relatively high compared to typical-ability peers. For example, a student who has traditionally made as in math class may become unmotivated in Algebra after they experience their first B on a report card and feel a lower sense of self-efficacy. This phenomenon is discussed in further detail in the section on perfectionism later in this chapter.

Expectancy-value theory

Expectancy-Value Theory (EVT) was developed to explain achievement motivation, and has been applied specifically to students in educational contexts (Eccles, 1983). In this model, people, and students, in particular, make achievement-related choices based upon two factors: (1) expectancies for success and (2) values of the task

EYE FOR DIVERSITY 7.1 MOTIVATION AND ENVIRONMENT ARE INTIMATELY CONNECTED

Dante D. Dixson

In America, society sends millions of messages, both implicit and explicit, to high ability students over the course of their academic careers. Many of these messages directly target high ability students' perceived competence across the academic domain. These messages can be positive and engender high intrinsic and extrinsic motivation (e.g., encouragement, incentives, and high expectations), or they can be negative and engender low intrinsic and extrinsic motivation (e.g., discouragement, lack of incentives [even for outstanding performance], and low expectations). Previous research indicates that students from diverse backgrounds (e.g., minority students, poor students, English language learners, and women) receive a disproportionate number of negative messages compared to their majority counterparts (e.g., sexism, racism, and classism). As a result, compared to those of the majority, students from diverse backgrounds may (a) be more at-risk for having depressed academic motivation, (b) be more likely to underachieve, and (c) require more intense interventions and activities to exhibit high intrinsic and extrinsic motivation within the academic domain.

(Eccles, 1983). In general, a student's self-efficacy, or perceptions of their competence for a task, and their self-concept, or perceptions of their abilities within a specific content domain, determine the student's expectancy for success. Students have higher motivation for completing tasks on which they perceive a high expectancy for success.

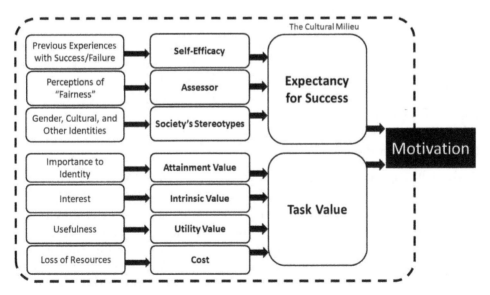

FIGURE 7.4 Simplified Expectancy-Value Theory (Eccles, 1983)

Although expectations are mostly internal, environmental and social factors can also play a role in expectancy, for example, if a teacher is viewed as an unfair assessor. Task value is subjective and individual for each student. Eccles (1983) categorized task value into four categories: (1) attainment value (importance to identity), (2) intrinsic value (interest), (3) utility value (usefulness), and (4) cost (loss of resources and negative influences).

The EVT has been shown to model math achievement and motivation among high-ability students in math (Fong & Kremer, 2019). For educators and families, this model offers intricacies that can explain various facets of the motivational differences between students. It again highlights the importance of self-efficacy and self-concept, and consequently, previous experiences with achievement, in motivation toward academic tasks. This expectancy for success is also mediated by the child's perception of their environment, such as the perceived fairness of their assessor or teacher, and their perception of cultural roles within society.

Among high-ability learners expectancy for success might be inflated, due to the combination of high aptitude toward academic tasks and unchallenging coursework. This expectancy can lead to perfectionism, as discussed in the previous section and detailed further in the perfectionism section of this chapter. However, EVT expands on these ideas by including the context within which students are making these judgements about their potential for success. For high ability children, who may develop an awareness of justice and fairness earlier than their age-peers, they may be affected by these environmental factors to a greater extent, or on a different developmental trajectory than their typically-developing peers.

The task value component of Expectancy-Value Theory includes the idea of intrinsic value, or interest, and adds concepts of utility and attainment value. Teachers already are familiar with utility value in the form of the question, "when are we going to use this in real life?" Expectancy-Value Theory predicts that by providing students with opportunities for success in achievement, presenting activities that connect clearly to areas of interest, and making relevance explicit, students will experience increases in achievement motivation. For children with high abilities who are passionate about a narrow range of topics, teachers, and families may need to increase the utility and attainment value of tasks to make them relevant to this population of learners.

Goal orientation theory

Tangentially related to motivation is Goal-Orientation Theory, which describes how a person validates their own ability in achievement settings (Van deWalle, 1997). Traditionally, goal orientation has been conceptualized as having two dimensions: (1) mastery goal orientation and (2) performance goal orientation (Dweck, 1986; Elliott & Dweck, 1988). Mastery orientation, sometimes called learning orientation, is associated with motivation to learn or master new skills, whereas performance orientation is associated with motivation to seek approval from others and avoid negative judgements. Connecting back to other theories, mastery orientation might be more closely aligned with intrinsic motivation, and performance orientation may be more aligned with the reinforcements and punishments of behaviorism and extrinsic motivation.

Some also have postulated a third dimension, performance-avoidance orientation, which is the motivation to avoid failure and centers on a lack of confidence (Van deWalle, 1997). This orientation is risk-averse and generally leads to worse academic outcomes, including anxiety and fear of failure. For high-ability learners, performance-avoidance orientation may be a cause of underachievement (via unwillingness to take academic risks or engage in academic pursuits) and may be a result of perfectionism (having unrealistic expectations for one's own performance).

Goal Orientation Theory suggests that these dimensions (mastery orientation, performance orientation, and performance-avoidance orientation) are separate, and thus a person can have a range of both performance and mastery aspects with regard to the same goal (Eison et al., 1986). In general, mastery goal orientation is associated with greater achievement and academic success (Güler, 2017; National Research Council, 2000). In other words, students who are motivated by learning and intrinsic reward tend to have greater academic achievement than those students who are motivated by the praise that they receive or by external rewards such as grades.

For parents and educators, Goal-Orientation Theory provides insights into how a child might be thinking about achievement in school. Many high ability children have a high mastery goal orientation and exhibit curiosity with motivation to learn. High ability children tend to also display high performance and achievement in school, which can lead to performance orientation, the seeking of outside validation of their skills and work. The phenomenon will be discussed more in the section below on perfectionism.

EDUCATIONAL AND COUNSELING IMPLICATIONS

Regarding the motivation of high ability children, two conditions (underachievement and perfectionism) have become primary concerns of parents, educators, and counselors who work with these learners. This section discusses the relationship of each condition to motivation and to models that seek to explain these phenomena.

The high ability child and underachievement

Underachievement typically is defined as achievement that is substantially lower than the potential or ability of the student would predict. However, among the population of children with high abilities, even typically acceptable levels of achievement could technically be considered underachievement, if the student is maintaining adequate levels of achievement (Matthews & McBee, 2007). Therefore, many researchers define underachievement in this population as levels of achievement that are measurably lower than levels of ability and that interfere with life or academic goals and outcomes (e.g., Peterson, 2001). Thus, for some high-ability students, earning a "B" in a Biology class may not be considered underachievement, if their interests and passions lie in other areas, but for a student who is considering becoming a doctor, this may represent underachievement.

There can be multiple causes of underachievement in high-ability students, and these can interact with one another. High ability children with another exceptionality (e.g., twice-exceptional children) may underachieve in part due to their exceptionality, such as dyslexia or Attention Deficit Hyperactivity Disorder (ADHD). Additionally, their negative experiences with achievement may lead to decreased motivation, which further exacerbates their underachievement. However, many researchers who study underachievement within the high-ability population explicitly exclude students with exceptionalities from definitions of underachievement (e.g., Reis & McCoach, 2002). Also, high-ability students sometimes may lack basic executive functioning skills that are fundamental to academic success, such as note-taking, time management, reading comprehension, or study skills, and this too can be a cause of underachievement. This lack of skills can cause students to experience failure, leading to a negative impact on their motivation, furthering their underachievement. However, most of the research into underachievement in the high-ability population has focused on motivation as the primary cause.

Achievement orientation model of underachievement

In the Achievement Orientation Model of Underachievement (see Figure 7.5; Ritchotte et al., 2014; Rubenstein et al., 2012; Siegle et al., 2017), underachievement is explained by both a students' skills to complete a task and the influence of the interaction of their goal valuation, self-efficacy, and environmental perceptions on their motivation to self-regulate, set goals, and, ultimately, to achieve on the task. Unpacking this model, motivation is a key element to understanding underachievement, and it is influenced not only by having the requisite skills but also by the three perception-related elements (goal valuation, self-efficacy, and environmental perceptions). Goal valuation refers to how important or relevant a

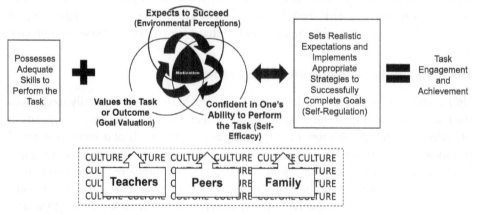

FIGURE 7.5 Achievement Orientation Model. Reprinted with permission of Del Siegle

child finds the task or area of achievement. Some research suggests that interventions focusing on this factor can be instrumental in improving achievement for high-ability, underachieving students (Rubenstein et al., 2012). Self-efficacy refers to how competent a child feels in completing the task. Environmental perceptions refer to the extent to which the child perceives the learning environment as a place in which they can be successful. These three elements of perceptions influence each other. Finally, these interactions provide a level of motivation that influences the degree of self-regulation to set goals, plan, and engage in the activities that lead to achievement. If this motivation is low, the corresponding lack of self-regulation leads to underachievement.

Person-centered, two-path model of underachievement

Snyder and Linnenbrink-Garcia (2013) took a different approach to explaining underachievement in the high-ability population, by framing it as two separate developmental pathways: Maladaptive Competence Beliefs and Declining Value Beliefs Pathways. In the Maladaptive Competence Beliefs pathway, when introduced to their gifted label early, high ability children develop an unhealthy perception of their own abilities, such that when faced with challenges they experience a significant drop in self-efficacy that leads to low motivation and underachievement. In the Declining Value Beliefs Pathway, high ability children have a healthy perception of their own abilities; however, when schoolwork is not challenging, they disengage with the curricula, experiencing a significant drop in goal valuation, leading to low motivation and underachievement. In both scenarios, high ability children do not develop a developmental understanding of the connection between effort and achievement, leading to underachievement in subsequent years.

Interventions for underachievement

There have been relatively few (a total of 14, recently) studies investigating the efficacy of underachievement interventions for high-ability students. Overall, the empirical studies show no evidence of academic improvement, but significant improvement in areas of psychosocial growth, such as self-efficacy and goal valuation (Steenbergen-Hu et al., 2020).

However, the models described earlier imply some approaches for parents and educators, and suggest that interventions with academic, rather than counseling, foci may be more effective in addressing psychosocial factors (Snyder et al., 2019). The Achievement Orientation Model implies that parents and teachers should focus on emphasizing goal valuation (e.g., relevance and utility) of tasks, providing opportunities for success to build self-efficacy, and creating environments in which children feel like they can be successful. In the Snyder and Linnenbrink-Garcia model (2013), an academic intervention is implied in which early educational experiences allow high ability children to experience developmentally-appropriate challenge. These experiences help children to draw connections between effort and achievement, while framing their high abilities in the context of skills development that facilitates achievement and engagement with the curricula. However, more research is needed to provide support for specific interventions that will be effective in reversing underachievement for high ability children (Snyder et al., 2019; Steenbergen-Hu et al., 2020).

The high ability child and perfectionism

Perfectionism "generally refers to setting unreasonably high expectations of oneself, including an intolerance of mistakes" (Adelson & Wilson, 2020, p. 9). Although perfectionism is sometimes divided into adaptive and maladaptive types, it is conceptualized for the purposes of this chapter as a continuum of problematic patterns of thinking and behaviors that range from minimally impactful to clinically important. This approach was chosen both because perfectionism is most commonly portrayed as a negative trait in popular culture and because adaptive perfectionism can be better classified as appropriate goal valuation and motivation. By conceptualizing perfectionism as maladaptive the various dimensions of how it is manifested can be organized clearly, without the need to consider normal or adaptive behaviors.

Perfectionism can be divided into three categories: self-oriented, socially prescribed, and other-oriented. Self-oriented perfectionists tend to hold themselves to high standards, often impossibly high, and become self-critical when they are unable to meet those expectations. However, this category of perfectionism is associated with the best outcomes, overall. Socially prescribed perfectionism is associated with feelings that others (e.g., peers, teachers, parents, society) hold an individual to high expectations. This category of perfectionism is associated with low self-esteem, and is generally more resistant to interventions. Finally, other-oriented perfectionism is the least studied type, and involves holding other people to high standards; at clinical levels it is associated with narcissism and sociopathy. These types of perfectionism are not mutually exclusive; for example, a person may exhibit signs of both self-oriented and socially prescribed perfectionism.

This framing of perfectionism has direct parallels to goal orientation theory. Specifically, self-orientated perfectionism can be viewed as an extreme end of the mastery goal orientation continuum. By holding high expectations for their own learning and mastery of material, self-oriented perfectionists may hold adaptive patterns of thought and behaviors. However, when those expectations of the self become overly focused on performance and become unrealistic, they become maladaptive and in need of interventions. Similarly, socially prescribed perfectionism focuses on the evaluation of one's performance by others, which closely aligns with performance goal orientation. As in performance goal orientation, socially prescribed perfectionism is associated with poor psychosocial and achievement outcomes.

Perfectionism is also connected with a lack of motivation, in that children who hold impossibly high standards will often decide not to engage in activities if they feel they are not able to meet their own high expectations (Siegle & McCoach, 2005). Essentially, perfectionism can cause a distortion of perception of one's own abilities, or self-efficacy to complete a task, causing a decrease in motivation. This can manifest in disengagement from activities, procrastination in beginning activities, or burnout from the increased effort needed to meet high expectations (Adelson & Wilson, 2020).

While perfectionism often is discussed in the context of high ability children, there is little evidence to support the hypothesis that perfectionism is more common among this population (Speirs Neumeister, 2017). However, due to the proclivity of high ability children toward academic pursuits, it may be that perfectionism among this group is more likely to manifest within academic and school-related tasks, as opposed to in other areas (e.g., body image or sports).

As mentioned earlier, perfectionism can be viewed on a continuum of severity, ranging from mild to clinical-level symptoms. At the clinical level, a child may need the help of a mental health professional (e.g., therapist, counselor, or psychologist) or even in-patient treatment. Perfectionism has been associated with eating disorders, such as anorexia and bulimia, suicidal ideation, substance abuse, and low self-esteem. These outcomes are serious, and when a child exhibits warning signs, it is vital to seek the advice and help of a mental health professional.

Among the strongest connections with perfectionism in the research base are those to anxiety and depression. However, across various fields (e.g., sports psychology, eating disorder psychology, educational psychology, and clinical psychology) few models have come to a consensus on the antecedent(s) of these behaviors. In other words, does perfectionism cause anxiety and depression, or vice versa? It is likely that the two are in a reciprocal relationship, in which each condition contributes to the development of the other.

While some promising research has begun to show effective whole-group interventions for perfectionism among high-ability students (e.g., Mofield & Chakraborti-Ghosh, 2010), the most research-supported intervention for reversing perfectionism is Cognitive Behavioral Therapy (CBT) in individual settings. This approach focuses on changing thought patterns in a manner that will result in changes to behaviors and higher quality of life. For high ability children, CBT may be particularly effective due to these learners' increased capacity for thinking and reasoning skills.

FINAL THOUGHTS

In this chapter, I have explored motivation and high ability children. The field of psychology has developed various models to explain both intrinsic and extrinsic motivations of people, and each of these models offer explicit or implicit contributions to understanding the development of high ability children. Ranging from models of external motivation, such as Behaviorism and Drive Theory, to those models that emphasize the importance of intrinsic motivations, such as Self-Determination Theory and Expectancy-Value Theory, these models of motivation indicate ways in which families and educators can support high-ability learners' development.

Additionally, both underachievement and perfectionism, which are often associated with the population of high ability children, are directly related to concepts of motivation. Underachievement among high ability children may be related to academic and psychosocial factors in school contexts, and as the models surrounding underachievement become more developed, the effectiveness of interventions for this population will be better substantiated. Similarly, models of perfectionism for high-ability learners will be subject to further development, and will likely incorporate learning from the research that has been conducted among other populations, so that more effective interventions can be developed and studied.

REFERENCES

Adelson, J. L., & Wilson, H. E. (2020). *Letting go of perfectionism: Overcoming perfectionism in kids* (2nd ed.). Prufrock Press, Inc.

Dweck, C. S. (1986). Motivational processes affecting learning. *American Psychologist, 41*(10), 1040–1048. https://doi.org/10.1037/0003-066X.41.10.1040

Eccles, J. (1983). Expectancies, values, and academic behaviors. In J. T. Spence (Ed.), *Achievement and achievement motives: Psychological and sociological approaches* (pp. 75–146). H. Freeman.

Eison, J. A., Pollio, H. R., & Milton, O. (1986). Educational and personal characteristics of four different types of learning-and grade-oriented students. *Contemporary Educational Psychology, 11*(1), 54–67. https://doi.org/10.1016/0361-476X(86)90012-3

Elliott, E. S., & Dweck, C. S. (1988). Goals: An approach to motivation and achievement. *Journal of Personality and Social Psychology, 54*(1), 5–12. https://doi-org.proxy.library.vcu.edu/10.1037/0022-3514.54.1.5

Fong, C. J., & Kremer, K. P. (2019). An expectancy-value approach to math underachievement: Examining high school achievement, college attendance, and STEM interest. *Gifted Child Quarterly, 64*(2), 67–84. https://doi.org/10.1177/0016986219890599

Garn, A., Matthews, M. S., & Jolly, J. L. (2010). Parental influences on the academic motivation of gifted students: A self-determination theory perspective. *Gifted Child Quarterly, 54*(4), 263–272. https://doi.org/10.1177/0016986210377657

Gottfried, A. E., & Gottfried, A. W. (2004). Toward the development of a conceptualization of gifted motivation. *Gifted Child Quarterly, 48*(2), 121–132. https://doi.org/10.1177/001698620404800205

Güler, M. (2017). The effect of goal orientation on student achievement. In *The factors effecting student achievement* (pp. 291–307). Springer. https://doi.org/10.1007/978-3-319-56083-0_18

Hull, C. L. (1952). *A behavior system.* Yale University Press.

Madden, G. J., Dube, W. V., Hackenberg, T. D., Hanley, G. P., & Lattal, K. A. (2013). *APA handbook of behavior analysis, Vol. 2: Translating principles into practice.* American Psychological Association.

Matthews, M. S., & McBee, M. T. (2007). School factors and the underachievement of gifted students in a talent search summer program. *Gifted Child Quarterly, 51*(2), 167–181. https://doi.org/10.1177/0016986207299473

McCoach, D. B., & Siegle, D. (2003). The school attitude assessment survey-revised: A new instrument to identify academically able students who underachieve. *Educational and Psychological Measurement, 63*(3), 414–429. https://doi.org/10.1177/0013164403063003005

Mofield, E. L., & Chakraborti-Ghosh, S. (2010). Addressing multidimensional perfectionism in gifted adolescents with affective curriculum. *Journal for the Education of the Gifted, 33*(4), 479–513. https://doi.org/10.3390/educsci6030021

National Research Council. (2000). *How people learn: brain, mind, experience, and school.* National Academy Press.

Peterson, J. S. (2001). Successful adults who were once adolescent underachievers. *Gifted Child Quarterly*, *45*(4), 236–250. https://doi.org/10.1177/001698620104500402

Reis, S. M., & McCoach, D. B. (2002). Underachievement in gifted and talented students with special needs. *Exceptionality*, *10*(2), 113–125. https://doi.org/10.1207/S15327035EX1002_5

Ritchotte, J. A., Matthews, M. S., & Flowers, C. P. (2014). The validity of the achievement-orientation model for gifted middle school students: An exploratory study. *Gifted Child Quarterly*, *58*(3), 183–198. https://doi.org/10.1177/0016986214534890

Ritchotte, J., Rubenstein, L., & Murry, F. (2015). Reversing the underachievement of gifted middle school students: Lessons from another field. *Gifted Child Today*, *38*(2), 103–113. https://doi.org/10.1177/1076217514568559

Rubenstein, L. D., Siegle, D., Reis, S. M., McCoach, D. B., & Burton, M. G. (2012). A complex quest: The development and research of underachievement interventions for gifted students. *Psychology in the Schools*, *49*(7), 678–694. https://doi.org/10.1002/pits.21620

Ryan, R. M. & Deci, E. L. (2000). Self-Determination Theory and the facilitation of intrinsic motivation, social development, and well-being. *American Psychologist*, *55*(1), 68–78. https://doi.og/10.1037/0003-066X.55.1.68

Siegle, D., & McCoach, D. B. (2005). *Motivating gifted students*. Prufrock Press, Inc.

Siegle, D., McCoach, D. B. & Roberts, A. (2017) Why I believe I achieve determines whether I achieve. *High Ability Studies*, *28*(1), 59–72. https://doi.og/10.1080/13598139.2017.1302873

Snyder, K. E., Fong, C. J., Painter, J. K., Pittard, C. M., Barr, S. M., & Patall, E. A. (2019). Interventions for academically underachieving students: A systematic review and meta-analysis. *Educational Research Review*, *28*, 1–22. https://doi.org/10.1016/j.edurev.2019.100294

Snyder, K., & Linnenbrink-Garcia, L. (2013). A developmental, person-centered approach to exploring multiple motivational pathways in gifted underachievement. *Educational Psychologist*, *48*(4), 209–228. https://doi.org/10.1080/00461520.2013.835597

Speirs Neumeister, K. L. S. (2017). Perfectionism in gifted students. *The psychology of perfectionism: Theory, research, applications*, 134–154. Routledge.

Spielman, R. M., Jenkins, W. J., & Lovett, M. D. (2020). Motivation. In *Psychology 2e*. OpenStax. https://openstax.org/books/psychology-2e/pages/10-1-motivation

Steenbergen-Hu, S., Olszewski-Kubilius, P., & Calvert, E. (2020). The effectiveness of current interventions to reverse the underachievement of gifted students: Findings of a meta-analysis and systematic review. *Gifted Child Quarterly*, *64*(2), 132–165. https://doi.org/10.1177/0016986220908601

Van deWalle, D. (1997). Development and validation of a work domain goal orientation instrument. *Educational and Psychological Measurement*, *8*(6), 995–1015. https://doi.org/10.1177/0013164497057006009

CHAPTER 8

Individual differences in personality among cognitively advanced learners

Sakhavat Mammadov

Defining personality is not easy. No single definition is widely accepted. At its most basic, personality refers to a set of relatively stable and organized psychological traits and mechanisms within the person (Larsen & Buss, 2002). These traits and mechanisms define and describe ways in which individuals are similar to or different from each other. Individual differences in personality, although dismissed by many, are highly correlated with life outcomes, including academic attainment, school success, and social and emotional well-being (Friedman & Kern, 2014; McAbee & Oswald, 2013; Steel et al., 2008). Therefore, understanding the interactions of fundamental traits, their origins, structures, correlations, and consequences is an important task in the field that is meant to genuinely support the development of students with advanced cognitive ability. In view of this, the primary purpose of this chapter is to inform practitioners, researchers, and educators about the essential role of personality in student achievement, affective competencies, and psychosocial outcomes in the context of the development and education of students with advanced academic abilities. An additional purpose is to suggest strategies and educational applications for nurturing intellectual and social-emotional development of these students. This chapter begins with a brief sketch of the trait approach to personality. Then, it focuses on the relevance of personality in understanding advanced cognitive ability and reviews findings from studies that have investigated personality traits of individuals who have been identified for gifted education programming. The pivotal role of personality in important learning outcomes is discussed along with the ways positive personality development among exceptional children could be facilitated.

DOI: 10.4324/9781003025443-9

THE TRAIT APPROACH TO PERSONALITY

The scientific field of personality psychology dates back to when Allport (1937) published his book, *Personality: A Psychological Interpretation*. The field has developed since then, and diverse perspectives have emerged that continue to coexist. During this time, psychologists have been concerned with identifying the basic dimensional constructs that make up personality. A plethora of personality models and taxonomies have been proposed for this purpose. Some have endured, while others have faded. Only a few taxonomies have built solid theoretical and statistical justifications. The Big Five or the five-factor model (Goldberg, 1981; John & Srivastava, 1999; McCrae & Costa, 1996) is the one on which this chapter focuses.

There are two research traditions upon which the Big Five model built: (1) the psycholexical approach and (2) the questionnaire approach (John & Srivastava, 1999). The Big Five model was first recognized and originally verified in psycholexical studies that are based on the lexical hypothesis, which states that all personality traits are encoded within the natural language (Cattell, 1943; Goldberg, 1981, 1990). Trait terms used in the lexical approach are exactly the same with the words that we use in daily language to describe individual differences in behavior. Those terms are identified through two criteria: (1) *synonym frequency* (i.e., a particular attribute is an important dimension of individual difference if many synonyms with some nuanced differences are used to describe it) and (2) *cross-cultural universality* (i.e., the most phenotypic and universally important attributes are described in many cultures and languages with corresponding terms; Saucier & Goldberg, 1996). Factor analysis, a statistical method used for dimensionality reduction, was the main tool applied in efforts to reduce large sets of words referring to personality attributes to smaller sets of basic personality traits (Strus et al., 2014).

The questionnaire approach played a significant role in the expansion of the Big Five model, both conceptually and empirically. In this line of research, personality dimensions were operationalized in the questionnaires to study their relationships with other important theoretical concepts (Digman, 1990; John & Srivastava, 1999). While the conceptualizations of personality dimensions within the psycholexical and questionnaire approaches differ slightly, a strong convergence on factor structures with nearly identical traits is observed between different models of the Big Five (De Raad & Perugini, 2002; Goldberg, 1990; John & Srivastava, 1999). The Big Five personality traits have traditionally been labeled as openness, conscientiousness, extraversion, agreeableness, and neuroticism (see Table 8.1 for trait descriptions).

Openness

Openness (or intellect), in a broad sense, refers to individual characteristics leading to positive attitudes towards challenging learning experiences as opposed to being simple and narrow-minded (McCrae & Costa, 1999). Openness is at the center of the major controversy between the lexical approach and the questionnaire approach.

TABLE 8.1 Descriptions of the Big Five Personality Traits

Personality Trait	Description	Low Scorers	High Scorers
Openness (O)	O refers to individual characteristics such as a positive attitude towards challenging learning experiences as opposed to being simple and narrow-minded.	Traditional, pragmatic, narrow-interests, and unanalytical.	Curious, unconventional, imaginative, and creative.
Conscientiousness (C)	C refers to the tendency to be organized, planful, disciplined, and reliable.	Laidback, careless, negligent, and unreliable.	Disciplined, fastidious, reliable, scrupulous, and persevering.
Extraversion (E)	E refers to the degree to which an individual is sociable, assertive, and outgoing. It contrasts such traits as talkativeness, assertiveness, and activity level with traits such as silence, passivity, and reserve.	Aloof, reserved, and independent, dominant, competitive, and frank.	Sociable, active, talkative, fun-loving, and assertive.
Agreeableness (A)	A refers to the tendency to be prosocial, cooperative, empathetic, compassionate, and trusting rather than antagonistic.	Hostile, indifferent, self-centered, spiteful, and jealous.	Altruistic, tender-hearted, trusting, empathetic, and modest.
Neuroticism (N)	N refers to individual differences in negative emotionality, anxiety, and emotional reactivity.	Emotionally stable, calm, relaxed, secure, and self-satisfied.	Emotionally distressed, nervous, insecure, and worrying.

In the lexical approach, openness is labeled as *intellect* (Goldberg, 1990, 1992) or *imagination* (Saucier, 1992, 1994) and conceptualized to represent a set of traits such as intellectuality, curiosity, creativity, and originality. Personality measures developed in the lexical tradition, such as the International Personality Item Pool (IPIP, Goldberg, 1999) and Goldberg's (1992) unipolar markers, include items primarily associated with intellectual orientation, and exclude several facets of the broader openness construct such as artistic interest and liberalism (McAbee & Oswald, 2013). Within the framework of the questionnaire approach, openness is labeled as *openness to experience* and covers a "wide range of loosely related traits" (McCrae, 2004; p. 707). It involves lower-order facets such as intellectual curiosity, imagination, independence of judgment, and aesthetic sensitivity. Despite differences, the models from these two distinct traditions have sufficient overlap to assume that they refer to the same domain of personality (DeYoung et al., 2005). The controversy should be considered as useful complementarity.

Conscientiousness

Conscientiousness refers to individual differences in the propensity to be responsible, self-controlled, organized, and deliberate (Goldberg, 1993). Individuals who score high on this personality trait are typically persistent, dependable, and achievement oriented (Raymark et al., 1997). Almost all facets of conscientiousness (i.e., competence, dutifulness, order, achievement striving, self-discipline, and deliberation) seem to be theoretically linked to positive academic outcomes (Chamorro-Premuzic & Furnham, 2003). Some studies examining the relationship between conscientiousness and cognitive ability have reported statistically significant negative associations (Wood & Englert, 2009). While both constructs are positively related to the same outcomes such as academic achievement (Poropat, 2009), this negative association seems somewhat interesting. Moutafi et al. (2004) have sought to clarify this observed contradiction by distinguishing crystallized intelligence (g_c) and fluid intelligence (g_f). Fluid intelligence refers to one's intellectual resources that are innate and based on biological factors such as heredity and basic sensory structures, whereas crystallized intelligence refers to the accumulation of knowledge, experiences, and skills throughout life. Moutafi et al. found that the association of conscientiousness with fluid intelligence is stronger than with crystallized intelligence; it is hypothesized that relatively less able individuals are likely to be more organized and use conscientiousness as a coping strategy to compensate for their relative lack of cognitive ability.

Extraversion

Extraversion contrasts such traits as talkativeness, assertiveness, and activity level with traits such as silence, passivity, and reserve (Goldberg, 1993). People scoring high on extraversion tend to be sociable, active, and assertive (John & Srivastava, 1999), as well as dominant, competitive, and frank (Digman, 1990). Those with low scores in extraversion tend to be aloof, reserved, and independent (Costa & Widiger, 2002). In a learning context, extraverts are expected to have focus on socialization rather than being committed to task completion, which may lead them to have lower levels of academic performance. Lower extraversion, on the contrary, is associated with a higher threshold for distractibility and better study habits. The ability to concentrate on tasks may be advantageous in academic contexts.

FIELD NOTE 8.1

Joe and Bill are twin brothers attending the same middle school in Seattle, USA. They were born and raised in the same home and have spent all their years together. They both have been identified to receive Highly Capable Program (The Washington State term for gifted programming) services in school. Ms. Hanson, their math teacher, knows her students well and adapts her instruction to students' needs. She says that Joe and Bill are very bright in math and are motivated to solve challenging problems beyond what students typically tackle according to a regular curriculum. The ways they learn math and approach problem solving diverge to a great extent. Joe prefers a quiet space where he can concentrate on a task, whereas Bill enjoys interacting with others and would rather work as a team when possible. Ms. Hanson believes that these distinct patterns of behavioral tendencies are reflective of their personalities. Although Joe and Bill are twins coming from the same environment and share similar strengths in the same domain, they differ in how they learn perhaps due to differences in where they stand along the introversion-extraversion continuum, noted Ms. Hanson.

Agreeableness

Agreeableness refers to the tendency to be prosocial and cooperative toward others. Agreeable people are described as being altruistic, tender-hearted, trusting, empathetic, and modest (Costa & Widiger, 2002). Like extraversion, agreeableness is an interpersonal personality trait. Agreeable behaviors play an essential role in managing social relationships and possible interpersonal conflicts within group activities (Watson & Clark, 1997). Agreeable students are likely to be good team players and perform well in assessments that involve collaborative group activities.

Neuroticism

Neuroticism includes traits such as nervousness, moodiness, and temperamentality (Goldberg, 1993). The opposite of neuroticism is *emotional stability*, which reflects the tendency to be calm, relaxed, and stable (Goldberg, 1990). Neuroticism includes not only negative affect but also the disturbed behaviors that accompany emotional distress (McCrae & Costa, 1987). Studies have shown that individuals who score high on neuroticism tend to be more anxious (De Raad & Schouwenburg, 1996), which may interfere with their attention to the task and thereby lead to negative academic outcomes.

PERSONALITY AND EXCEPTIONAL ABILITY

An interest in the personality traits of individuals with exceptional cognitive ability started as early as Terman's (1925) pioneering study of 1,528 children with high IQ scores in which he found that as adults these individuals were well adjusted socially and had above-average curiosity and eagerness. Olszewski-Kubilius et al. (1988) studied personality dimensions of adolescents who had been identified as gifted and compared them to the same-age and chronologically older non-identified groups. The gifted identified group had higher emotional stability, dominance, cheerfulness, conformity, warmth, and lower tension and apprehension than their peers of the same age. In a recent study, gifted adolescents were reported to score higher in openness and motivation and had better school grades than adolescents who were not identified as gifted (Wirthwein et al., 2019). These findings support the *harmony hypothesis*, which assumes that gifted individuals typically excel in various domains. Although results from accumulated research over decades are by no means homogeneous, there is convincing evidence that individuals who participate in gifted programming are not only more academically successful than the general population, but they are also better emotionally and socially adjusted (Plucker & Callahan, 2008).

The dominant view among laypeople on giftedness diverges from what research suggests. Baudson and Preckel (2013) used an experimental approach to investigate teachers' implicit personality theories about the gifted. Teachers perceived gifted students as more open to new experience, more introverted, less emotionally stable, and less agreeable. Their implicit theories about personalities of gifted students were in line with the *disharmony hypothesis*, which proposes that deficits that gifted students experience in socioemotional domains are due to giftedness. Media representation and popular culture, too, often provide a negative portrayal by focusing on socioemotional downsides of giftedness (Baudson, 2016). Some research studies may have contributed to the support of the disharmony hypothesis (see Becker, 1978; Gallagher, 1990; Neihart, 1999). These hypotheses, despite being contradictory and mutually opposed, have led to assumptions in the field that gifted students possess unique personalities that set them apart from their counterparts (Wirthwein et al., 2019).

There are both conceptual and empirical reasons for framing an understanding of the personality-giftedness relationship. Multidimensional conceptualizations of giftedness identify cognitive variables as important for the development of gifted behaviors (e.g., Gagné, 2004; Renzulli, 1978). Types of cognitive functioning are also recognized to be central ingredients of personality. According to Eysenck (1970), the interplay between three overarching behavioral systems, namely those of conative behavior (will), affective behavior (emotion), and cognitive behavior (intelligence) characterizes personality and determines one's interaction with the environment. The growing evidence of links between personality traits and cognitive functions such as intelligence (Judge et al., 2007) sheds a partial light on the personality-intellectual giftedness link.

Findings from studies of the Big Five-intelligence relationship illuminate some aspects of personality traits associated with exceptional academic performance. Of the Big Five, openness has shown consistent positive associations with intelligence (e.g., Limont et al., 2014; McCrae et al., 2002; Zeidner & Shani-Zinovich, 2011). Judge et al. (2007) reported positive meta-analytic correlation between openness and intelligence ($r = .22$). Higher intelligence was also found to be associated with a lesser degree of neuroticism (Zeidner & Shani-Zinovich, 2011). This negative association of intelligence with neuroticism was assumed to be due to anxiety, which is one of the sub-traits characterizing neuroticism. As it is well known, anxiety may impair an individual's cognitive performance (Eysenck, 1994). Therefore, the negative correlation of neuroticism is with intelligence test performance, rather than with actual intelligence (Stolarski et al., 2013).

It has been observed that openness correlates more specifically with crystallized intelligence (g_c; the ability to use skills, knowledge, and experience in new situations) rather than with fluid intelligence (g_f; the ability to use learned knowledge and experience; Moutafi et al., 2005; Zeidner & Matthews, 2000). Individuals who are highly open to experience usually are intellectually curious such that their motivation to engage in intellectual pursuits may lead to an increase in their crystallized intelligence (Ackerman, 1996; Matthews et al., 2009).

The basis of the relationship between openness and intelligence lies in the nature of this particular personality trait. The Big Five taxonomy was developed empirically rather than theoretically (John et al., 2008). The statistical identification of five factors makes the interpretation process contentious. By far, openness has been the factor surrounded by the most extensive debate. A widely accepted view is that openness reflects the shared variance of the two lower-level traits: openness to experience and intellect (DeYoung et al., 2014). "Intellect reflects the ability and tendency to explore abstract information through reasoning, whereas openness reflects the ability and tendency to explore sensory and aesthetic information through perception, fantasy, and artistic endeavor" (DeYoung et al., 2012, p. 2). Openness is consistently associated with intelligence, because descriptors of intelligence fall within this personality trait. Recall that Eysenck (1970) described personality as a broad concept that covers conative, affective, and cognitive behaviors.

Findings from many studies within and beyond the Big Five framework consistently demonstrate that negative stereotypes portraying gifted students as possessing maladaptive personality traits lack empirical support (Francis et al., 2016; Mammadov, 2020; Martin et al., 2010; Olszewski-Kubilius et al., 1988; Zeidner & Shani-Zinovich, 2011). In a recent study, Mammadov (2020) investigated personality types among adolescents who were identified for gifted programming using a person-centered approach. The main focus of this approach is on the within-person organization of personality traits. The analyses revealed three profiles: (1) Flexibles, (2) Resilients, and (3) Averages. The profile *Flexibles* was so named for its members' high openness and extraversion. Students in this profile had average scores on the other Big Five personality traits: (1) *Resilients* were characterized as highly open, (2) extraverted, (3) conscientious, (4) agreeable, and (5) emotionally stable. The profile *Averages* had average scores on most personality traits. As it is evident from profile descriptions, no maladaptive personality profile emerged through the analyses. More interestingly, these profiles, except Resilients, did not resemble the *Overcontrolled* and *Undercontrolled* personality types that have widely been replicable across studies with the general population (Donnellan & Robins, 2010). Overcontrolled individuals typically score high on neuroticism and low on extraversion, and tend to be introverted, emotionally brittle, and tense. Undercontrolled individuals report low scores on all positive Big Five traits. They tend to be disagreeable and lack self-control. Cross et al. (2018a) took a similar approach to examine personality profiles of honors college students. Of the five emerged profiles, only one, *Possible Misfits*, had less favorable personality characteristics (i.e., high neuroticism and low agreeableness). This profile consisted of a small percent (8%) of the overall sample. These results support the harmony hypothesis, suggesting that gifted individuals overall exhibit high scores on positive psychosocial qualities and show fewer indications of personality maladjustments.

OTHER TRAIT-LEVEL INDIVIDUAL DIFFERENCES

Overexcitability

One of the theoretical personality constructs popular in the field of gifted education is *overexcitability*, which was introduced by Kazimierz Dabrowski (1964) as part of his Theory of Positive Disintegration (TPD). Overexcitability can be described as "an enhanced and intensified mental activity distinguished by characteristic forms of expression, which are above common and average" (Piechowski et al., 1985, p. 540). Dabrowski distinguished five dimensions of overexcitability: psychomotor (high levels of physical activity and frenetic energy), sensual (enriched experience of sensual pleasure), imaginational (heightened imagination with rich associations of images and impressions), emotional (intense emotions and feelings), and intellectual (deep pursuit of knowledge, analysis, and problem solving). The most dominant overexcitability in persons determines the way they respond to different situations. Dabrowski viewed and interpreted overexcitabilities as the overall developmental potential rather than emotional extremes (Bouchard, 2004). As Piechowski and Cunningham (1985) put it, "the richer and more complex their expression, the stronger the potential for development" (p. 156).

A considerable number of studies examined overexcitabilities in the samples of individuals with different talents, abilities, and achievements (Falk et al., 1997;

Limont et al., 2014; Piechowski et al., 1985; Piirto et al., 2008). Several findings are summarized here. C. M. Ackerman (1997) conducted an exploratory study to determine the potential of overexcitability as a method for identifying giftedness. Intellectually gifted students (n = 42) reported higher scores on all five dimensions of overexcitability than students in the nongifted group (n = 37). The discriminant analysis identified three overexcitabilities (psychomotor, intellectual, and emotional) as discriminating between the two groups. Yakmaci-Guzel and Akarsu (2006) compared overexcitabilities of Turkish high school students (n = 711) across three intellectual ability groups identified by Raven Advanced Progressive Matrices Test (APM). Statistically significant differences were found in imaginational and intellectual dimensions in favor of the group of students with a high intellectual ability. As part of the Marburg Giftedness Project Wirthwein & Rost (2011) compared a sample of adults (n = 96) who had exceptional IQ scores at grades 3 and 9 to a sample of demographically matched adults of average intelligence (n = 91) in five dimensions of overexcitability. The high intellectual ability group scored significantly higher only on intellectual overexcitability. Bouchet and Falk (2001) found significant differences in the sample of undergraduate college students. Students who had attended a program for gifted students or advanced placement courses scored higher in emotional and intellectual overexcitabilities compared to students who did not participate in any specialized program. In a study situated in a tracked educational system, De Bondt et al. (2020) found no difference in the degree or nature of overexcitability between students attending a technical secondary education program (n = 132) in comparison with general secondary education (n = 356) students. Overall, findings suggest that gifted students differ from the general population in dimensions of overexcitabilities in varying patterns depending on age, gender, culture, gifted identification method, and among other factors. Winkler and Voight (2016) conducted a meta-analysis to summarize previously reported differences. The calculated effect sizes for intellectual and imaginational overexcitabilities were medium. The effect sizes for emotional and sensual overexcitabilities were small. Samples designated as gifted were found to have higher meta-analytic means in these four dimensions. No statistical effect size was found in the psychomotor dimension.

    Although the TPD has drawn considerable attention from the gifted education researchers, it has not often been applied in the broader field of personality psychology. There are two main reasons for that. First, the TPD lacks empirical support (Mendaglio, 2012). Its assumptions regarding the over-reactive nervous system have not been validated. Second, overexcitability and openness seem to be the same underlying construct with different names (Vuyk et al., 2016). Self-report measures used for the Big Five (e.g., NEO Five-Factor Inventory [NEO-FFI], Costa & McCrae, 1992) and overexcitabilities (Overexcitability Questionnaire-Two [OEQII], Falk et al., 1999) have several similar items (Limont et al., 2014). Gallagher (2013) pointed out that the descriptions of overexcitability dimensions, except that of psychomotor overexcitability, are strongly similar with subtraits of openness. Vuyk et al. (2016) examined the similarity of overexcitabilities to corresponding openness facets using exploratory structural equation modeling. The joint-factor model was found to be a better model, suggesting that openness and overexcitability represent largely the same construct.

Grit

Another trait-level individual difference construct is grit. It is conceptualized and defined as "trait-level perseverance and passion for long-term goals" by Duckworth and colleagues (Duckworth et al., 2007, p. 1087). Unlike overexcitability, grit has become increasingly popular in psychology and drawn attention from popular press, educational policymakers, and researchers and practitioners from various disciplines. Grit has not been specifically studied with samples with high cognitive ability. There is no evidence that gifted children are more or less "gritty" than non-identified children. Implications that could be drawn from the grit research with the general population are most likely to be relevant to gifted individuals. Many studies have reported an essential predictive role of grit in mental health (Kleiman et al., 2013), learning motivation (Myers et al., 2016), and academic and workplace success (Cosgrove et al., 2018; Eskreis-Winkler et al., 2014).

Grit was operationalized to have three components: (1) goal directedness (i.e., to set clear goals to achieve), (2) perseverance of effort (i.e., to continue working hard to achieve those goals), and (3) consistency of interest (i.e., to have commitment and passion toward the goals). Similarities between grit and some other constructs such as self-control, self-regulation, and intrinsic motivation are evident in the literature. Oriol et al. (2017) reported high correlation with self-control. Muenks et al. (2017) found that grit empirically overlapped with self-report, self-regulation, and engagement. Credé et al. (2017) argued that "the conceptual similarities between these constructs and grit raises the possibility that the proponents of grit may have fallen victim to... the 'jangle fallacy'—the belief that two things are different simply because they have different names" (p. 495). Ponnock et al. (2020) examined if grit is empirically distinct from its conceptual neighbor, conscientiousness. They went beyond simply examining correlations. Using item-level factor analysis, they found that grit and conscientiousness are not separate constructs.

PIVOTAL ROLE OF PERSONALITY IN LEARNING OUTCOMES

As briefly outlined above, empirical evidence suggests that both overexcitability and grit are a relabeling of two Big Five traits, openness and conscientiousness, respectively. The Big Five model seems to be rightly acknowledged as a comprehensive taxonomy capturing the majority of individual differences in behavioral patterns (McCrae & Costa, 1999). In this section, the pivotal role of personality, specifically the Big Five traits, in two important learning outcomes, creative performance and academic achievement, is briefly illustrated by reviewing and discussing recent findings.

Creative performance

Creativity is considered as a key facet of many theories regarding the development of children with high cognitive ability into professionally successful adults. Several gifted education scholars have argued that creativity should be used as part of identification of children for advanced academic services (Renzulli, 1978; Sternberg & Lubart, 1993; Torrance, 1984). For example, Renzulli (1978) identifies creativity as one of the three interlocking traits essential for the manifestation of creative-productive gifted behavior. The other traits that are part of his theory are above average ability and task commitment. Creativity is a widely used concept and is not restricted to education or psychology. It spreads across many other fields and disciplines and is a part of everyday life (Runco & Richards, 1997). In this chapter, it is only possible to review briefly some of the most important aspects of the relationship between creativity and personality in the context of giftedness research.

The Big Five personality traits predict various aspects of creativity such as creative interests (Wolfradt & Pretz, 2001), originality of thinking (Eysenck, 1995), achievement (Batey et al., 2010; Silvia et al., 2009), activities (Jauk et al., 2013), and creative cognitive style and engagement (Mammadov et al., 2019). Openness to experience is of special interest in creativity research. It has been widely considered as an important individual difference characteristic that contributes to creative outcomes. Empirical results support this assumption, showing openness to be consistently associated with creative achievement across different measures, particularly on divergent thinking tests, story creativity measures, metaphors, and autobiographical photo essays (Batey et al., 2010; Kaufman et al., 2018; Silvia & Beauty, 2012; Silvia et al., 2011). The openness/intellect (O/I) subfactors allowed researchers to better understand and interpret the openness-creativity relationship. Nusbaum and Silvia (2011) examined the relationships between openness and intellect with creativity and fluid intelligence. Openness, but not intellect, predicted self-reported creativity. Intellect, but not openness, predicted fluid intelligence. To further clarify the openness-creativity relationship, S. B. Kaufman (2013) used a four-factor model of openness to new experience and examined its associations with creative achievement in the arts and sciences. A factor analysis of a battery of measures of cognitive ability, working memory, intellect, openness, affect, and intuition revealed four factors: (1) explicit cognitive ability, (2) intellectual engagement, (3) affective engagement, and (4) aesthetic engagement. Affective engagement and aesthetic engagement independently predicted creative achievement in the arts. Explicit cognitive ability and intellectual engagement independently predicted creative achievement in the sciences but not the arts. No relationship was found between aesthetic engagement and creative achievement in the sciences. Interestingly, affective engagement was negatively related to creative achievement in the sciences.

Agreeableness has been reported to have slight negative correlations with creativity (Batey & Furnham, 2006; Furnham et al., 2009; King et al., 1996). Creative individuals were found to be less norm adherent (Feist, 1998). Other personality traits have not shown consistent relationships, most likely due to domain specificity.

Conscientiousness, for example, has shown positive correlations with creativity in science and business (Feist, 1998; Larson et al., 2002), but negative correlation with creativity in the arts (Furnham et al., 2006). In some studies, neuroticism was found to have negative associations with creativity-related outcomes (Batey & Furnham, 2006; Guo et al., 2017; Mammadov et al., 2019). Other studies reported positive correlations (Batey et al., 2010). Although neurotic tendencies were argued to have a beneficial effect on creativity among artists (Feist, 1998), emotional stability may be more important for creative productivity in other domains.

Academic achievement

Most of the research on the relationship between personality traits and academic achievement has been structured around the Big Five model. Of the Big Five personality traits, conscientiousness has consistently been reported as the strong and robust predictor of academic achievement, even when cognitive ability is controlled (Gatzka & Hell, 2018; Poropat, 2009). Conscientious students tend to be effective at carrying out tasks and typically are self-disciplined and well-organized (McCrae & John, 1992). These are important individual characteristics that are expected to enhance student performance in examinations, tests, and other types of evaluation measures. Another personality trait showing consistent association with achievement is openness, but not as strong as that of conscientiousness. Studies reported from weak to moderate positive correlations for openness (Caprara et al., 2011; Carretta & Ree, 2019; Gerbino et al., 2018). Even some studies found negative associations between openness and achievement (Furnham et al., 2006; Schmitt et al., 2011; Steinmayr & Kessels, 2017). Openness is also closely linked to other achievement-related constructs, such as approach to learning (Vermetten et al., 2001), autonomous motivation (Mammadov et al., 2021), and critical thinking (Bidjerano & Dai, 2007). These associations provide an empirical support for the importance of openness for student success. The findings regarding the associations of other personality traits with academic achievement are mixed and inconclusive.

Any attempt to understand the underlying mechanisms of the personality-achievement relationship should include motivational processes, in concert with individual and environmental factors. For example, one empirically supported hypothesis for the conscientiousness-achievement relationship has been that the predictive role of conscientiousness is transmitted through mediating variables (e.g., Mammadov et al., 2018; Noftle & Robins, 2007; Trautwein et al., 2009). For example, Trautwein et al. found that academic effort plays a mediation role in the relationship between conscientiousness and mathematics achievement among middle school students. Mammadov et al. (2018) investigated associations of the Big Five personality traits with academic achievement and underlying mechanisms in the sample of gifted students. Conscientiousness was reported to have an indirect effect on academic achievement through students' beliefs of their self-regulatory skills for learning (i.e., self-regulatory efficacy) and autonomous motivation. Although these and other studies hypothesized conscientiousness as a distant predictor and achievement as a criterion variable, we should not ignore the possibility of the causal mechanism running in the opposite direction. It is plausible that students with high academic success are better motivated and have stronger self-efficacy, which leads them to exhibit more conscientious behaviors such as staying focused on tasks and persisting in learning behaviors.

EDUCATIONAL AND COUNSELING IMPLICATIONS

The pervasive influence of personality traits on individual difference outcomes goes beyond creative and academic performance. As reviewed in this chapter, albeit briefly, many traits play pivotal roles in shaping students' educational and life experiences. Each of the Big Five do matter. Openness is important in creative and intellectual engagement. Conscientiousness fuels task commitment. Extraversion and agreeableness benefit collaborative activities. And emotional stability allows one to perform well under pressure.

As described in this chapter, many studies have reported that gifted individuals, on average, are more open and less neurotic than the general population. They score higher on positive psychosocial qualities. They also show fewer indications of personality maladjustments. These findings are important to further break widespread misconceptions and stereotypes about the personality of the gifted. As noted earlier, teachers perceived gifted students as less emotionally stable, more introverted, and less agreeable (Baudson & Preckel, 2013). These perceptions are not supported by the empirical evidence. The findings should also be interpreted cautiously. The mean-level, or average, difference is a basic statistical concept, but sometimes can get confused. When we say, for example, gifted students are more open compared to others, we should be aware that not all gifted students are open. Gifted students are not a homogeneous group, nor is the "gifted" a homogeneous label. Educators should create learning environments that are sensitive to individual differences.

Studies focusing on social and emotional needs of gifted students do not necessarily show personality-related factors as the reason for possible psychological vulnerabilities. Stress, fear of failure, and other distractions that gifted students may experience are more likely to occur due to outside factors such as peer pressure, excessive parental involvement, and teacher expectations (Schultz & Delisle, 2003; Stoeber & Otto, 2006). In addition, being identified as gifted may lead gifted students to feel stereotyped and experience limited social latitude (Cross et al., 2018b). In the gifted education literature, this phenomenon has been termed "the stigma of giftedness" (Coleman, 1985). Gifted students may employ coping strategies to reduce the effect of perceived stigma (Cross et al., 2015, 2019; Swiatek, 2001). Students using avoidance strategies (e.g., denying giftedness) may be specifically susceptible to psychological distress due to being more vulnerable to identity confusion (Mammadov, in press; Striley, 2014). Educators and counselors should help students redefine the meanings of "giftedness," "normal," and "fitting in."

Personality can be malleable (Roberts & DelVecchio, 2000). Openness and conscientious behaviors can be reinforced by teachers, parents, and counselors. For example, teachers can help their students to become more open by strategically encouraging them to think beyond the confines of curricular topics and integrating focuses and creative ideas on a broad exposure. Similarly, students could be taught the qualities of conscientiousness. Various modeling and instructional approaches are available for helping students improve their self-regulatory skills, self-discipline, and achievement striving (Peeters et al., 2014). Findings on the role of motivational and self-regulative processes help to further shift our focus from relatively fixed individual differences to potentially malleable personal and environmental factors and student-initiated strategies. A better understanding of the effects of personality and motivational and self-regulative processes, in concert with students' gifts and talents, may help educators design optimal learning environments that facilitate individual student functioning.

REFERENCES

Ackerman, C. M. (1997). Identifying gifted adolescents using personality characteristics. *Roeper Review*, 19, 229–236.

Ackerman, P. L. (1996). Intelligence as process and knowledge: An integration for adult development and application. In W. Rogers, & A. Fisk, et al. (Eds.), *Aging and skilled performance: Advances in theory and application* (pp. 139–156). Erlbaum.

Allport, G. (1937). *Personality: A psychological interpretation*. Henry Holt and Company.

Batey, M. & Furnham, A. (2006). Creativity, intelligence, and personality: A critical review of the scattered literature. *Genetic, Social and General Psychology Monographs*, 132, 355–429. http://dx.doi.org/10.3200/MONO.132.4.355-430

Batey, M., Furnham, A., & Safiullina, X. (2010). Intelligence, general knowledge and personality as predictors of creativity. *Learning and Individual Differences*, 20, 532–535. http://dx.doi.org/10.1016/j.lindif.2010.04.008

Baudson, T. G. (2016). The mad genius stereotype: Still alive and well. *Frontiers in Psychology*, 7, 1–9. http://dx.doi.org/10.3389/fpsyg.2016.00368

Baudson, T. & Preckel, F. (2013). Teachers' implicit personality theories about the gifted: An experimental approach. *School Psychology Quarterly*, 28, 37–46. http://dx.doi.org/10.1037/spq0000011

Becker, G. (1978). *The mad genius debate*. SAGE.

Bidjerano, T. & Dai, D. Y. (2007). The relationship between the Big-Five model of personality and self-regulated learning strategies. *Learning and Individual Differences*, 17, 69–81. http://dx.doi.org/10.1016/j.lindif.2007.02.001

Bouchard, L. (2004). An instrument for the measure of Dabrowskian overexcitabilities to identify gifted elementary students. *Gifted Child Quarterly*, 48, 339–350. http://dx.doi.org/10.1177/001698620404800407

Bouchet, N. & Falk, R. (2001). The relationship among giftedness, gender, and overexcitability. *Gifted Child Quarterly*, 45, 260–267. http://dx.doi.org/10.1177/001698620104500404

Caprara, G. V., Vecchione, M., Alessandri, G., Gerbino, M., & Barbaranelli, C. (2011). The contribution of personality traits and self-efficacy beliefs to academic achievement: A longitudinal study. *British Journal of Educational Psychology*, 81, 78–96. http://dx.doi.org/10.1348/2044-8279.002004

Carretta, T. R. & Ree, M. J. (2019). The relations between cognitive ability and personality: Convergent results across measures. *International Journal of Selection and Assessment*, 26, 133–144. http://dx.doi.org/10.1111/ijsa.12224

Cattell, R. B. (1943). The description of personality. I. Foundations of trait measurement. *Psychological Review*, 50, 559–594. http://dx.doi.org/10.1037/h0057276

Chamorro-Premuzic, T. & Furnham, A. (2003). Personality predicts academic performance: Evidence from two longitudinal university samples. *Journal of Research in Psychology*, 37, 319–338. http://dx.doi.org/10.1016/S0092-6566(02)00578-0

Coleman, L. J. (1985). *Being gifted in school*. Addison-Wesley.

Cosgrove, J. M., Chen, Y. T., & Castelli, D. M. (2018). Physical fitness, grit, school attendance, and academic performance among adolescents. *BioMed Research International*, 2018, 9801258. http://dx.doi.org/10.1155/2018/9801258

Costa, P. T., Jr. & McCrae, R. R. (1992). *Revised NEO personality inventory (NEO-PI-R) and NEO five-factor inventory (NEO-FFI): Professional manual*. Psychological Assessment Resources.

Costa, P. T. & Widiger, T. A. (2002). *Personality disorders and the five-factor model of personality* (2nd ed.). American Psychological Association.

Credé, M., Tynan, M. C., & Harms, P. D. (2017). Much ado about grit: A meta-analytic synthesis of the grit literature. *Journal of Personality and Social Psychology*, 113, 492–511. http://dx.doi.org/10.1037/pspp0000102

Cross, J. R., O'Reilly, C., Kim, M., Mammadov, S., & Cross, T. L. (2015). Social coping and self-concept among young gifted students in Ireland and the United States: A cross-cultural study. *High Ability Studies*, 26, 39–61. http://dx.doi.org/10.1080/13598139.2015.1031881

Cross, J. R., Vaughn, C. T., Mammadov, S., Cross, T. L., Kim, M., O'Reilly, C., Spielhagen, F. R., Da Costa, M. P., & Hymer, B. (2019). A cross-cultural study of the social experience of giftedness. *Roeper Review*, 41, 224–242. http://dx.doi.org/10.1080/02783193.2019.1661052

Cross, T. L., Cross, J. R., Mammadov, S., Ward. T. J., Neumeister, K. S., & Andersen, L. (2018a). Psychological heterogeneity among honors college students. *Journal for the Education of the Gifted*, 41, 242–272. http://dx.doi.org/10.1177/0162353218781754

Cross, T. L., Andersen, L., Mammadov, S., & Cross, J. R. (2018b). Social and emotional development of students with gifts and talents. In J. L. Roberts, T. F. Inman, & J. H. Robins (Eds.), *Introduction to gifted education* (pp. 77–95). Prufrock Press.

Dabrowski, K. (1964). *Positive disintegration*. Little, Brown and Company.

De Bondt, N., Donche, V., & Van Petegem, P. (2020). Are contextual rather than personal factors at the basis of an anti-school culture? A Bayesian analysis of differences in intelligence, overexcitability, and learning patterns between (former) lower and higher-track students. *Social Psychology of Education*, 23(6), 1627–1657. https://doi.org/10.1007/s11218-020-09597-5

De Raad, B. & Schouwenburg, H. C. (1996). Personality in learning and education: A review. *European Journal of Personality*, 10, 303–336. http://dx.doi.org/10.1002/(SICI)1099-0984(199612)10:5%3C303::AID-PER262%3E3.0.CO;2-2

De Raad, B. & Perugini, M. (2002). *Big Five Assessment*. Hogrefe and Huber Publishers.

DeYoung, C. G., Peterson, J. B., & Higgins, D. M. (2005). Sources of openness/intellect: Cognitive and neuropsychological correlates of the fifth factor of personality. *Journal of Personality*, 73, 825–858. http://dx.doi.org/10.1111/j.1467-6494.2005.00330.x

DeYoung, C. G., Grazioplene, R. G., & Peterson, J. B. (2012). From madness to genius: The openness/intellect trait domain as a paradoxical simplex. *Journal of Research in Personality*, 46, 63–78. http://dx.doi.org/10.1016/j.jrp.2011.12.003

DeYoung, C. G., Quilty, L. C., Peterson, J. B., & Gray, J. R. (2014). Openness to experience, intellect, and cognitive ability. *Journal of Personality Assessment*, 96, 46–52. http://dx.doi.org/10.1080/00223891.2013.806327

Digman, J. M. (1990). Personality structure: Emergence of the five-factor model. *Annual Review of Psychology, 41*, 417–440. http://dx.doi.org/10.1146/annurev.ps.41.020190.002221

Donnellan, M. B. & Robins, R. W. (2010). Resilient, overcontrolled, and undercontrolled personality types: Issues and controversies. *Social and Personality Psychology Compass*, 11(4), 1070–1083. https://doi-org.proxy.library.vcu.edu/10.1111/j.1751-9004.2010.00313.x

Duckworth, A. L., Peterson, C., Matthews, M. D., & Kelly, D. R. (2007). Grit: Perseverance and passion for long-term goals. *Journal of Personality and Social Psychology, 92*, 1087–1101. http://dx.doi.org/10.1037/0022-3514.92.6.1087

Eskreis-Winkler, L., Shulman, E. P., Beal, S. A., & Duckworth, A. L. (2014). The grit effect: Predicting retention in the military, the workplace, school and marriage. *Frontiers in Psychology, 5*, 36. http://dx.doi.org/10.3389/fpsyg.2014.00036

Eysenck, H. J. (1970). *The structure of human personality* (3rd Ed.). Methuen.

Eysenck, H. J. (1994). Personality and intelligence: Psychometric and experimental approaches. In R. J. Sternberg & P. Ruzgis (Eds.), *Personality and intelligence* (pp. 3–31). Cambridge University Press.

Eysenck, H. J. (1995). Creativity as a product of intelligence and personality. In D. H. Saklofske & M. Zeidner (Eds.), *International handbook of personality and intelligence* (pp. 231–247). Plenum Press. https://dx.doi.org /10.1007/978-1-4757-5571-8_12

Falk, R. F., Manzanero, J. B., & Miller, N. B. (1997). Developmental potential in Venezuelan and American artists: A cross cultural validity study. *Creativity Research Journal, 10*, 201–206. http://dx.doi.org/10.1207/s15326934crj1002&3_8

Falk, R. F., Lind, S., Miller, N. B., Piechowski, M. M., & Silverman, L. K. (1999). *The Overexcitability Questionnaire-two (OEQII): Manual, scoring system, and questionnaire.* Institute for the Study of Advanced Development.

Feist, G. J. (1998). A meta-analysis of personality in scientific and artistic creativity. *Personality and Social Psychology Review, 4*, 290–309. http://dx.doi.org/10.1207/s15327957pspr0204_5

Francis, R., Hawes, D. J., & Abbott, M. (2016). Intellectual giftedness and psychology in children and adolescents: A systematic literature review. *Exceptional Children, 82*, 279–302.

Friedman, H. S. & Kern, M. L. (2014). Personality, well-being, and health. *Annual Review of Psychology, 65*, 719–742. http://dx.doi.org/10.1146/annurev-psych-010213-115123

Furnham, A., Zhang, J., & Chamorro-Premuzic, T. (2006). The relationship between psychometric and self-estimated intelligence, creativity, personality, and academic achievement. *Imagination, Cognition, and Personality, 25*, 119–145. http://dx.doi.org/10.2190/530V-3M9U-7UQ8-FMBG

Furnham, A., Monsen, J., & Ahmetoglu, G. (2009). Typical intellectual engagement, Big Five personality traits, approaches to learning and cognitive ability predictors of academic performance. *British Journal of Educational Psychology, 79*, 769–782.

Gagné, F. (2004). Transforming gifts into talents: the DMGT as a developmental theory. *High Ability Studies, 15*, 119–147. http://dx.doi.org/10.1080/1359813042000314682

Gallagher, S. A. (1990). Personality patterns of the gifted. *Understanding Our Gifted, 3*, 11–13.

Gallagher, S. A. (2013). Building bridges: Research on gifted children's personalities from three perspectives. In C. S. Neville, M. M. Piechowski, & S. S. Tolan (Eds.), *Off the charts: Asynchrony and the gifted child* (pp. 48–98). Royal Fireworks Press.

Gatzka, T., & Hell, B. (2018). Openness and postsecondary academic performance: A meta-analysis of facet-, aspect-, and dimension-level correlations. *Journal of Educational Psychology, 110*(3), 355–377. https://doi.org/10.1037/edu0000194

Gerbino, M., Zuffiano, A., Eisenberg, N., Castellani, V., Kanacri, B. P. L., Pastorelli, C., & Caprara, G. V. (2018). Adolescents' prosocial behavior predicts good grades beyond intelligence and personality traits. *Journal of Personality, 86*, 247–260. http://dx.doi.org/10.1111/jopy.12309

Goldberg, L. R. (1981). Language and individual differences: The search for universals in personality lexicons. *Review of Personality and Social Psychology, 2*, 141–165.

Goldberg, L. R. (1990). An alternative "description of personality": The big-five factor structure. *Journal of Personality and Social Psychology, 59*, 1216–1229. http://dx.doi.org/10.1037/0022-3514.59.6.1216

Goldberg, L. R. (1992). The development of markers for the Big-Five factor structure. *Psychological Assessment, 4*, 26–42. http://dx.doi.org/10.1037/1040-3590.4.1.26

Goldberg, L. R. (1993). The structure of phenotypic personality traits. *American Psychologist, 48*, 26–34. http://dx.doi.org/10.1037/0003-066X.48.1.26

Goldberg, L. R. (1999). A broad-bandwidth, public-domain, personality inventory measuring the lower-level facets of several five-factor models. In I. Mervielde, I. Deary, F. De Fruyt, & F. Ostendorf (Eds.), *Personality psychology in Europe* (pp. 7–28). Tilburg University Press.

Guo, J., Su, Q., & Zhang, Q. (2017). Individual creativity during the ideation phase of product innovation: An interactional perspective. *Creativity and Innovation Management, 26*, 31–48. http://dx.doi.org/10.1111/caim.12205

Jauk, E., Benedek, M., Dunst, B., & Neubauer, A. C. (2013). The relationship between intelligence and creativity: New support for the threshold hypothesis by means of empirical breakpoint detection. *Intelligence, 41*, 21–221. http://dx.doi.org/10.1016/j.intell.2013.03.003

John, O. P. & Srivastava, S. (1999). The Big-Five trait taxonomy: History, measurement, and theoretical perspectives. In L. A. Pervin & O. P. John (Eds.), *Handbook of personality: Theory and research* (2nd ed., pp. 102–138). Guilford Press.

John, O. P., Naumann, L. P., & Soto, C. J. (2008). Paradigm shift to the integrative Big Five trait taxonomy: History: measurement, and conceptual issue. In O. P. John, R. W. Robins, & L. A. Pervin (Eds.), *Handbook of personality: Theory and research* (pp. 114–158). Guilford.

Judge, T. A., Jackson, C. L., Shaw, J. C., Scott, B. A., & Rich, B. L. (2007). Self-efficacy and work-related performance: The integral role of individual differences. *Journal of Applied Psychology, 92*, 107–127. http://dx.doi.org/10.1037/0021-9010.92.1.107

Kaufman, J. C., Luria, S. R., & Beghetto, R. A. (2018). Creativity. In S. I. Pfeiffer (Ed.), *APA handbook of giftedness and talent* (pp. 287–298). American Psychological Association.

Kaufman, S. B. (2013). Opening up openness to experience: A four-factor model and relations to creative achievement in the arts and sciences. *Journal of Creative Behavior, 47*, 233–255. http://dx.doi.org/10.1002/jocb.33

King, L. A., Walker, L. M., & Broyles, S. J. (1996). Creativity and the five-factor model. *Journal of Research in Personality, 30*, 189–203. http://dx.doi.org/10.1006/jrpe.1996.0013

Kleiman, E. M., Adams, L. M., Kashdan, T. B., & Riskind, J. H. (2013). Gratitude and grit indirectly reduce risk of suicidal ideations by enhancing meaning in life: Evidence for a mediated moderation model. *Journal of Research in Personality, 47*, 539–546. http://dx.doi.org/10.1016/j.jrp.2013.04.007

Larsen, R. J. & Buss, D. M. (2002). *Personality psychology: Domains of knowledge about human nature.* McGraw-Hill.

Larson, L. M., Rottinghaus, P. J., & Borgen, F. H. (2002). Meta-analyses of Big Six interests and Big Five personality factors. *Journal of Vocational Behavior, 61*, 217–239. http://dx.doi.org/10.1006/jvbe.2001.1854

Limont, W., Dreszer-Drogorób, J., Bedyńska, S., Śliwińska, K., & Jastrzębska, D. (2014). 'Old wine in new bottles'? Relationships between overexcitabilities, the Big Five personality traits and giftedness in adolescents. *Personality and Individual Differences, 69*, 199–204. http://dx.doi.org/10.1016/j.paid.2014.06.003

Mammadov, S. (2020). A comparison of creativity-relevant personal characteristics in adolescents across personality profiles. *The Journal of Creative Behavior.* Advance online publication. http://dx.doi.org/10.1002/jocb.451

Mammadov, S. (2021). Social coping. In T. L. Cross and J. R. Cross (Eds.). *Handbook for counselors serving students with gifts and talents.* Prufrock Press.

Mammadov, S., Cross, T. L., & Ward, T. J. (2018). The Big Five personality predictors of academic achievement in gifted students: Mediation by self-regulatory efficacy and academic motivation. *High Ability Studies, 29,* 111–133. http://dx.doi.org/10.1080/135 98139.2018.1489222

Mammadov, S., Cross, T. L., & Cross, J. R. (2019). In search of temperament and personality predictors of creativity: A test of a mediation model. *Creativity Research Journal, 31,* 174–187. http://dx.doi.org/10.1080/10400419.2019.1577085

Mammadov, S., Cross, T. L., & Olszewski-Kubilius, P. (2021). A look beyond aptitude: The relationship between personality traits, autonomous motivation, and academic achievement in gifted students. *Roeper Review, 43*(3), 161–172, http://dx.doi.org/10.10 80/02783193.2021.1923595

Martin, L. T., Burns, R. M., & Schonlau, M. (2010). Mental disorders among gifted and non-gifted youth: A selected review of the epidemiologic literature. *Gifted Child Quarterly, 54,* 31–41. http://dx.doi.org/10.1177/0016986209352684

Matthews, G., Deary, I., & Whiteman, A. (2009). *Personality traits.* Cambridge University Press.

McAbee, S. T. & Oswald, F. L. (2013). The criterion-related validity of personality measures for predicting GPA: A meta-analytic validity competition. *Psychological Assessment, 25,* 532–544. http://dx.doi.org/10.1037/a0031748

McCrae, R. R. (2004). Openness to Experience. In C. Spielberger (Ed.), *Encyclopedia of applied psychology* (pp. 707–709). Elsevier.

McCrae, R. R. & Costa, P. T., Jr. (1987). Variation of the five-factor model of personality across instruments and observers. *Journal of Personality and Social Psychology, 52,* 81–90. http://dx.doi.org/10.1037//0022-3514.52.1.81

McCrae, R. R. & Costa, P. T., Jr. (1996). Toward a new generation of personality theories: Theoretical contexts for the Five-Factor Model. In J. S. Wiggins (Ed.), *The Five-Factor Model of personality: Theoretical perspectives* (pp. 51–87). Guilford Press.

McCrae, R. R. & Costa, P. T. Jr. (1999). A five-factor theory of personality. In L. A. Pervin & O. P. John (Eds.), *Handbook of personality* (pp. 139–153). Guilford Press.

McCrae, R. R., Costa P. T. Jr., Terracciano, A., Parker, W. D., Mills, C. J., De Fruyt, F., & Mervielde, I. (2002). Personality trait development from age 12 to age 18: Longitudinal, cross-sectional and cross-cultural analyses. *Journal of Personality and Social Psychology, 83,* 1456–1468. http://dx.doi.org/10.1037/0022-3514.83.6.1456

McCrae, R. & John, O. (1992). An introduction to the five-factor model and its applications. *Journal of Personality, 60,* 175–215. http://dx.doi.org/10.1111/j.1467-6494.1992.tb00970.x

Mendaglio, S. (2012). Overexcitabilities and giftedness research: A call for paradigm shift. *Journal for the Education of the Gifted, 35,* 207–219. http://dx.doi.org/10.1177/0162353212451704

Moutafi, J., Furnham, A., & Paltiel, L. (2004). Why is conscientiousness negatively correlated with intelligence? *Personality and Individual Differences, 37,* 1013–1022. http://dx.doi.org/10.1016/j.paid.2003.11.010

Moutafi, J., Furnham, A., & Paltiel, L. (2005). Can personality factors predict intelligence? *Personality and Individual Differences, 38,* 1021–1033. http://dx.doi.org/10.1016/j.paid.2004.06.023

Muenks, K., Wigfield, A., Yang, J. S., & O'Neal, C. R. (2017). How true is grit? Assessing its relations to high school and college students' personality characteristics, self-regulation, engagement, and achievement. *Journal of Educational Psychology, 109,* 599–620. http://dx.doi.org/10.1037/edu0000153

Myers, C. A., Wang, C., Black, J. M., Bugescu, N., & Hoeft, F. (2016). The matter of motivation: Striatal resting-state connectivity is dissociable between grit and growth mindset. *Social Cognitive and Affective Neuroscience, 11,* 1521–1527. http://dx.doi.org/10.1093/scan/nsw065

Neihart, M. (1999). The impact of giftedness on psychological well-being: What does the empirical literature say? *Roeper Review, 22,* 10–17.

Noftle, E. E. & Robins, R. W. (2007). Personality predictors of academic outcomes: Big Five correlates of GPA and SAT scores. *Journal of Personality and Social Psychology, 93,* 116–130. http://dx.doi.org/10.1037/0022-3514.93.1.116

Nusbaum, E. C. & Silvia, P. J. (2011). Are openness and intellect distinct aspects of openness to experience? A test of the O/I model. *Personality and Individual Differences, 51,* 571–574. http://dx.doi.org/10.1016/j.paid.2011.05.013

Olszewski-Kubilius, P. M., Kulieke, M. J., & Krasney, N. (1988). Personality dimensions of gifted adolescents: A review of the empirical literature. *Gifted Child Quarterly, 32,* 347–352. http://dx.doi.org/10.1177/001698628803200403

Oriol, X., Miranda, R., Oyanedel, J. C., & Torres, J. (2017). The role of self-control and grit in domains of school success in students of primary and secondary school. *Frontiers in Psychology, 8,* 1–9. http://dx.doi.org/10.3389/fpsyg.2017.01716

Peeters, J., De Backer, F., Reina, V. R., Kindekens, A., Buffel, T., & Lombaerts, K. (2014). The role of teachers' self-regulatory capacities in the implementation of self-regulated learning practices. *Procedia - Social and Behavioral Sciences, 116,* 1963–1970. http://dx.doi.org/10.1016/j.sbspro.2014.01.504

Piechowski, M. M. & Cunningham, K. (1985). Patterns of overexcitability in a group of artists. *Journal of Creative Behavior, 19,* 153–174.

Piechowski, M. M., Silverman, L. K., & Falk, R. F. (1985). Comparison of intellectually and artistically gifted on five dimensions of mental functioning. *Perceptual and Motor Skills, 60,* 539–549. http://dx.doi.org/10.2466/pms.1985.60.2.539

Piirto, J., Montgomery, D., & May, J. (2008). A comparison of Dabrowski's overexcitabilities by gender for American and Korean high school gifted students. *High Ability Studies, 19,* 141–153. http://dx.doi.org/10.1080/13598130802504080

Plucker, J. A. & Callahan, C. M. (Eds.). (2008). *Critical issues and practices in gifted education: What the research says.* Prufrock Press.

Ponnock, A., Muenks, K., Morell, M., Yang, J. S., Gladstone, J. R., & Wigfield, A. (2020). Grit and conscientiousness: Another jangle fallacy. *Journal of Research in Personality, 89,* 104021. http://dx.doi.org/10.1016/j.jrp.2020.104021

Poropat, A. E. (2009). A meta-analysis of the five-factor model of personality and academic performance. *Psychological Bulletin, 135,* 322–338. http://dx.doi.org/10.1037/a0014996

Raymark, P., Schmit, M., & Guion, R. (1997). Identifying potentially useful personality constructs for employee selection. *Personnel Psychology, 50,* 723–736. http://dx.doi.org/10.1111/j.1744-6570.1997.tb00712.x

Renzulli, J. S. (1978). What makes giftedness? Reexamining a definition. *Phi Delta Kappan, 60,* 180–184. http://dx.doi.org/10.1177/003172171109200821

Roberts, B. W. & DelVecchio, W. F. (2000). The rank-order consistency of personality traits from childhood to old age: A quantitative review of longitudinal studies. *Psychological Bulletin, 126,* 3–25. http://dx.doi.org/10.1037/0033-2909.126.1.3

Runco, M. A. & Richards, R. (1997). *Eminent creativity: Everyday creativity, and health.* Ablex.

Saucier, G. (1992). Openness versus intellect: Much ado about nothing? *European Journal of Personality, 6,* 381–386. http://dx.doi.org/10.1002/per.2410060506

Saucier, G. (1994). Trapnell versus the lexical factor: More ado about nothing? *European Journal of Personality, 8,* 291–298. http://dx.doi.org/10.1002/per.2410080406

Saucier, G. & Goldberg, L. R. (1996). The language of personality: Lexical perspectives on the five-factor model. In J. S. Wiggins (Ed.), *The five-factor model of personality: Theoretical perspectives* (pp. 21–50). Guilford Press.

Schmitt, N., Golubovich, J., & Leong, F. T. L. (2011). Impact of measurement invariance of construct correlations, mean differences, and relations with external correlates: An illustrative example using Big Five and RIASEC measures. *Assessment*, *18*, 412–427. http://dx.doi.org/10.1177/1073191110373223

Schultz, R. A. & Delisle, J. A. (2003). Gifted adolescents. In N. Colangelo & C. A. Davis (Eds.), *Handbook of gifted education* (3rd ed., pp. 483–492). Allyn & Bacon.

Silvia, P. J. & Beauty, R. E. (2012). Making creative metaphors: The importance of fluid intelligence for creative thought. *Intelligence*, *40*, 343–351. http://dx.doi.org/10.1016/j.intell.2012.02.005

Silvia, P. J., Kaufman, J. C., Reiter-Palmon, R., & Wigert, B. (2011). Cantankerous creativity: Honesty– humility, agreeableness, and the HEXACO structure of creative achievement. *Personality and Individual Differences*, *51*, 687–689. http://dx.doi.org/10.1016/j.paid.2011.06.011

Silvia, P. J., Nusbaum, E. C., Berg, C., Martin, C., & O'Connor, A. (2009). Openness to experience, plasticity, and creativity: Exploring lower order, higher order, and interactive effects. *Journal of Research in Personality*, *43*, 1087–1090. http://dx.doi.org/10.1016/j.jrp.2009.04.015

Steel, P., Schmidt, J., & Shultz, J. (2008). Refining the relationship between personality and subjective well-being. *Psychological Bulletin*, *134*, 138–161. http://dx.doi.org/10.1037/0033-2909.134.1.138

Steinmayr, R. & Kessels, U. (2017). Good at school = successful on the job? Explaining gender differences in scholastic and vocational success. *Personality and Individual Differences*, *105*, 107–115. http://dx.doi.org/10.1016/j.paid.2016.09.032

Sternberg, R. J. & Lubart, T. I. (1993). Creative giftedness: A multivariate investment approach. *Gifted Child Quarterly*, *37*, 7–15. http://dx.doi.org/10.1177/001698629303700102

Stoeber, J. & Otto, K. (2006). Positive conceptions of perfectionism: Approaches, evidence, challenges. *Personality and Social Psychology Review*, *10*, 295–319. http://dx.doi.org/10.1207/s15327957pspr1004_2

Stolarski, M., Zajenkowski, M., & Meisenberg, G. (2013). National intelligence and personality: Their relationships and impact on national economic success. *Intelligence*, *41*, 94–101. http://dx.doi.org/10.1016/j.intell.2012.11.003

Striley, K. M. (2014). The stigma of excellence and the dialectic of (perceived) superiority and inferiority: Exploring intellectually gifted adolescents' experiences of stigma. *Communication Studies*, *65*, 139–153. http://dx.doi.org/10.1080/10510974.2013.851726

Strus, W., Cieciuch, J., & Rowinski, T. (2014). The circumplex of personality metatraits: A synthesizing model of personality based on the Big Five. *Review of General Psychology*, *18*, 273–286. http://dx.doi.org/10.1037/gpr0000017

Swiatek, M. A. (2001). Social coping among gifted high school students and its relationship to self-concept. *Journal of Youth and Adolescence*, *30*, 19–39. http://dx.doi.org/10.1023/A:1005268704144

Terman, L. M. (1925). *Genetic studies of genius: Mental and physical traits of a thousand gifted children*. Stanford University Press.

Torrance, E. P. (1984). The role of creativity in identification of the gifted and talented. *Gifted Child Quarterly*, *28*, 153–156. http://dx.doi.org/10.1177/001698628402800403

Trautwein, U., Ludtke, O., Roberts, B. W., Schnyder, I., & Niggli, A. (2009). Different forces, same consequences: Conscientiousness and competence beliefs are independent predictors of academic effort and achievement. *Journal of Personality and Social Psychology*, *97*, 1115–1128. http://dx.doi.org/10.1037/a0017048

Vermetten, Y. J., Lodewijks, H. G., & Vermunt, J. D. (2001). The role of personality traits and goal orientations in strategy use. *Contemporary Educational Psychology*, *26*, 149–170. http://dx.doi.org/10.1006/ceps.1999.1042

Vuyk, M. A., Krieshok, T. S., & Kerr, B. A. (2016). Openness to experience rather than overexcitabilities: Call it like it is. *Gifted Child Quarterly*, *60*, 192–211. http://dx.doi.org/10.1177/0016986216645407

Watson, D. & Clark, L. A. (1997). Extraversion and its positive emotional core. In R. Hogan, J. Johnson, & S. Briggs (Eds.), *Handbook of personality psychology* (p. 767–793). Academic Press.

Winkler, D. & Voight, A. (2016). Giftedness and overexcitability: Investigating the relationship using meta-analysis. *Gifted Child Quarterly*, *60*, 243–257. http://dx.doi.org/10.1177/0016986216657588

Wirthwein, L. & Rost, D. H. (2011). Focusing on overexcitabilities. Studies with intellectually gifted and academically talented adults. *Personality and Individual Differences*, *51*, 337–342.

Wirthwein, L., Bergold, S., Preckel, F., & Steinmayr, R. (2019). Personality and school functioning of intellectually gifted and nongifted adolescents: Self-perceptions and parents' assessments. *Learning and Individual Differences*, *73*, 16–29. http://dx.doi.org/10.1016/j.lindif.2019.04.003

Wolfradt, U. & Pretz, J. E. (2001). Individual differences in creativity: Personality, story writing, and hobbies. *European Journal of Personality*, *4*, 297–310. http://dx.doi.org/10.1002/per.409

Wood, P. & Englert, P. (2009). Intelligence compensation theory: A critical examination of the negative relationship between conscientiousness and fluid and crystallized intelligence. *The Australian and New Zealand Journal of Organisational Psychology*, *2*, 19–29. http://dx.doi.org/10.1375/ajop.2.1.19

Yakmaci-Guzel, B. & Akarsu, F. (2006). Comparing overexcitabilities of gifted and nongifted 10th grade students in Turkey. *High Ability Studies*, *17*, 43–56. http://dx.doi.org/10.1080/13598130600947002

Zeidner, M. & Matthews, G. (2000). Intelligence and personality. In R. Sternberg (Ed.), *Handbook of intelligence* (pp. 581–610). Cambridge University Press.

Zeidner, M. & Shani-Zinovich, I. (2011). Do academically gifted and nongifted students differ on the Big-Five and adaptive status? Some recent data and conclusions. *Personality and Individual Differences*, *51*, 566–570. http://dx.doi.org/10.1016/j.paid.2011.05.007

The psychological adjustment of gifted children and individuals with high intellectual ability

Andrea Esperat Lein

There is a long history of debate regarding the psychological adjustment of gifted children and individuals with high intellectual ability. As with other developmental issues discussed in this book, one's examination of mental health issues in the gifted population must be considered in the context of the definition of giftedness being used. In this chapter, I review studies conducted by researchers who conceptualize giftedness through both the "gifted child" and "talent development" lens. Much of the literature in the field of mental health and giftedness has been written by clinicians describing their clinical experience with this population. Conversely, empirical studies completed in non-clinical settings (i.e., educational) often fail to include gifted children who may, for a variety of reasons, not be identified as such. Finally, twice-exceptional individuals have unique challenges given the potential for interactions among their exceptional abilities and disabilities, that may impact mental health and social-emotional development.

After a brief review of the primary factors that impact mental health, I review the complex issues surrounding psychiatric diagnosis of gifted children, commonly referenced social and emotional traits of the gifted, and the literature regarding psychopathology and giftedness. Finally, I offer an overview of these issues' implications related to mental health prevention and intervention, including proposed models of counseling geared toward gifted individuals.

METHODOLOGY ISSUES

As Webb et al. (2016) aptly summarized, there are two groups of researchers who have added to this body of literature: one group who views gifted children as being more vulnerable to mental health problems and thus, needing special interventions

DOI: 10.4324/9781003025443-10

to overcome those challenges (e.g., Lovecky, 2004; Silverman, 1994), and another group who views gifted children as no more or less vulnerable to mental health issues as their non-gifted peers (e.g., Janos et al., 1985; Neihart et al., 2002; 2015; and Robinson et al., 2007). One of the first exhaustive reviews of the literature on the social-emotional development of gifted children (Neihart et al., 2002), concluded that gifted children were similar to other children in regard to their risk of suffering from social and emotional difficulties.

In the early 2000s, it was clear that there were more questions than answers when it came to the social and emotional development of children with exceptional cognitive ability, and Neihart et al. (2002) recommended that more research be completed to explore these issues. Indeed, in the last two decades, there has been a clear effort to fill gaps in the literature, though much of the findings have been conflicting. As Webb et al. (2016) pointed out, these apparent contradictions can best be understood through a closer examination of the groups of children being studied, driven by the foundational assumptions and definitions of giftedness being used, as well as sampling bias. Many of the studies concluding that gifted children are more at risk for social and emotional challenges stem from clinical observation, case studies, and anecdotal evidence in clinical practice, wherein the gifted individuals are, by definition, presenting with serious difficulties needing treatment. It is obvious, then, that these studies are impacted by self-selection bias and would logically result in high percentages – potentially reflecting an over-incidence – of gifted children presenting with mental, emotional, and behavioral issues.

On the other hand, studies that conclude that gifted children are more or less similar to their typically developing peers in this regard have often been based on samples of identified gifted students being served in academic settings. Children identified as gifted for school services are, by the nature of the selection process, a particular group of children who share similar characteristics. It is logical to conclude, then, that the behavior of these students are in greater alignment with the behaviors that schools and gifted programs reward – namely, academic achievement and motivation– which is often not manifested when there are mental, emotional, and/or behavioral issues at play (Webb et al., 2016). Using this methodological design, samples likely underestimate the finding of any serious social or emotional difficulties. Even at a young age, children with exceptional cognitive potential who are struggling may be overlooked because their behavior does not readily make them identifiable for gifted programs – and indeed, their behavior may preclude them from gaining access to such programs. Understanding these key methodological and sampling concerns is fundamental in analyzing conflicting findings.

DIAGNOSTIC CHALLENGES FOR THE GIFTED

Unfortunately, a comprehensive understanding of the mental health needs of gifted individuals is complicated by diagnostic issues. Many assert that gifted individuals are often diagnosed with mental health problems for behaviors that are better explained by giftedness itself (Edwards, 2009; Pfeiffer, 2009; Webb et al., 2016; Wellisch & Brown, 2013). Because healthcare professionals are trained to examine and evaluate individuals for pathology, they may find what they are looking for even when there may be a better explanation for behaviors or symptoms. The effect of professionals' confirmation bias is not limited to the diagnosis of gifted individuals, of course, but some argue this is a more widespread concern for the gifted population given that their behavior, by definition, is different from their peers.

Obtaining an accurate mental health diagnosis for children and adolescents, in general, can be challenging for a variety of reasons (Merten et al., 2017), as many psychiatric disorders cannot be detected by genetic, neuronal, or physiological correlates. There are no external criteria by which to measure validity; therefore, reliability is used as a measure of accuracy. Even within the field of psychiatry, substantial criticism has been directed at poor diagnostic reliability rates (Frances, 2012). Rates of detection and low inter-rater agreement can be influenced by treatment setting, training, and professional background of the person making the diagnosis, their clinical experience, and the age of the patient (Vermani et al., 2011).

There is ample evidence showing rates of mental health diagnoses in children and adolescents have risen in recent years, with some suggesting that certain disorders are being overdiagnosed (Gnaulati, 2013; Merten et al., 2017; Schlesinger, 2012). For example, some studies suggest that as many as 20% of children in the United States – or nearly one million – diagnosed with ADHD are misdiagnosed due to relative immaturity compared to their peers (Elder, 2010). Similar findings have been replicated in Canada (Morrow et al., 2012), Sweden (Halldner et al., 2014), and Iceland (Zoëga et al., 2012). Researchers also have found evidence of misdiagnosis of bipolar disorder, estimating that it is correctly diagnosed less than 50% of the time (Zimmerman et al., 2008). It is also likely that the COVID-19 pandemic will result in an increase of mental health needs due to the stresses related to the global tragedy. It is reasonable to assume that these diagnostic problems affect the gifted and non-gifted alike.

In fact, gifted children and adolescents may be more at risk for misdiagnosis or overdiagnosis by professionals (Bishop & Rinn, 2019; Webb et al., 2016), though there remains little empirical data to support this concern. As stated by Webb et al. (2016, p.55):

> Misdiagnosis is a mismatch between the gifted child's actual learning and health needs and the perception of those needs by others. More specifically, this mismatch results in either (a) a labeled mental health diagnosis and/or learning disorder being placed on the child when the behaviors or concerns can be better explained by giftedness, and/or (b) a health disorder and/or learning need being overlooked, which may also be referred to as a missed diagnosis.

Misdiagnosis can have serious consequences for a child or adolescents, including receiving inappropriate treatment (e.g., psychopharmacological interventions) and negatively impacting the child's sense of developing identity. For example, as related to the age-related effects of misdiagnosis of ADHD previously discussed, these concerns have serious implications for gifted children who are younger than their classmates due to grade or subject acceleration.

Not only does misdiagnosis affect treatment decisions and outcomes (Elder, 2010; Walker & Shapiro, 2010), it makes it difficult to obtain an accurate assessment of how many gifted children suffer from mental health issues. Misdiagnosis and overdiagnosis of gifted individuals are the result of a variety of factors. These may include cultural and societal norms and stereotypes about high IQ youth, reliance on heuristics, misleading endorsement of symptoms by caregivers, and disregarding differential causes of behavior, all of which affect overdiagnosis in the general population (Merten et al., 2017). Compounding these issues are the fact that most healthcare, mental health providers, school counselors, and teachers receive little to no training related to the specific needs of a student with advanced cognitive abilities (Evans, 1996; Ford & Harris, 1995; Peterson, 2006; Peterson & Morris, 2010; Webb et al., 2016). Without a foundational understanding of the characteristics of this group, professionals are more prone to label certain behaviors as pathological, without considering the element of giftedness in their decision-making (Hartnett et al., 2004; Silverman, 1998; Webb, 2014). Many have called for better school counseling training to prepare them to work with high IQ youth (Colangelo, 2002; Colangelo & Wood, 2015; Davis & Rimm, 1998; Kerr, 1986; Muratori & Smith, 2015; Myers & Pace, 1986; Parker, 1988; Tolbert, 1982). Others, such as the SENG Misdiagnosis Initiative, have focused a great deal on educating healthcare and mental health professionals on the issues of misdiagnosis related to gifted individuals (SENG, 2015).

While these concerns abound within the clinical community focused on gifted individuals, little empirical data have been gathered to examine the extent of the problem. To address this gap in the literature, Bishop and Rinn (2019) conducted a mixed-methods study in which they presented mental health professionals in the United States with case vignettes, with and without guided prompts, to test the possibility of misdiagnosis of high IQ youth. Of the 330 professionals who responded, the majority (82.9% for unguided vs. 78.4% for guided) leaned toward diagnosing a disorder even when presented with high IQ as a possible explanation of presenting issues. The prompt seemed to benefit in the combination disorder/high IQ combined assessment (9.5% unguided vs. 60.0% guided). These findings appear to justify concerns of misdiagnosis of high IQ youth in mental health settings, though more empirical research is needed in this area.

Dual-diagnoses (2e)

Gifted individuals may well be overdiagnosed in certain cases, but they are also not exempt from experiencing (and being accurately diagnosed with) additional learning, medical, or psychological issues. The case of twice-exceptionality (2e) – giftedness in addition to another diagnosable condition–offers yet another level of diagnostic complexity and many children and adolescents are not accurately identified as such. Indeed, it is difficult to determine how many cases of 2e exist given the heightened challenges of making accurate dual-diagnoses (Pfeiffer, 2013), and the diagnostic difficulties previously discussed. For example, a twice-exceptional child's high cognitive ability may mask their disability, or vice versa, so that the child's intellectual and academic needs go unidentified. In some cases, both the exceptionality and disability mask one another, so that a child's gifts and struggles go unnoticed altogether. In these circumstances, the child may be struggling but, to the untrained observer, appear "normal" because their high ability allows them to mask their struggles to a large degree. This unique set of challenges poses obvious risk to the developing child should the conditions be unrecognized or untreated.

GIFTED CHARACTERISTICS RELATED TO MENTAL HEALTH

Previous chapters of this text have presented common social, emotional, and behavioral characteristics of students with advanced academic ability, creativity, and intelligence, many of which may affect the trajectory of their mental health. These characteristics are not believed to be the cause of social and emotional issues, per se, but problems are more likely to stem from a mismatch between children's traits and the familial, school, peer, or cultural expectations placed upon them (Coleman et al., 2015). This "poorness of fit" between individual and environment explains many social and emotional problems associated with high IQ youth (Mueller & Winsor, 2018). However, some traits are thought to more directly increase the probability of problems, regardless of the environment, as summarized by Webb et al. (2016, p. 22):

- Drive to use one's abilities.
- Drive to understand, to search for consistency.
- Ability to see possibilities and alternatives.
- Emotional intensity (focus; intrinsic motivation; persistence).
- Concern with social and moral issues (idealism; sensitivity).
- Different rates or levels of physical and emotional development.

These traits can present as beneficial or problematic aspects of a child's personality, and parents may misinterpret some of these traits when they seek professional help. Webb et al. (2016) describe several common presenting issues for gifted children referred to health care professionals, including: high activity level and questions of ADHD, intense emotional reactions and outbursts, existential anxiety and depression, poor judgment relative to intelligence, high sensitivity to stimuli, difficulty relating to same-age peers, underachievement, and concerns about learning disabilities. Again, without a thorough understanding of giftedness, professionals may be apt to misinterpret some of these behaviors as disorders rather than variations among gifted children or issues related to environmental conditions. Common misdiagnoses include Attention-Deficit Hyperactivity Disorder (ADHD), Asperger's Disorder, Oppositional Defiant Disorder, Conduct Disorder, Obsessive-Compulsive Disorder, Sleep Terror Disorder, Narcissistic Personality Disorder, and Bipolar Disorder (Webb et al., 2016). Errors in diagnosis are heightened for gifted children from minority groups and/or twice-exceptional students, as their giftedness may not be identified and therefore, problematic behaviors are seen largely through the lens of pathology (Beljan, 2011; Davis, 2010; Grantham, 2012).

The following section reviews the research findings to date related to commonly cited social and emotional traits of the gifted.

Asynchrony

Asynchronous development refers to the inter- and intra-personal variations of abilities of gifted individuals. The theory is that cognitive abilities can develop at a rate much faster than physical, social, or emotional capacities, potentially leading to frustration, anxiety, a feeling of being different, and isolation (Cross & Cross, 2015). If this theory is correct, then gifted children may feel out-of-sync, not only within themselves but with others as well (Silverman, 2002). These feelings often arise whether or not they are identified as gifted or self-identify with the label (Coleman et al., 2015). This internal sense of "different-ness" often increases with the level of exceptionality in cognitive ability (Mueller, 2009; Neihart et al., 2002; Rogers, 2007; Silverman, 2012; Webb & Kleine, 1993; Wiley, 2020). Other factors, including gender, ethnicity, sexual identity, and culture or environment can also exacerbate the feeling of being out-of-sync (Ford, 2002; Reis, 2002). Asynchrony is perhaps most pronounced among twice-exceptional students, whose high abilities coupled with disabilities represent extreme differences often misunderstood by self and others (Webb et al., 2016).

Being identified as gifted, by definition, indicates that a child is different from their peers on one or more measurable traits. The experience of being identified as gifted, in and of itself, is thought to influence the development of a child's sense of self and their social-emotional experiences. The act of being identified and acknowledged as "different" may impact gifted children in myriad ways and at differing points along their development, whether due to being placed in special programming separate from their peers; being treated differently by others in light of their higher intelligence or achievement scores; or their lived experiences and the realization of inherent differences from peers (see Mendaglio & Peterson, 2007). Being different is thought to be a risk factor for some gifted students. For example, Coleman et al. (2015) described the "clash" (p. 366) that can occur between the unique learning needs of gifted students and the academic environments in which they tend to find themselves, many of which do not offer appropriately differentiated curricula for the gifted (Mueller & Winsor, 2016; Tomlinson et al., 2003). This clash between the individual and environment can lead to several negative outcomes: feelings of frustration, academic avoidance or resistance, and problematic interactions with peers (e.g., bullying) (Coleman et al., 2015).

Social competence

Related to asynchrony is the concern that gifted children have more difficulty finding and making friends. In fact, research suggests that gifted students are no less adept socially than their non-gifted peers (Pfeiffer, 2013). However, some key differences have been noted in the literature which may impact gifted youth's social and emotional development. Some researchers, for instance, have found that while identified gifted students did not differ on measures of social competence, loneliness, or empathy, broadly assessed, as compared to their non-identified peers, they scored higher on measures of assertiveness and cognitive empathy (Shechtman & Silektor, 2012). Similarly, in a study of self-perceptions of social competence among gifted students in grades 5-12, researchers found that the students had positive perceptions about their ability to make and keep friends, and being identified as gifted was not viewed negatively from a social perspective (Lee et al., 2012). The results of both of these studies seem to support the social benefits of placing gifted students with their cognitive peers. The findings of other studies (Kosir et al., 2016), including a meta-analysis conducted by Francis et al. (2016), support the notion that gifted students are not viewed any less positively than their nongifted peers in terms of social acceptance.

Self-concept

The self-concept of gifted students, when examined as individual dimensions (e.g., academic, social, and physical) rather than a global self-concept measure, has been shown to be significantly different than non-identified peers. Litster and Roberts' (2011) seminal meta-analysis, which compared various dimensions of self-concept across 40 studies, found that gifted students demonstrated higher global self-concept. They also exhibited higher perceived competencies in areas of academics and behavior. These gifted students, however, did not perceive their physical or appearance competencies to be as high; their scores were significantly lower than non-identified peers in these domains. Additional research has supported these findings, particularly that gifted students tend to score higher in global, academic, and behavior self-concepts (Kosir et al., 2016; Sarouphim, 2011; Shechtman & Silektor, 2012), but lower in the physical domain (Shechtman & Silektor, 2012). Importantly, self-concept among the gifted seems to be positively influenced by academic acceleration (Hoogeveen et al., 2012; Lee et al., 2012).

Perfectionism

Perfectionism has long been held as a common characteristic among the gifted, if not the one most often associated with intellectually gifted youth (Silverman, 1999). Further designated into functional and dysfunctional types (Locicero & Ashby, 2000; Parker et al., 2001; Wiley, 2020), perfectionism is often associated with test anxiety, academic satisfaction, and performance (Eum & Rice, 2011; Hanchon, 2010; Miquelon et al., 2005; Vansteenkiste et al., 2010) and is not always problematic. Unhealthy manifestations of perfectionism can become debilitative for gifted youth, hindering their ability to function at optimal levels. However, most of the studies do not support higher rates of unhealthy perfectionism among intellectually gifted students (Baker, 1996; Margot & Rinn, 2016; Parker & Mills, 1996: Parker et al., 2001; Roberts & Lovett, 1994; Schuler, 2000). Additionally, recent comparison studies examining perfectionism in gifted students find that identified students engage in unhealthy forms of perfectionism less frequently than their non-identified peers (Locicero & Ashby, 2000; Parker et al., 2001; Parker & Mills, 1996). These findings were further supported by a recent meta-analysis of 32 studies, which concluded that intellectually gifted students do not differ from their nongifted peers on this dimension (Stricker et al., 2019).

Underachievement

Underachievement has been widely studied in the field of gifted education, the premise being that some gifted students are not fulfilling their intellectual potential. Due to varying definitions, identification of underachievement in high-ability youth can be challenging (Siegle & McCoach, 2018). Underachievement generally refers to a discrepancy between a gifted student's measured aptitude and achievement, as measured by standardized achievement testing or grades. However, the process of determining such discrepancy is not always clear or exact, as school districts and professionals often use different procedures (Rimm, 2008; Ziegler et al., 2012).

White et al. (2018) reviewed nine studies and concluded that gifted achievement is related to individual factors (i.e., motivation and emotion). Underachievement may be influenced by a variety of factors and situations, including test anxiety, poor placement, lack of challenge, poor instruction, failure to be identified as gifted, social pressure, and deprived communities (Baum et al., 1995; Reis, 2004; Rimm, 2008; Robinson, 2002). Several strategies have been shown to help reverse underachievement include assessing student readiness and ensuring a better curricular fit, minimizing a focus on grades or evaluation, and allowing for more student interest-driven learning (Rimm, 2008).

Collectively, these social-emotional traits, while not shared by all gifted students, can impact healthy development in a variety of ways. Taken together with the common risk and resiliency factors known to influence the mental health of *all* children, a percentage of gifted students will find themselves at increased risk for developing mental health issues.

FIELD NOTE 9.1

Carole, clinical social worker, NY

I worked with a young, teenage girl who was incredibly gifted and talented in multiple areas: math, science, language arts, music composition, leadership, and so forth. Daria had struggled for several years and often compared herself to her older brother who she viewed as "the smart one" in the family. Everyone in her family was highly educated and accomplished, and whether it was intentional or not, she felt burdened by the weight of high expectations for academic success. She went to school and lived in an affluent community also known for its high value on achievement. On top of that, she placed an immense burden on herself, setting very aspirational goals for herself at a young age. Over time, she seemed to crack under the pressure of it all. Every area of her life began to break down, even as she worked harder and harder to keep up the facade of success. She had been in outpatient psychotherapy and tried psychotropic medications but, due to extreme anxiety and increasing self-destructive behavior, eventually needed more intensive treatment. Her parents were at a loss as to how they could help her, though they continued to try everything that was recommended. After a psychiatric hospitalization following a suicide attempt, she ended up in long-term residential treatment.

Daria was clearly bright and full of potential, but her extreme perfectionism often got in the way. She began to dread school, even though she had always loved learning. Unbeknownst to her parents, she was also struggling with her sexual and gender identity, and this exacerbated her already entrenched social anxiety. She also struggled with obsessive-compulsive disorder, but for a long time, never had a name for this. She thought maybe she was just weirdly wired and beat up on herself for compulsive thoughts that she found repulsive and shameful. Finally, her family, while well-intentioned, had engaged in long-standing patterns that resulted in prolonged, painful emotional disconnection. This young girl alienated herself from her family and her peers, during a time when she needed their support the most.

I remember the day I gave her an article on giftedness and mental health. It was written by a psychiatrist, and it articulated some of the common struggles that gifted youth experience. I had a feeling that she would resonate with it, both from an intellectual and emotional standpoint. As I suspected, she felt incredibly validated by this information. With wide-eyed disbelief, she asked me more questions about this construct, "giftedness," as if I had just opened up a new door into understanding herself at a pretty basic level. She had never heard that her intellectual giftedness and heightened creativity may have played a role in how she developed as a child, and some of the struggles she was currently facing. She was so excited about this new information that she asked to share the article with a friend who she thought might also benefit from reading it. From that point on, she began to develop more self-compassion and understanding of her particular quirks, interests, and struggles. While it didn't solve all of her problems immediately, understanding the complexity of her personality development and mental health issues in the context of her giftedness helped her embark on a new path of identity exploration and development. This new framework helped shape the treatment goals and process, and she was able to effectively engage in this therapeutic work.

THE MENTAL HEALTH OF THE GIFTED

Continued debate surrounds the notion that gifted individuals are more vulnerable to psychological maladjustment, and much of the investigation in this area has been based on the gifted child paradigm perspective, with the assumption that gifted individuals are more susceptible given their inherent gifted traits. The evidence is mixed and does not necessarily support this assumption, though some suggest otherwise (Mendaglio & Peterson, 2007 Webb, 1993). Rather, there is a substantial body of research to support the notion that gifted students are comparable to their peers in terms of psychological adjustment (Bain & Bell 2004; Bracken & Brown, 2006; Cross et al., 2008; Mueller, 2009). It should be noted that much of the research in this area has historically focused on adults, though there is a growing focus on the psychological well-being of gifted children and adolescents. The following section provides an overview of the literature to date examining the related, but different, constructs of psychological well-being and psychopathology (e.g., depression and anxiety) among gifted individuals.

Psychological well-being

Longitudinal research dating back to the earliest beginnings of the study of gifted individuals (Terman, 1925) has long indicated that highly intelligent individuals report higher life satisfaction over time as compared to average-able peers. In contemporary research, including an ongoing longitudinal study by Lubinski et al. (2014) spanning over 40 years, findings confirm this positive correlation between high IQ and life satisfaction. Several recent reviews of studies, including a meta-analysis of 33 studies (n = 49,378) also support this relationship (Gonzalez-Mule et al., 2017, Rinn & Bishop, 2015).

Other studies have found limited or no differences between identified gifted and non-identified individuals in terms of life satisfaction and well-being (Bergold et al., 2015; Chmiel et al., 2012; Wirthwein & Rost, 2011). However, some suggest that there may be qualitatively different assessments of life satisfaction for exceptional vs. typically developing adults. For example, compared to adults who had not been identified as gifted, gifted-identified adults' general life satisfaction was more heavily influenced by their satisfaction with work relative to other areas such as self and friends (Wirthwein & Rost, 2011).

In the relatively scant literature focused on the psychological well-being of gifted children and adolescents, findings are mixed. Bergold et al. (2015) examined well-being and life satisfaction among gifted and typically developing adolescents and found no meaningful differences between them. Gubbels et al. (2018) studied fifth-grade children (n = 513) and found that while gifted children scored higher on self-concept measures, they reported similar levels of well-being as their same age peers. Similarly, in a recent small scale meta-analysis of six studies (n = 1632) examining differences in happiness between 713 identified gifted and 919 non-identified students, no meaningful differences were found between the two groups (Zeidner, 2020).

Other studies point to a positive advantage for gifted children and adolescents as it relates to psychological well-being. In a systematic literature review, Francis et al. (2016) concluded that gifted children and adolescents were superior in psychological adjustment compared to their peers. Another recent meta-analysis of 21 studies examined the relationship between giftedness and emotional intelligence, which has been shown to be positively linked to mental health and well-being outcomes (Alabbasi et al., 2020). The findings indicated small but significant outperformance by gifted students in various areas of emotional intelligence. More specifically, gifted students tended to score higher on adaptability and general mood skills, and they were more optimistic and happier than their average ability peers. The authors noted their findings were consistent with earlier conclusions drawn by Neihart (1999).

Taken together, current research suggests that gifted individuals experience well-being and life satisfaction at rates at least comparable, if not higher, than their non-identified peers. These findings are in alignment with much of the findings discussed in this book thus far.

EYE FOR DIVERSITY 9.1 EFFECT OF STRESS, RACISM, AND CLASSISM ON MENTAL HEALTH

Dante D. Dixson

Students from minority and low-income backgrounds are at a higher risk of developing mental health disorders compared to their peers from the majority and high-income backgrounds due to their lived experiences. Specifically, research indicates that students from minority and low-income backgrounds perpetually experience an added tax on their mental capacity due to them enduring detrimental forces like stress, racism, and classism to a higher degree, and on a more consistent basis, than their majority and high-income student counterparts. This line of research has three implications for gifted students from minority and low-income backgrounds. First, it indicates that gifted students from minority and low-income backgrounds are more likely to develop mental health disorders compared to their majority and high-income student peers due to reasons unrelated to their advanced cognitive abilities. Second, it indicates that gifted students from minority and low-income backgrounds have to put forth more mental effort than their majority and high-income counterparts to achieve the same academic goals due to the additional tax on their mental capacity. Third, it indicates that teachers and parents should make a consistent and concerted effort to reduce the detrimental forces prevalent in the environments surrounding their children.

Psychopathology

There has been no shortage of interest in the link between high intelligence and psychopathology, the so-called "mad genius theory" (Haynes, 2016; MacCabe et al., 2010; Saltz, 2017), with questions circulating as far back as ancient Greek times. In the *Problemata* XXX.1 Aristotle (as quoted in Akiskal & Akiskal, 2007) posed the question, "Why is it that all those who become eminent in philosophy or politics or poetry or the arts are clearly melancholics?..." Contemporary clinical accounts have described the many paths of psychological suffering for individuals with high IQ scores, even if the research is mixed as to whether high IQ individuals do, in fact, suffer more than is typical for humans in general. As noted earlier, defining the criterion is important in placing the current review of the literature into proper context. For example, while some studies have found a link between high creativity and bipolar disorder or depression (e.g., Andreasen, 2008; Jamison, 1996; Ludwig, 1995; Misset, 2013; and Piirto, 2004), the majority of studies reviewed here will center primarily on intellectual giftedness and/or high IQ (not creativity). Keeping that in mind, this section reviews what is known to date about various psychological disorders in the intellectually gifted population.

General psychiatric illness

Much of the research on intelligence and psychiatric illness has demonstrated a negative relationship (Francis et al., 2016; Harrison et al., 2015; Khandaker et al., 2011; 2018; Midouhas et al., 2018), supporting the notion once again that higher IQ appears to serve as a protective factor for mental health. However, as Rinn (2020) pointed out, much of this research has been conducted with samples that do not include individuals with exceptionally high IQs, and therefore, the findings may not necessarily be generalizable to the gifted population. To examine this link more closely, Karpinski et al. (2018) conducted a study that included individuals with IQ scores in the gifted range (>130). However, the study had fatal methodological flaws. The sample was drawn from a group of American Mensa members (and therefore, likely affected by self-selection bias.). Additionally, participants in the study were asked to self-report medically-given diagnoses, but were also asked to self-diagnose if a particular disease, symptom, or disorder was suspected.

Matta et al. (2019), operating under the assumption that gifted individuals are more vulnerable to psychopathology than nongifted, found significant differences on certain measures of subclinical personality traits between high-IQ ($n = 70$) and average-IQ adults ($n = 166$). They concluded that the unique social and emotional needs and challenges specific to gifted adults may put them at greater risk of developing psychopathological disorders. However, the gifted adult sample in this study was also a self-selected group of Mensa members, and the gifted sample was 80% male, limiting its generalizability as well.

Finally, in a large, prospective, longitudinal study examining the prevalence of sleep problems and mental health issues in children with high cognitive ability (IQ > 120), Cook et al. (2020) found no significant differences between these children and children with lower IQ scores on sleep problems assessed at ages 1, 2, 3, and 11. Sleep problems often coincide with other mental health and behavioral issues. In this study, the children with higher IQ scores were found to have significantly fewer symptoms of mental health difficulties, as assessed over time at ages 5, 7, and 11 years, with 66% reduced odds for problem presentation in the clinical range at 11 years of age. Similarly, as noted earlier, Francis et al. (2016) reviewed 18 studies examining the relationship between intellectual giftedness and mental health in children and adolescents, and concluded that gifted children exhibited fewer social, emotional, and behavioral issues compared to their nongifted peers.

Mood disorders

Mood disorders, such as major depressive disorder and bipolar disorder, are a group of mental health issues that, as referenced earlier, affect a large percentage of young people across the globe. Depression and bipolar disorder can manifest differently, particularly in children, and for different underlying causes. The specific differences are beyond the scope of this chapter, but should be noted as specificity of diagnosis is an important factor in analyzing the research. Some have observed that highly intelligent persons may be more at risk for existential depression (Webb, 2013), though it's unclear based on available empirical data. The vast majority of empirical evidence available suggests that persons with exceptional cognitive ability are no more likely to suffer from depression than typically developing individuals (Wiley, 2020), or at the very least, the evidence is inconclusive (Cross & Andersen, 2016). Indeed, some research supports that higher cognitive ability is a protective factor, incurring greater mental health benefits for those with high intelligence (IQ > 130) (Missett, 2013; Neihart, 1999).

Neihart (1999) examined early research that had been conducted to date, and concluded that there was overwhelming support showing that gifted individuals were at similar or lower risk for depression compared to non-gifted peers. She looked at several studies that included high IQ individuals who were diagnosed with specific mental disorders (e.g., depression, bipolar disorder, eating disorders, obsessive-compulsive disorder, and anxiety). The existing literature at that time indicated that high-IQ children showed lower rates of traits linked to emotional problems across various measures of mental health; however, results were more mixed when examining high IQ individuals with respect to specific disorders (e.g., eating disorders and obsessive-compulsive disorder) (Neihart, 1999).

Others have since conducted similar reviews and found confirming evidence that individuals with high IQ scores do not necessarily suffer from mood disorders any more than the average population. For example, Missett (2013) reviewed literature examining both high intelligence and high creative abilities as they relate to mood disorders, and found that most studies found no conclusive evidence that high IQ was linked to higher rates of depression but, rather, high IQ appeared to serve as a protective factor (Martin et al., 2010; Mueller, 2009; Ryland et al., 2010). In other studies examining gifted children and adolescents, specifically, both groups were significantly less depressed than their non-identified peers (Mueller, 2009; Richards et al., 2003). In a meta-analysis by Martin et al. (2010), studies involving identified gifted and non-identified students showed no significant difference between the two groups. A review of 18 studies by Francis et al. (2016), examining the relationship between intellectual giftedness and psychopathology in children and adolescents, likewise found that gifted students were not at greater risk for depression or anxiety, and in fact, demonstrated "superior social-emotional adjustment" compared to non-gifted peers (p. 279). Finally, a study by Bolland et al. (2019) examined hopelessness among low-income gifted students and found that identified gifted students generally had lower levels of hopelessness compared to their peers.

While several studies indicate high IQ as a protective factor, this may not hold up in certain cases (e.g., twice-exceptional, low income, minority status). Antshel et al. (2009) examined depression in high-IQ adults (Full Scale IQ > 120) diagnosed with and without attention-deficit hyperactivity disorder (ADHD), and found that high-IQ adults with ADHD were significantly more likely than high-IQ adults without ADHD to be diagnosed with major depressive disorder. Similar results were found in a study involving high-IQ (Full Scale IQ > 120) youth with ADHD. Antshel et al. (2008) found that, like the high-IQ adults with ADHD, the youth had higher rates of mood disorders, including depression. Interaction effects have been noted in other cases. Most notably, Francis et al. (2016) found giftedness to be a risk factor for depression for youth in juvenile detention facilities, and Mueller (2009) found that giftedness was a risk factor for depression in Hispanic youth. These findings suggest that high intelligence may not be enough to protect gifted individuals from depression or other mood disorders when other risk variables are taken into account.

The literature regarding bipolar disorder and intellectual giftedness is mixed, and nearly nonexistent with gifted and nongifted youth in particular (Martin et al., 2010). Given the diagnostic challenges specific to accurate evaluation of bipolar disorder in children and adolescents, this may be inevitable. A longitudinal study that followed 1,037 participants for 25 years, found that high-IQ individuals (IQ > 115), assessed at ages 7, 9, and 11, experienced significantly lower rates of mental disorders, such as schizophrenia, major depression, and anxiety disorders (Koenen et al., 2009). However, higher childhood IQ was found to predict an increased risk of mania in adulthood. Additional studies by Antshel et al. (2008, 2009) also found that high-IQ individuals with ADHD were at greater risk for bipolar disorder; this association was not significant for those without ADHD. MacCabe et al. (2010) examined 900,000 Swedish students, using grades as an indicator of cognitive ability, and found that high-ability participants had a statistically significant increased risk for adult bipolar disorder diagnoses. Finally, Smith et al. (2015), in a large prospective UK birth cohort study ($n = 1881$), examined children who were assessed at age 8 and 22–23 years. They concluded that higher childhood IQ scores, particularly verbal IQ, may be a marker of risk for developing bipolar disorder. Overall, while some research exists to support a link between bipolar disorder and high IQ, more research is warranted to fully understand the impact of intelligence, and possibly specific aspects of intelligence, in the development of this disorder.

Suicide

While it is widely accepted that gifted students are not immune to severe mental distress, suicidal ideation, and even completed suicide, there exists no empirical evidence suggesting that suicide is more prevalent among gifted students compared to typically developing students (Cross et al., 2008; Martin et al., 2010). Some suggest, though, that gifted students are more successful at completing their first suicide attempts (Cross & Andersen, 2016). Additionally, personality variables such as neuroticism and self-criticism have been found to be associated with depression and suicidal ideation in suicidal adolescents (Enns et al., 2003), which may have important implications for gifted adolescents with these particular personality traits (Cross & Cross, 2020). Finally, as is true for many suicidal nongifted youth, gifted students who are struggling with severe emotional conflict, suicidal ideation, gestures, and attempts are more likely to be dealing with a complex interaction of multiple variables, including personal, interpersonal, familial, and environmental challenges (Cross & Cross, 2015; Mueller & Winsor, 2018).

Anxiety disorders

Anxiety disorders manifest in a variety of ways, such as generalized anxiety disorder, obsessive compulsive disorder, and eating disorders, to name a few. In their discussion of anxiety issues for gifted individuals, Webb et al. (2016) also grouped related ideational disorders, centered on interpersonal relations, such as obsessive-compulsive personality disorder, social anxiety disorder, schizoid personality disorder, and schizotypal personality disorder. Other clinicians might also add compulsive disorders, such as those related to technology, gaming, sex, and even substance abuse, under the umbrella of anxiety-related disorders, given that many conceptualize compulsive behavior as a particular method of self-soothing anxiety. Unhealthy perfectionism is also often linked to anxiety-based issues, though it is not, in and of itself, a diagnosable condition. There is a paucity of research as it relates to these specific anxiety-related disorders and giftedness. The majority of research, which has largely already been reviewed here, relates to perfectionism.

Earlier studies examining the relationship between intelligence and anxiety also found a negative correlation in healthy subjects (Feldhusen & Klausmeier, 1962; Spielberger, 1958, as cited in Coplan et al., 2012). For example, Feldhusen and Klausmeier (1962) studied anxiety among three groups of children, those with: (1) low (IQ = 56–81); (2) average (IQ = 90–110); and (3) high IQ (IQ = 120–146), with 40 children in each group. The study found significantly higher mean anxiety scores for low IQ children as compared to both average and high-IQ children. There were no significant differences between the average and high-IQ groups.

Several studies have documented high intelligence as a factor contributing to eating disorders (Lopez et al., 2010; Neihart, 1999), though others have not found such a relationship (Touyz et al., 1986). In a study of adolescents, high intelligence was again predictive of eating disordered behavior (Blanz et al., 1997). Eating disorders have been linked to other anxiety-related issues, such as perfectionism and obsessiveness, and commonly co-occur with other mental health issues (e.g., depression, substance abuse, OCD, and personality disorders) (Webb et al., 2016).

In summary, the preponderance of empirical evidence to date indicates that rates of anxiety and depression in gifted children are not significantly different from the general population, as was articulated by earlier reviewers (Cross & Cross, 2015; Neihart, 1999). More research is warranted with regards to specific anxiety-related diagnoses, such as eating disorders and obsessive-compulsive disorders, to determine if there are any meaningful differences for gifted individuals. Additionally, research closely examining the impact of co-occurring disorders and contextual variables (i.e., personality, family, or school variables) is needed to better understand the complex interplay of giftedness with other risk and protective factors.

STRATEGIES & IMPLICATIONS FOR SUPPORTING MENTAL HEALTH

Many clinicians who specialize in working with the gifted population support the view that identified gifted students struggling with mental health issues are best served by those who have at least some foundational knowledge about giftedness (Webb et al., 2016). While a full description of mental health prevention and intervention strategies for gifted students is beyond the scope of this chapter (see Mendaglio & Peterson, 2007; Cross & Cross, 2015), a general overview of best practices will be provided here.

Prevention

Mental health professionals recognize that preventative measures should include systemic, holistic, developmentally-appropriate responses that support mental health on multiple levels: individual, family, school-wide, and community (Cross, 2018). Much of the general advice given to parents to help support mental health is applicable to gifted children as well. For example, on the individual level, parents and professionals can help young gifted people learn and implement important therapeutic lifestyle choices regarding nutrition, physical exercise, sleep, social connections, and general healthcare, as these all have important implications for emotional and mental well-being. Teaching mindfulness practices to gifted students can be particularly helpful in developing brain-body awareness and emotional regulation. Drawing upon the field of positive psychology, many social and emotional skill-sets can be nurtured and developed at home, even from a very young age. For example, positive psychology practices related to increasing gratitude, fostering resiliency, focusing on growth rather than deficits, cultivating positive self-talk, understanding the role of meaning and purpose, and nurturing positive relationships are examples of ways that adults can teach and support gifted youth in building foundational skills that support good mental health.

Parents and other guiding adults can help by teaching and implementing appropriate boundaries around activities and relationships that may be potentially risky or traumatic events for a child. For example, teaching young people how to set healthy boundaries around technology use, social media, relationships, and even school work can help a gifted student develop self-awareness and self-discipline. More and more youth, gifted or not, are exposed to sexually inappropriate and violent material at younger ages, putting them at risk for later emotional or behavioral issues. Guiding young gifted people so that they understand and can, ultimately, avoid these risks is another way parents and other trusted adults can assist them.

Families play an important role in the lives of gifted children and adolescents, not only in advocating for appropriate education, but in helping them to develop the social and emotional skills they need to succeed in life. Primary caregivers are the first to model and teach emotional intelligence, healthy boundaries, and safe, trusting relationships. Strong, healthy attachment forms a foundation for healthy psychological development for all children, and gifted children are no exception. A healthy parental structure and an authoritarian parenting style have also been shown to positively influence the emotional development of gifted children, whereas over-empowerment may lead to underachievement, anger, and depression. Overparenting – being overly intrusive, overprotective, or taking on responsibilities that are developmentally appropriate for the child to learn–is another problematic pattern that can have ill effects on any child or adolescent. One of the best investments a parent can make is in his or her own development of parenting or social-emotional skills if they are limited in some way.

On a school-wide level, social-emotional learning initiatives, including the teaching of psychosocial skills, character development, and positive education frameworks are all ways that schools can help support the healthy development of all children including gifted youth. Specifically, offering appropriately challenging, differentiated curriculum can prevent many academic and emotional issues down the road, including boredom, frustration, underachievement, and school avoidance or dropout. School counselors and school psychologists are particularly qualified to help support both students and families in recognizing, understanding, and supporting the social and emotional needs of gifted students.

Finally, on a community level, gifted children's psychological development is supported and nurtured when they engage in volunteering and community service, peer mentoring, social activism, formal or informal mentoring, as well as extracurricular activities that support the whole child (e.g., sports, interest-groups, religious, or spiritual communities). Finding like-minded peers, regardless of age, is an important aspect of creating a sense of belonging for a gifted child, an important element of social-emotional well-being. These kinds of communities increasingly can be found through online searches, an advantage for gifted Gen Z students, particularly those who live in rural or low-income communities.

Intervention

In cases when a gifted student's social, emotional, or behavioral difficulties begin to impact his or her functioning on a subclinical level, and/or when the issues warrant a psychiatric diagnosis, counseling or psychotherapy by a trained mental health professional is recommended. Therapists are trained to consider a variety of factors when joining with a new client, conceptualizing the therapeutic needs and goals, and choosing the best course of treatment. Exceptional cognitive ability is an important factor for any therapist to consider. However, most professionals who would be in a role to support distressed gifted youth have had no education or training related to giftedness (Bishop & Rinn, 2019; Webb et al., 2016). A key priority, then, is to facilitate this training on a broad scale.

Several models of counseling, strategies, and perspectives on psychological treatment for gifted individuals have been proposed in the literature (see Cross & Cross, 2015; Mendaglio & Peterson, 2007; Silverman, 2012). Most contend that a differentiated approach, taking cognitive ability into account, be used in counseling intellectually gifted students. A brief overview of some of the most commonly referenced approaches and models follows.

Cross (2018) outlined a continuum of psychological services, which denotes various intervention points where a gifted student may receive help (e.g., advising, guidance, counseling, therapy, and psychopharmacology). While this continuum of services is similar to those available to the general population, Cross tailors the discussion to how various adults (i.e., parents, teachers, counselors, and psychiatrists) might specifically help gifted youth along this continuum. Mendaglio and Peterson (2007) outlined four stages of counseling when working with gifted clients: (1) conceptual; (2) action; (3) evaluation; and (4) termination. Again, while these stages parallel those that would be used in counseling typically developing clients, Mendaglio discusses them in the context of an affective-cognitive therapy approach to working with the gifted. Others have described their approaches to counseling gifted individuals using a systems approach (Thomas & Ray, 2006), a developmentally-informed approach (Peterson, 2006), and a family-systems-based approach (Peterson, 2006). Mahoney (1998) created the Gifted Identity Formation model, developed specifically for gifted children and adolescents. It focuses primarily on identity development and questions of meaning and purpose, and outlines 12 systems that the client is supported in applying throughout their process of self-exploration. Each of these counseling approaches draw upon well-developed frameworks already in use in the field of counseling. In their descriptions, however, the authors offer case examples along with the theoretical assumptions for how these approaches can be effectively utilized for the gifted population (Mendaglio & Peterson, 2007).

Created specifically for depressed and suicidal gifted youth, the *Integrated Model for Depression and Suicide Applied to Gifted Students* (Mueller & Winsor, 2018) is a developmental approach that draws from Gagne's Differentiated Model of Giftedness and Talent Development (DMGT; Gagne, 2013) and Person-Environment Fit Theory (P-E fit; Eccles et al., 1993). It consists of three interrelated factors – intrapersonal, interpersonal, and environment – which interact and intersect along a developmental continuum. This ecological approach supports the therapist in considering intervention strategies that might be effective at various developmental stages and entry points, whether it's intrapersonal (e.g., reflection and mindfulness), interpersonal (e.g., psychoeducation and group therapy), or contextual (e.g., therapeutic programming).

Other commonly used therapeutic approaches, such as bibliotherapy, cinematherapy, narrative therapy, cognitive behavioral therapy, dialectical behavior therapy, psychodynamic therapy, group therapy, and family therapy, all have a place in working with intellectually gifted youth depending on the presenting problem. Pfeiffer (2020) has taken a somewhat different approach to counseling the gifted compared to others in the field. Rather than focusing on creating a counseling model unique to gifted individuals, Pfeiffer discusses guiding principles for working with the gifted and recommends that counselors rely on widely supported, evidence-based clinical practice as a core feature in treating gifted clients. He describes this integrated approach as using "the best available empirically supported treatment protocol on the presenting disorder or disorders, in conjunction with establishing and maintaining a strong therapeutic relationship with the client, and finally, clinical expertise in the context of considerable supervised experience and a deep understanding working with this unique population" (Pfeiffer, 2020, p. 4).

Mental health professionals have an important role to play in educating the gifted child, the child's family members, teachers, or other important adults in the child's life. For example, teaching mindfulness strategies to combat anxiety and stress, supporting parents in developing positive discipline approaches, or communicating with a gifted child's coaches and mentors are all practical ways to support the mental health trajectory of the child. School psychologists, for instance, can create small peer-group settings at school to facilitate practicing social skills, sharing common interests, or learning emotional regulation skills. They might advocate for a more nuanced approach to identifying and serving gifted children who may be more at risk due to being twice-exceptional or coming from minority or low-income backgrounds (Wiley, 2020). Finally, all adults – parents, teachers, and mental health professionals– can support the emotional lives of gifted children by recognizing and addressing the *whole* child, rather than solely seeing a child through the lens of their gifts and talents or any given label, "gifted" or otherwise. Helping them to develop their social and emotional intelligence, through modeling and experience at a young age, will provide an important foundation for developing more complex skills as they grow and mature.

CONCLUSION

As demonstrated through this book, gifted children may be different than their non-gifted peers in certain respects, but they are normal in the sense that their mental health is influenced by the same variables that hold true for all developing human beings. There is mixed evidence as to whether gifted children are indeed more vulnerable to mental ill-health, with most evidence suggesting that identified students are *not* at greater risk. In fact, being identified as intellectually gifted appears to serve as a protective factor in many, though not all, cases. However, it is also true that gifted children are not exempt from developing mental, emotional, and behavioral disorders. Like their nongifted peers, we should not presume that gifted students' basic psychological needs – and vulnerability to risk factors–are any different. When gifted children are struggling, parents and professionals should consider best practices regarding intervention strategies while also taking into consideration their giftedness (Pfeiffer, 2020). Mental health professionals are encouraged to develop a greater understanding of the nuances and unique challenges that can arise from both being labeled as "gifted," as well as particular family dynamics that may occur as a result. Finally, parents should neither be alarmed nor overly confident simply because their child has been identified as gifted. Supportive, effective parenting practices serve as the bedrock foundation for healthy child development and attachment, under-standing that each child is unique – gifted or not – and will require attunement and attentiveness on the parent's part. When parents and professionals educate themselves about the social-emotional and mental health needs of gifted children – as well as the unique needs of a gifted child, in particular – they create the best chance for optimal mental health outcomes for that child.

REFERENCES

Akiskal, H. S., & Akiskal, K. K. (Eds.). (2007). In search of Aristotle: Temperament, human nature, melancholia, creativity and eminence. *Journal of Affective Disorders, 100*, 1–6.

Alabbasi, A., Ayoub, A., & Ziegler, A. (2020). Are gifted students more emotionally intelligent than their non-gifted peers? A meta-analysis. *High Ability Studies*. https://doi.org/10.10 80/13598139.2020.1770704

Andreasen, N. C. (2008). The relationship between creativity and mood disorders. *Dialogues in Clinical Neuroscience, 10*(2), 251–255. https://doi.org/10.31887/DCNS.2008.10.2/ncandreasen

Antshel, K. M., Faraone, S. V., Maglione, K., Doyle, A., Fried, R., Seidman, L., & Biederman, J. (2008). Temporal stability of ADHD in the high-IQ population: Results from the MGH longitudinal family studies of ADHD. *Journal of the American Academy of Child and Adolescent Psychiatry, 47*(7), 817–825. https://doi.org/10.1097/CHI.0b013e318172eecf

Antshel, K.M, Faraone, S.V., Maglione, K., Doyle, A., Fried, R., Seidman, & L., Biederman, J. (2009). Is adult attention deficit hyperactivity disorder a valid diagnosis in the presence of high IQ? *Psychological Medicine, 39*(8), 1325–35. https://doi.org/10.1017/S0033291708004959

Bain, S. K., & Bell, S. M. (2004). Social self-concept, social attributions, and peer relationships in fourth, fifth, and sixth graders who are gifted compared to high achievers. *Gifted Child Quarterly, 48*(3), 168–178. https://doi.org/10.1177/001698620404800302

Baker, J. (1996). Everyday stressors of academically gifted adolescents. *Journal of Secondary Gifted Education, 7*, 356–368.

Baum, S. M., Renzulli, J. S., & Hebert, T. P. (1995). Reversing underachievement: Creative productivity as a systematic intervention. *Gifted Child Quarterly, 39*, 224–235. https://doi.org/10.1177/001698629503900406

Beljan, P. (2011). Misdiagnosis of culturally diverse students. In J. A. Castellano & A. D. Frazier (Eds.), *Special populations of gifted education: Understanding from our most able students from diverse backgrounds*. Prufrock Press, Inc.

Bergold, S., Wirthwein, L., Rost, D. H., & Steinmayr, R. (2015, October). Are gifted adolescents more satisfied with their lives than their non-gifted peers? *Frontiers in Psychology, 6,* 1623. https://doi.org/10.3389/fpsyg.2015.01623

Bishop, J. C., & Rinn, A. N. (2019). The potential of misdiagnosis of high IQ youth by practicing mental health professionals: A mixed methods study. *High Ability Studies.* https://doi.org/10.1080/13598139.2019.1661223

Blanz, B. J., Detzner, U., Lay, B., Rose, F., & Schmidt, M. H. (1997). The intellectual functioning of adolescents with anorexia nervosa and bulimia nervosa. *European Child and Adolescent Psychiatry, 6*(3), 129–135.

Bolland, A. C., Besnoy, K. D., Tomek, S., & Bolland, J. M. (2019). The effects of academic giftedness and gender on developmental trajectories of hopelessness among students living in economically disadvantaged neighborhoods. *Gifted Child Quarterly, 63,* 225–242. https://doi.org/10.1177/0016986219839205

Bracken, B. A. & Brown, E. F. (2006). Behavioral identification and assessment of gifted and talented students. *Journal of Psychoeducational Assessment, 24*(2), 112–122. https://doi.org/10.1177/0734282905285246

Chmiel, M., Brunner, M., Keller, U., Schalke, D., Wrulich, M., & Martin, R. (2012). Does childhood general cognitive ability at age 12 predict subjective well-being at age 52? *Journal of Research in Personality, 46*(5), 627–631. https://doi.org/10.1016/j.jrp.2012.06.006

Colangelo, N. & Wood, S. W. (2015). Introduction to the special section: Counseling the gifted individual. *Journal of Counseling and Development, 93,* 131–133.

Colangelo, N. (2002). *Counseling gifted and talented students.* The National Research Center on the Gifted and Talented.

Coleman, L. J., Micko, K. J., & Cross, T. L. (2015). Twenty-five years of research on the lived experience of being gifted in school: Capturing the students' voices. *Journal for the Education of the Gifted, 38*(4), 358–376. https://doi.org/10.1177/0162353215607322

Cook, F., Hippmann, D., & Omerovic, E. (2020). The sleep and mental health of gifted children: A prospective, longitudinal, community cohort study. *Gifted and Talented International, 35*(1), 16–26. http://doi.org/10.1080/15332276.2020.1758977

Coplan, J. D., Hodulik, S., Mathew, S. J., Mao, X., Hof, P. R., Gorman, J. M., & Shungu, D. C. (2012). The relationship between intelligence and anxiety: An association with subcortical white matter metabolism. *Frontiers in Evolutionary Neuroscience, 3,* 8–14. http://doi.org/10.3389/fnevo.2011.00008

Cross, T. L. (2018). *On the social and emotional lives of gifted children* (5th ed.). Prufrock Press, Inc.

Cross, T. L. & Andersen, L. (2016). Depression and suicide among gifted children and adolescents. In M. Neihart, S. I. Pfeiffer, & T. L. Cross (Eds.), *The social and emotional development of gifted children: What do we know?* (2nd ed.) (pp. 79–90). Prufrock Press, Inc.

Cross, J. R. & Cross, T. L. (2015). Clinical and mental health issues in counseling the gifted individual. *Journal of Counseling & Development, 93*(2), 163–172. http://doi.org/10.1002/j.1556-6676.2015.00192.x

Cross, T. L. & Cross, J. R. (2020). An ecological model of suicidal behavior among students with gifts and talents. *High Ability Studies,* 1–19. https://doi.org/10.1080/13598139.2020.1733391

Cross, T. L., Cassady, J. C., Dixon, F. A., & Adams, C. M. (2008). The psychology of gifted adolescents as measured by the MMPI-A. *Gifted Child Quarterly, 52*(4), 326–339. https://doi.org/10.1177/0016986208321810

Davis, J. L. (2010). *Bright, talented, and black: A guide for families of African American gifted learners.* Great Potential Press.

Davis, G. & Rimm, S. B. (1998). *Education of the gifted and talented* (4th ed.). Allyn & Bacon.

Eccles, J. S., Midgley, C., Wigfield, A., Buchanan, C. M., Reuman, D., Flanagan, C., & Mac Iver, D. (1993). Development during adolescence: The impact of stage-environment fit on young adolescents' experiences in schools and in families. *American Psychologist*, 48(2), 90–101. https://doi.org/10.1037/0003-066X.48.2.90

Edwards, K. (2009). Misdiagnosis, the recent trend in thinking about gifted children with ADHD. *APEX*, 15(1), 29–44. http://www.giftedchildren.or.nz/apex

Elder, T. E. (2010). The importance of relative standards in ADHD diagnoses: Evidence based on exact birth dates. *Journal of Health Economics*, 29(5), 641–656. https://doi.org/10.1016/j.jhealeco.2010.06.003

Enns, M.W., Cox, B.J., & Inayatulla, M. (2003). Personality predictors of outcomes for adolescents hospitalized for suicidal ideation. *Journal of the American Academy of Child and Adolescent Psychiatry*, 42, 720–727. https://doi.org/10.1097/01.CHI.0000046847.56865.B0

Eum, K. & Rice, K. G. (2011). Test anxiety, perfectionism, goal orientation, and academic performance. *Anxiety, Stress, & Coping*, 23, 1–12. https://doi.org/10.1080/10615806.2010.488723

Evans, K. M. (1996). Counseling gifted women of color. In K. D. Arnold, K. D. Noble, & R. F. Subotnik (Eds.), *Remarkable women: Perspectives on female talent development* (pp. 367–381). Hampton Press, Inc.

Feldhusen, J. & Klausmeier, H. (1962). Anxiety, intelligence, and achievement in children of low, average, and high intelligence. *Child Development*, 33(2), 403–409. http://doi.org/10.2307/1126453

Ford, D. Y. (2002). Racial identity among gifted African American students. In M. Neihart, S. M. Reis, N. M. Robinson, & S. M. Moon (Eds.), *The social and emotional development of gifted children: What do we know?* (pp.155–163). Prufrock Press, Inc.

Ford, D. Y. & Harris, J. J. (1995). Underachievement among gifted African American students: Implications for school counselors. *School Counselor*, 42(3), 196–203. https://www.jstor.org/stable/23901325

Frances, A. (2012, May 8). *Newsflash from APA meeting: DSM-5 has flunked its reliability tests.* http://www.huffingtonpost.com/allen-frances/dsm-5-reliability-tests_b_1490857.html

Gnaulati, E. (2013). *Back to normal: Why ordinary childhood behavior is mistaken for ADHD, bipolar disorder, and autism spectrum disorder.* Beacon Press.

Gonzalez-Mule, E., Carter, K. M., Mount, & M. K. (2017). Are smarter people happier? Meta-analyses of the relationships between general mental ability and job and life satisfaction. *Journal of Vocational Behavior*, 99, 146–164. https://doi.org/10.1016/j.jvb.2017.01.003

Grantham, T. C. (2012). Eminence-focused gifted education. *Gifted Child Quarterly*, 56(4), 215–220. https://doi.org/10.1177/0016986212456074

Gubbels, J., Segers, E., & Verhoeven, L. (2018). How children's intellectual profiles relate to their cognitive, socio-emotional, and academic functioning, *High Ability Studies*, 29(2), 149–168. http://doi.org/10.1080/13598139.2018.1507902

Halldner, L., Tillander, A., Lundholm, C., Boman, M., Långström, N., Larsson, H., & Lichtenstein, P. (2014). Relative immaturity and ADHD: Findings from nationwide registers, parent- and self-reports. *The Journal of Child Psychology and Psychiatry*, 55(8), 897–904. https://doi.org/10.1111/jcpp.12229

Hanchon, T. A. (2010). The relations between perfectionism and achievement goals. *Personality and Individual Differences*, 49, 885–890. https://doi.org/10.1016/j.paid.2010.07.023

Harrison, S. L., Sajjad, A., Bramer, W. M., Ikram, M. A., Tiemeier, H., & Stephan, B. C. M. (2015). Exploring strategies to operationalize cognitive reserve: A systematic review of reviews. *Journal of Clinical and Experimental Neuropsychology*, 37(3), 253–264. https://doi.org/10.1080/13803395.2014.1002759

Hartnett, D. N., Nelson, J. M., & Rinn, A. N. (2004). Gifted or ADHD? The possibilities of misdiagnosis. *Roeper Review*, 26(2), 73–76.

Haynes, R. D. (2016). Whatever happened to the 'mad, bad' scientist? Overturning the stereotype. *Public Understanding of Science*, 25(1), 31–44. https://doi.org/10.1177/0963662514535689

Hoogeveen, L., van Hell, J. G., & Verhoeven, L. (2012). Social-emotional characteristics of gifted accelerated and non-accelerated students in the Netherlands. *British Journal of Educational Psychology*, 82, 585–605. https://doi.org/10.1111/j.2044-8279.2011.020247.x

Jamison, K. R. (1996). *Touched with fire: Manic-depressive illness and the artistic temperament.* Simon & Schuster.

Janos, P. M., Fung, H. C., & Robinson, N. M. (1985). Self-concept, self-esteem, and peer relations among gifted children who feel "different." *Gifted Child Quarterly*, 29, 78–82. https://doi.org/10.1177/001698628502900207

Karpinski, R. I., Kinase Kolb, A. M., Tetreault, N. A., & Borowski, T. B. (2018). High intelligence: A risk factor for psychological and physiological overexcitabilities. *Intelligence*, 66, 8–23. https://doi.org/10.1016/j.intell.2017.09.001

Kerr, B. A. (1986). Career counseling for the gifted: Assessments and interventions. *Journal of Counseling and Development*, 64, 602–604. https://doi.org/10.1002/j.1556-6676.1986.tb01215.x

Khandaker, G. M., Barnett, J. H., White, I. R., & Jones, P. B. (2011). A quantitative meta-analysis of population-based studies of premorbid intelligence and schizophrenia. *Schizophrenia Research*, 132(2–3), 220–227. https://doi.org/10.1016/j.schres.2011.06.017

Khandaker, G. M., Stochl, J., Zammit, S., Goodyer, I., Lewis, G., & Jones, P. B. (2018). Childhood inflammatory markers and intelligence as predictors of subsequent persistent depressive symptoms: A longitudinal cohort study. *Psychological Medicine*, 48(9), 1514–1522. https://doi.org/10.1017/S0033291717003038

Koenen, K. C., Moffitt, T. E., Roberts, A. L., Martin, L. T., Kubzansky, L., Harrington, H., Poulton, R., & Caspi, A. (2009). Childhood IQ and adult mental disorders: A test of the cognitive reserve hypothesis. *The American Journal of Psychiatry*, 166(1), 50–57. https://doi.org/10.1176/appi.ajp.2008.08030343

Kosir, K., Horvat, M., Aram, U., & Jurinec, N. (2016). Is being gifted always an advantage? Peer relations and self-concept of gifted students. *High Ability Studies*, 27, 129–148. https://doi.org/10.1080/13598139.2015.1108186

Lee, S. Y., Olszewski-Kubilius, P., & Thomson, D. T. (2012). Academically gifted students' perceived interpersonal competence and peer relationships. *Gifted Child Quarterly*, 56, 90–104. https://doi.org/10.1177/0016986212442568

Litster, K. & Roberts, J. (2011). The self-concepts and perceived competencies of gifted and non-gifted students: A meta-analysis. *Journal of Research in Special Educational Needs*, 11(2), 130–140. https://doi.org/10.1111/j.1471-3802.2010.01166.x

Locicero, K. A. & Ashby, J. S. (2000). Multidimensional perfectionism in middle school age gifted students: A comparison to peers from the general cohort. *Roeper Review*, 22, 182–185. https://doi.org/10.1080/02783190009554030

Lopez, C., Stahl, D., & Tchanturia, K. (2010). Estimated intelligence quotient in anorexia nervosa: A systematic review and meta-analysis of the literature. *Annals of General Psychiatry*, 9, 40. https://doi.org/10.1186/1744-859X-9-40

Lovecky, D. V. (2004). *Different minds: Gifted children with ADHD, Asperger syndrome, and other learning deficits.* Jessica Kingsley.

Lubinski, D., Benbow, C. P., & Kell, H. J. (2014). Life paths and accomplishments of mathematically precocious males and females four decades later. *Psychological Science*, 25(12), 2217–2232. https://doi.org/10.1177/0956797614551371

Ludwig, A. M. (1995) *The price of greatness: Resolving the creativity and madness controversy.* Guilford Press.

MacCabe, J. H., Lambe, M. P., Cnattingius, S., Sham, P. C., David, A. S., Reichberg, A., & Hultman, C. M. (2010). Excellent school performance at age 16 and risk of adult bipolar disorder: National cohort study. *The British Journal of Psychiatry*, *196*(2), 109–115. https://doi.org/10.1192/bjp.bp.108.060368

Mahoney, A. S. (1998). In search of the gifted identity: From abstract concept to workable counseling constructs. *Roeper Review: A Journal on Gifted Education*, *20*(3), 222–226. https://doi.org/10.1080/02783199809553895

Margot, K. C. & Rinn, A. N. (2016). Perfectionism in gifted adolescents: A replication and extension. *Journal of Advanced Academics*, *27*, 190–209. https://doi.org/10.1177/1932202X16656452

Martin, L. T., Burns, R. M., & Schonlau, M. (2010). Mental disorders among gifted and nongifted youth: A selected review of the epidemiologic literature. *Gifted Child Quarterly*, *54*(1), 31–41. https://doi.org/10.1177/0016986209352684

Matta, M., Gritti, E. S., & Lang, M. (2019). Personality assessment of intellectually gifted adults: A dimensional trait approach. *Personality and Individual Differences*, *140*, 21–26. https://doi.org/10.1016/j.paid.2018.05.009

Mendaglio, S. & Peterson, J. (2007). *Models of counseling gifted children, adolescents, and young adults*. Prufrock Press, Inc.

Merten, E. C., Cwik, J. C., Margraf, J., & Schneider, S. (2017). Overdiagnosis of mental disorders in children and adolescents (in developed countries). *Child and Adolescent Psychiatry and Mental Health*, *11*(5). https://doi.org/10.1186/s13034-016-0140-5

Midouhas, E., Flouri, E., Papachristou, E., & Kokosi, T. (2018). Does general intelligence moderate the association between inflammation and psychological distress? *Intelligence*, *68*, 30–36. https://doi.org/10.1016/j.intell.2018.03.002

Miquelon, P., Vallerand, R. J., Grouzet, F. M. E., & Cardinal, G. (2005). Perfectionism, academic motivation, and psychological adjustment: An integrative model. *Personality and Social Psychology Bulletin*, *31*, 913–924. https://doi.org/10.1177/0146167204272298

Missett, T. (2013). Exploring the relationship between mood disorders and gifted individuals. *Roeper Review*, *35*, 47–57. https://doi.org/10.1080/02783193.2013.740602

Morrow, R. L., Garland, E. J., Wright, J. M., Maclure, M., Taylor, S., & Dormuth, C. R. (2012). Influence of relative age on diagnosis and treatment of attention-deficit/hyperactivity disorder in children. *Canadian Medical Association Journal*, *184*(7), 755–762. https://doi.org/10.1503/cmaj.111619

Mueller, C. E. (2009). Protective factors as barriers to depression among gifted and nongifted youth: A selected review of the epidemiological literature. *Gifted Child Quarterly*, *54*(1), 31–41. https://doi.org/10.1177/0016986209352684

Mueller, C. E. & Winsor, D. L. (2016). Math/Verbal academic self-concept: Subject-specificity across four distinctive groups of high ability adolescents. *Learning and Individual Differences*, *50*, 240–245. https://doi.org/10.1016/j.lindif.2016.08.002

Mueller, C. E. & Winsor, D. L. (2018). Depression, suicide, and giftedness: Disentangling risk factors, protective factors, and implications for optimal growth. In S. I. Pfeiffer (Ed.), *Handbook of giftedness in children* (2nd ed.). Springer. https://doi.org/10.1007/978-3-319-77004-8_15

Muratori, M. C., & Smith, C. K. (2015). Guiding the talent and career development of the gifted individual. *Journal of Counseling & Development*, *93*(2), 173–182. https://doi.org/10.1002/j.1556-6676.2015.00193.x

Myers, R. S. & Pace, T. M. (1986). Counseling gifted and talented students: Historical perspectives and contemporary issues. *Journal of Counseling & Development*, *64*, 548–551. https://doi.org/10.1002/j.1556-6676.1986.tb01199.x

Neihart, M. (1999). The impact of giftedness on psychological well-being: What does the empirical literature say? *Roeper Review*, *22*(1), 10–17. https://doi.org/10.1080/02783199909553991

Neihart, M., Pfeiffer, S. I., & Cross, T. L. (Eds.) (2015). *The social and emotional development of gifted children: What do we know?* (2nd ed.). Prufrock Press, Inc.

Neihart, M., Reis, S.M., Robinson, N.M., & Moon, S.M. (2002). *The social and emotional development of gifted children: What do we know?* Prufrock Press, Inc.

Parker, J. (1988). Differentiated Programs for the G/C/T ... Luxury or Necessity? *Gifted Child Today Magazine, 11*(1), 31–33. https://doi.org/10.1177/107621758801100109

Parker, W. D. & Mills, C. J. (1996). The incidence of perfectionism in gifted students. *Gifted Child Quarterly, 40*, 194–199. https://doi.org/10.1177/001698629604000404

Parker, W. D., Portesova, S., & Stump, H. (2001). Perfectionism in mathematically gifted and typical Czech students. *Journal for the Education of the Gifted, 25*, 138–1152. https://doi.org/10.1177/016235320102500203

Peterson, J. (2006). Addressing counseling needs of gifted students. *Professional School Counseling, 10*(1), 43–51. https://doi.org/10.1177/2156759X0601001S06

Peterson, J. S. & Morris, C. W. (2010). Preparing school counselors to address concerns related to giftedness: A study of accredited counselor preparation programs. *Journal for the Education of the Gifted, 33*(3), 311–336. https://doi.org/10.1177/016235321003300302

Pfeiffer, S. (2013). *Serving the gifted: Evidence-based clinical and psycho-educational practice.* Routledge/Taylor & Francis Group.

Pfeiffer, S. I. (2009). The gifted: Clinical challenges for child psychiatry. *Journal of the American Academy of Child & Adolescent Psychiatry, 48*, 787–790. https://doi.org/10.1097/CHI.0b013e3181aa039d

Pfeiffer, S. I. (2020). Optimizing favorable outcomes when counseling the gifted: A best practices approach. *Gifted Education International*, 1–16. https://doi.org/10.1177/0261429420969917

Piirto, J. (2004). *Understanding creativity.* Great Potential Press.

Reis, S. M. (2002). Gifted females in elementary and secondary school. In M. Neihart, S. M. Reis, N. M. Robinson, & S. M. Moon (Eds.), *The social and emotional development of gifted children: What do we know?* (pp. 125–135). Prufrock Press, Inc.

Reis, S. M. (2004). Social and emotional issues, underachievement, and counseling. In S. M. Moon (Ed.), *Social/emotional, issues, underachievement and counseling of gifted and talented students* (pp. xxiii–xxxviii). Corwin Press.

Richards, J., Encel, J., & Shute, R. (2003). The emotional and behavioural adjustment of intellectually gifted adolescents: A multi-dimensional, multi-informant approach. *High Ability Studies, 14*, 153–164. http://doi.org/10.1080/1359813032000163889

Rimm, S. (2008). Underachievement syndrome: A psychological defensive pattern. In S. I. Pfeiffer (Ed.), *Handbook of giftedness in children* (pp. 139–160). Springer.

Rinn, A. N. (2020). *Social, emotional, and psychosocial development of gifted and talented individuals.* Prufrock Press, Inc.

Rinn, A. N., & Bishop, J. (2015). Gifted adults: A systematic review and analysis of the literature. *Gifted Child Quarterly, 59*(4), 213–235. https://doi.org/10.1177/0016986215600795

Roberts, S. M. & Lovett, S. B. (1994). Examining the "F" in gifted: Academically gifted adolescents' physiological and affective response to scholastic failure. *Journal for the Education of the Gifted, 17*, 241–259. https://doi.org/10.1177/016235329401700304

Robinson, N. M. (2002). Introduction. In M. Neihart, S. M. Reis, N. M. Robinson, & S. M. Moon (Eds.), *The social and emotional development of gifted children: What do we know?* (pp. xi–xxiv). Prufrock Press, Inc.

Robinson, A., Shore, B. M., & Enersen, D. L. (2007). *Best practices in gifted education: An evidence-based guide.* Prufrock Press, Inc.

Rogers, K. B. (2007). What makes the highly gifted child qualitatively different? In K. Kay, D. Robson, & J. F. Brennemann, *High IQ kids: Collected insights, information, and personal stories* (pp. 90–100). Free Spirit.

Ryland, H. K., Lundervold, A. J., Elgen, I., & Hysing, M. (2010). Is there a protective effect of normal to high intellectual function on mental health in children with chronic illness? *Child and Adolescent Psychiatry and Mental Health, 4*. https://doi.org/10.1186/1753-2000-4-3

Saltz, G. (2017). *The power of different: The link between disorder and genius.* Flatiron Books.

Sarouphim, K. M. (2011). Gifted and non-gifted Lebanese youth: Gender differences in self concept, self-esteem and depression. *International Education, 41*, 26–41.

Schlesinger, J. (2012). *The insanity hoax: Exposing the myth of the mad genius.* Shrinktunes Media.

Schuler, P. A. (2000). Perfectionism and gifted adolescents. *Journal of Secondary Gifted Education, 11*, 183–196. https://doi.org//10.4219/jsge-2000-629

SENG. (2015). *SENG Misdiagnosis Initiative.* http://sengifted.org/programs/misdiagnosis-initiative/

Shechtman, Z. & Silektor, A. (2012). Social competencies and difficulties of gifted children compared to nongifted peers. *Roeper Review, 34*, 63–72. https://doi.org/10.1080/0278 3193.2012.627555

Siegle, D. & McCoach, D. B. (2018). Underachievement and the gifted child. In S. I. Pfeiffer, E. Shaunessy-Dedrick, & M. Foley-Nicpon (Eds.), *APA handbook of giftedness and talent* (pp. 559–574). American Psychological Association.

Silverman, L. K. (1994). The moral sensitivity of gifted children and the evolution of society. *Roeper Review: A Journal on Gifted Education, 17*(2), 110–116. https://doi.org/10.1080/02783199409553636

Silverman, L. K. (1998). The second child syndrome. *Mensa Bulletin, 320*, 18–120. http://spe.idv.tw/UploadFile/News/2013920162845/The%20second%20child%20syndrome.pdf

Silverman, L. K. (1999). Perfectionism: The crucible of giftedness. *Advanced Development, 8*, 47–61. https://doi.org/10.1177/026142940702300304

Silverman, L. K. (2002). Asynchronous development. In M. Neihart, S. M. Reis, N. M. Robinson, & S. M. Moon (Eds.), *The social and emotional development of gifted children: What do we know?* (pp. 31–37). Prufrock Press, Inc.

Silverman, L. K. (2012). *Using test results to support clinical judgment.* Retrieved from https://www.giftedchildren.dk/content.php?787-Using-test-results-to-support-clinical-judgment-linda-silverman

Smith, D., Anderson, J., Zammit, S., Meyer, T., Pell, J., & Mackay, D. (2015). Childhood IQ and risk of bipolar disorder in adulthood: Prospective birth cohort study. *BJPsych Open, 1*(1), 74–80. https://doi.org/10.1192/bjpo.bp.115.000455

Spielberger, C. D. (1958). On the relationship between manifest anxiety and intelligence. *Journal of Consulting Psychology, 22*(3), 220–224. https://doi.org/10.1037/h0044773

Stricker, J., Buecker, S., Schneider, M., & Preckel, F. (2019). Intellectual giftedness and multidimensional perfectionism: A meta-analytic review. *Educational Psychology Review, 31*, 1–24. https://doi.org/1007/s10648-019-09504-1

Terman, L. M. (1925). *Genetic studies of genius.* Stanford University Press.

Thomas, V., & Ray, K. E. (2006). Counseling exceptional individuals and their families: A systems perspective. *Professional School Counseling, 10*(1), 58–65. https://doi.org/10.1177/2156759X0601001S08

Tolbert, E. L. (1982). *An introduction to guidance: The professional counselor* (2nd ed.). Little, Brown & Company.

Tomlinson, C. A., Brighton, C., Hertberg, H., Callahan, C. M., Moon, T. R., Brimijoin, K., & Reynolds, T. (2003). Differentiating instruction in response to student readiness, interest, and learning profile in academically diverse classroom: A review of literature. *Journal for the Education of the Gifted, 27*(2–3), 119–145. https://doi.org/10.1177/016235320302700203

Touyz, S. W., Beumont, P. J., & Johnstone, L. C. (1986). Neuropsychological correlates of dieting disorders. *International Journal of Eating Disorders, 5*(6), 1025–1034. https://doi.org/10.1002/1098-108X(198609)5:6<1025::AID-EAT2260050606>3.0.CO;2-T

Vansteenkiste, M., Smeets, S., Soenens, B., Lens, W., Matos, L., & Deci, E. L. (2010). Autonomous and controlled regulation of performance-approach goals: Their relations to perfectionism and educational outcomes. *Motivation and Emotion, 34*, 333–353. https://doi.org/10.1007/s11031-010-9188-3

Vermani, M., Marcus, M., & Katzman, M. A. (2011). Rates of detection of mood and anxiety disorders in primary care: A descriptive, cross-sectional study. *The Primary Care Companion for CNS Disorders, 13*(2). https://doi.org/10.4088/PCC.10m01013

Walker, L. E. & Shapiro, D. L. (2010). Parental alienation disorder: Why label children with a mental diagnosis? *Journal of Child Custody, 7*, 266–286. https://nsuworks.nova.edu/cps_facarticles/397

Webb, J. T. & Kleine, P. A. (1993). Assessing gifted and talented children. In D. J. Willis & J. L. Culbertson (Eds.), *Testing young children* (pp. 383–407). PRO-ED.

Webb, J. T. (1993). Nurturing social-emotional development of gifted children. In K. A. Heler, F. J. Monks, & A. H. Passow (Eds.), *International handbook of research and development of giftedness and talent* (pp. 525–538). Pergamon Press.

Webb, J. (2013). *Searching for meaning: Idealism, bright minds, disillusionment, and hope.* Great Potential Press.

Webb, J. T. (2014). Gifted children and adults. Neglected areas of practice. The National Register of Health Service Psychologists. The Register Report, 18–27.

Webb, J. T., Amend, E. R., Beljan, P., Webb, N. E., Kuzujanakis, M., Olenchak, F., R., & Goerss, J. (2016). *Misdiagnosis and dual diagnosis of gifted children and adults.* Great Potential Press.

Wellisch, M. & Brown J. (2013). Many faces of a gifted personality: Characteristics along a complex gifted spectrum. *Talent Development & Excellence, 5*(2), 43–58. http://iratde.com/index.php/jtde/article/view/34

White, S. L., Graham, L. J., & Blass, S. (2018). Why do we know so little about the factors associated with gifted underachievement? A systematic literature review. *Educational Research Review, 24*, 55–66. https://doi.org/10.1016/j.edurev.2018.03.001

Wiley, K. R. (2020). The social and emotional world of gifted students: Moving beyond the label. *Psychology in the Schools, 57*(3), 1528–1541. https://doi.org/10.1002/pits.22340

Wirthwein, L. & Rost, D. H. (2011). Giftedness and subjective well-being: A study with adults. *Learning and Individual Differences, 21*(2), 182–186. https://doi.org/10.1016/j.lindif.2011.01.001

Zeidner, M. (2020). "Don't worry—be happy": The sad state of happiness research in gifted students, *High Ability Studies.* http://doi.org/10.1080/13598139.2020.1733392

Ziegler, A., Ziegler, A., & Stoeger, H. (2012). Shortcomings of the IQ-based construct of underachievement. *Roeper Review, 34*, 123–132. https://doi.org/10.1080/02783193.2012.660726

Zimmerman, M., Ruggero, C.J., Chelminski, I., & Young, D. (2008). Is bipolar disorder overdiagnosed? *Journal of Clinical Psychiatry, 69*, 935–940. https://doi.org/10.4088/jcp.v69n0608

Zoëga, H., Valdimarsdóttir, U. A., & Hernández-Díaz, S. (2012). Age, academic performance, and stimulant prescribing for ADHD: A nationwide cohort study. *Pediatrics, 130*(6), 1012–1018. https://doi.org/10.1542/peds.2012-0689

CHAPTER 10

Conclusions and implications for the future

Michael S. Matthews, Erin M. Miller,
and Dante D. Dixson

As should now be evident from this book's chapters, students identified for gifted programming and their cognitively advanced peers develop in a substantially similar if not identical manner as cognitively typical children across most aspects of human development. That said, some milestones may occur in a different order, or may be more or less influential on the learning and growth of cognitively advanced children than they are for typically developing children and youth.

Chapter 1 provided background knowledge to help readers more effectively interpret current and future research in light of its social context. Much can be learned from systematic inquiry, but the systems within which it is conducted should inform the reader's understanding of how much confidence to place in specific findings. McBee has identified more reasons for skepticism than for confidence in existing findings. In short, single findings should be understood as just that – suggestive, but not in any way conclusive. A body of evidence built up over time, conducted by varied authors, based on larger rather than smaller samples, and derived using a variety of modes of inquiry will always be stronger than any single individual study. Unfortunately, as the remainder of this book has demonstrated, there are very few areas of gifted development for which a strong, consistent body of evidence exists. This is not due to any one specific shortcoming, but rather to the small number of studies whose authors specifically have considered cognitively advanced learners as a unique comparison group. As new findings enter the literature and are reported in the popular press, we urge readers to look back at and apply McBee's nine strategies for "reading between the lines" to evaluate credibility.

Following this broad introduction, Jolly's chapter on physical development focused on specific similarities and differences between high-ability children and those who develop typically. A handful of landmark longitudinal studies have established that despite stubbornly persistent popular stereotypes, gifted children are no more fragile than typically developing children are. Rather, higher intelligence measured in childhood is associated with better life outcomes in a variety of areas that include physical health, though this may be due to the higher income in adulthood

DOI: 10.4324/9781003025443-11

(and correspondingly greater access to healthy lifestyles and medical care) that also is associated with higher intelligence. While of course correlation cannot be taken to mean that one causes the other, these foundational studies by Lewis Terman and others provide the best evidence we are likely to get regarding these relationships.

Other notable issues with regard to physical development reported in this chapter include that early motor ability does not appear to be associated with advanced academic abilities; that allergies and immune system disorders occur at the same rates as in typically developing children and youth; and that left-handedness probably is not associated with giftedness, though more work may be needed to confirm this. While there are some studies whose findings run contrary to these generalizations, they often either are not based on representative samples or they lack comparison groups.

In Chapter 3, Bishop and Hujar provided an overview of three major theories of learning – Behaviorism, Social Cognitive Theory, and Constructivism – that can be applied in working with children with high academic potential. These authors defined learning as "the process by which a person gains new insight, ability, or wisdom through practice or experience." Though each of these perspectives on learning builds on the prior theory, beginning with behaviorism, all three remain relevant to understanding the many and varied reasons why a student may engage – or not engage – with learning in the classroom and other settings. Social Cognitive Theory in particular addresses learner agency, and as a result this theory also helps explain some of the ways in which homogeneous ability grouping and mentoring can be particularly valuable in understanding and supporting the growth and development of high-ability learners. Constructivism includes both cognitive and social applications. Cognitive constructivism helps explain learners' internal processes in relating new knowledge to their existing knowledge and mental models, and supports the importance of providing challenging learning material and self-directed learning opportunities to advanced learners, while social constructivism's emphasis on how interaction between the learner and others supports the learning process highlights the value of providing meaningful collaborative activities for advanced (and likely, all) learners. Social constructivism also lends support for homogeneous learning environments in which learners of high ability can interact with others working at a similarly advanced level.

While there are relatively minimal differences between individuals with high cognitive ability and typically developing children and youth in either physical development or in how they learn, differences are clearly apparent in the areas of attention and memory, which Chapter 4 highlighted. This should not be surprising, because strengths in attention and memory are two of the areas that define high cognitive ability to begin with. Miller first discussed how attention works, and noted that with the exception of children diagnosed with an attention deficit disorder, attention works in the same fundamental manner in both cognitively advanced and typically developing children. Once one pays attention to something, the brain then can begin encoding it into memory. Information first goes into the temporary and limited storage provided by working memory, and then is encoded into long-term memory. Children identified as gifted can store and process more information than the typically developing child can, due to some combination of greater capacity, more efficient processing, and better available strategies. Of these, better strategies can be taught and learned, helping all children to improve their memory, whereas capacity and efficiency are likely due to a combination of genetic and environmental influences that are not yet fully understood.

Long-term memory may be encoded and recalled via semantic, episodic, procedural, or some combination of these mechanisms. Children identified as gifted tend to excel in semantic and episodic memory, and may or may not also excel in its procedural aspects. In terms of its physical mechanism, memories are encoded in the form of networks of connections within the brain; children identified as gifted likely have more complex networks with larger numbers of connections and greater activation of these networks, in comparison to typical children. Gifted children may be faster and more efficient at storing and retrieving memories, with the result that they may appear to the external observer to be learning almost effortlessly. These differences appear to be both innate and learned, which again supports the importance of the home and school environment in fostering high abilities, but how these differences arise is not yet well understood. For parents and teachers who work with gifted and advanced learners, explaining how the mind works (or in some cases, doesn't work) is key to helping children become comfortable with their own individual learning differences. Despite their typical strengths Miller points out that the gifted child's memory is not perfect, that they do make mistakes or forget things the same as everyone else, and that teachers and parents (and especially the child themselves) should not over-react when this occurs.

In addition to their more internally focused differences in attention and memory, language is perhaps the most obvious difference others see between cognitively advanced and typically developing children. Students identified as gifted in school frequently started speaking earlier than typical learners, began using advanced vocabulary at an early age, and often taught themselves how to read well before formally entering school. While their language skills progress in a similar manner and through the same stages as typical children do, advanced learners do so more rapidly and at earlier ages. As Slade explained in Chapter 5, because of these differences the general education curriculum alone is not enough to help these learners progress; it simply is not challenging enough. Students who are advanced readers benefit from more difficult vocabulary and more challenging content, from an accelerated pace, and from less repetition of content than typically developing children require to achieve mastery.

Slade's chapter also revisited the learning theories introduced in Chapter 3, and here they are connected specifically to language development. Behaviorism, in this context, suggests that imitation is one means through which learning occurs. It follows that advanced learners are more likely to learn from other similar-ability peers than from their typically developing peers, supporting the importance of homogeneous ability grouping for academically advanced students. Cognitive learning theory suggests that focused attention, strong memory, and faster processing all work together in specific ways to support the enhanced language learning that is characteristic of advanced learners. The discussion of constructivism focuses on Vygotsky's conception of the Zone of Proximal Development, which also supports the idea that children learn best from those whose abilities are just above their own, in a process of scaffolded learning. For the high-ability learner, this view implies that the traditional classroom practice in which high-ability learners are grouped with typically developing and less-able learners may help these learners, but is unlikely to help in their own learning process.

Chapter 5 also considered humanistic learning theory, which emphasizes that non-cognitive needs, such as physical comfort and safety also need to be met before optimal learning can occur. Slade described how humanistic learning environments support meeting the differentiated learning needs of advanced learners and of all children, such as interest-based learning and self-evaluation of progress by the learner. As such, the humanistic approach also supports equity in programming and fosters literacy instruction that supports both gap remediation and instruction focused on developing each child's specific learning strengths. Chapter 5 concluded with an extensive discussion of literacy education and vocabulary development strategies, with advice about how these should be differentiated to meet the needs of advanced learners.

Chapter 6 took a slightly different approach by having an advanced learner who also is a coauthor of the chapter reflect on her own problem-solving to illustrate directly the processes that research suggests occur. Both problem-finding and problem-solving are important aspects of the processes used by experts in diverse domains, and can be taught and practiced via a broad range of school- and home-based activities. As the authors note, advanced learners tend to display more of the same processes that typically developing learners do: They ask more questions, ask more complex questions, and are more likely to ask questions that teachers or parents cannot immediately answer.

Emma Birlean shared her science fair project experience as an example. In relating it to what is known about problem-solving among advanced learners, there are several connections that can be drawn to other chapters in this volume. The authors of Chapter 6 noted that these students typically have a larger and more connected knowledge base (as one would expect, given the earlier discussion of learning in Chapters 3 and 5). While advanced learners prefer to figure things out on their own, they also benefit from the support of adults and others who are more knowledgeable or more experienced than they are on a particular topic, which goes back to the discussion of Vygotsky's work in the previous chapter. Motivation and social context also tie back to the earlier discussion of these topics and especially to Chapter 7. The authors of Chapter 6 offer the additional realization that as a result of how group work commonly is misused in the classroom, gifted and advanced learners often prefer to work alone rather than being forced to work in a group; they here have provided some suggestions for addressing this concern in group work within the classroom setting.

Chapter 6 also tied the discussion of advanced cognitive ability to the literature on creativity, which is especially appropriate because effective problem-finding and problem-solving require both creativity and cognitive ability be brought to bear at different points in the process. Additional non-cognitive, process, and organizational skills are brought to bear as the need for commitment, planning, and progress monitoring become apparent in successfully addressing this kind of complex, long-term project. Flexibility – another important aspect of creative thought – together with discipline-based thinking and reflection on the process and outcomes also are key components of students' learning processes over the course of these kinds of high-level work. Focusing on engaging students in the manner described here is important training for the cognitively and behaviorally complex work in which many advanced learners will be expected to engage in their future education and as adults.

Chapter 7 addressed motivation and high-ability children through the lenses of several different general theories of motivation. Wilson then addressed two specific concerns that are often found among gifted and high-achieving children, perfectionism, and underachievement. Motivation most broadly can be divided into intrinsic, or internal, sources and extrinsic (external) motivators. In practice, however, there often is some overlap between these causes. High-ability students who also are high achievers tend to have greater intrinsic motivation in academic areas than typically developing learners do, and developing students' intrinsic motivation is a key goal for parents and teachers who wish to foster their child's long-term academic success.

Other theories of motivation have specific uses. Drive Reduction Theory is useful in understanding and helping to modify student behaviors. Self-Determination Theory focuses on intrinsic motivation in the areas of autonomy, connectedness, and self-efficacy, and lends support to specific instructional strategies that allow high-ability learners to satisfy their needs in each of these areas. Expectancy-Value Theory focuses on students' expectations that they can succeed on a task and the value they place on it, which are influenced by the child's perceptions of the learning environment, their interest in a specific task, and their perceptions of its importance to their identity and its usefulness balanced against the costs of completing it. Each of these areas suggests that parents and teachers can individualize tasks in ways that will increase their child's motivation for completing them.

One other theory, Goal Orientation, suggests that students may hold learning goals that are either related to mastery (i.e., intrinsic) or to performance (extrinsic). There may also be a third type of goal, performance-avoidance, which is the motivation to avoid failure. A performance-avoidance goal orientation can lead children to underachieve, because they prefer not trying at all to trying and possibly not succeeding. The Achievement-Orientation Model is based on this theory and on Expectancy-Value Theory, and seeks to model the causes of underachievement in a way that can help suggest specific strategies for how to address it. A second theoretical approach to explaining underachievement in high-ability populations is the two-pathway developmental model suggested by Snyder and Linnenbrink-Garcia. In this model, the Maladaptive Competence Beliefs pathway suggests that the child's inability to live up to the high expectations of their gifted label leads them to develop low self-efficacy that leads to low motivation and underachievement. In the Declining Value Beliefs Pathway, in contrast, the child's perception of their own abilities is appropriate, but low challenge in the school curriculum leads them to disengagement and low goal valuation that then lead to low motivation and academic underachievement. This model suggests that in both pathways, helping high-ability children to understand the connection between effort and achievement may help prevent underachievement from developing. Wilson observed that there have been relatively few studies of interventions to reverse underachievement, and that to date, academic interventions appear to have had more effect on psychosocial outcomes than on students' academic outcomes.

Chapter 7 closes with a discussion of perfectionism, which is tied closely to Goal Orientation approaches to understanding motivation. Perfection may be self-oriented, socially prescribed, or other-oriented, though here too there is some overlap across these categories within any individual. Perfectionism may be more obvious in high-achieving learners because of their greater participation in academically focused activities, but Wilson notes there is no evidence that perfectionism is more common among high-ability children than among typically developing learners. Perfectionism often occurs together with anxiety or depression, though there is not a clear cause-and-effect relationship or even good data on which of these may precede the others or whether they simultaneously influence each other. Parents and teachers should be aware that these behaviors often may be serious enough to warrant professional help in the form of Cognitive-Behavioral Therapy.

In Chapter 8, Mammadov addresses individual differences in personality. The five-factor model of personality, known informally as the Big Five model, is the best-supported model developed to categorize and explain these individual differences. The five areas are Openness, Conscientiousness, Extraversion, Agreeableness, and Neuroticism. Openness includes descriptive components, such as intellectual curiosity, imagination, and creativity. In addition to Openness traits, high-ability children, and adults tend to also be rated highly on Conscientiousness components, such as persistence, dependability, and academic achievement. Of these two areas, Conscientiousness has been shown to be a better predictor of academic achievement even than Openness is. Individuals with lower levels of Extraversion tend to have better study habits and a higher ability to concentrate, both of which are evident among high-ability individuals. Agreeableness relates to working well within a group, but it does not appear to have been well studied yet in high-ability learners. Neuroticism is essentially the opposite of emotional stability; some studies have suggested that high neuroticism is associated with high anxiety, and may produce negative academic outcomes, but again this does not appear to have been well studied among high-ability learners.

Mammadov explained that individuals identified as academically gifted appear overall to be better adjusted in social and emotional areas according to the available research, but noted that teachers, media, and popular culture tend to espouse the opposite view. For parents, teachers, and schools, these differences may also suggest that the gifted identification process is less likely to identify as gifted those children who have high ability but also are less well adjusted socially or emotionally, a possibility also mentioned by Lein in Chapter 9.

Chapter 7 also addressed Dabrowski's Theory of Positive Disintegration and his idea of overexcitability. While these ideas have been enthusiastically accepted by many in gifted education circles, parents and others should be aware that recent work suggests these explanations largely can be subsumed within the Openness factor in the Big Five model. Likewise, the construct of Grit – which was widely popular in education circles until recently – does not appear to be separable from Conscientiousness.

One other important takeaway from Chapter 7 is that personality factors are malleable to some extent. This means that school staff and parents can reinforce behaviors associated with Openness and Conscientiousness that are highly related to academic achievement.

Chapter 9 addresses mental health concerns as they relate to gifted and high-ability learners. As researchers who often speak with groups of parents and teachers, this is one of the areas in which we hear the most concern. Chapter author Lein noted the difficulty inherent both in obtaining an accurate mental health diagnosis, and in reconciling differing findings in the literature with attention to potential biases in sampling and related methods across studies. Preliminary studies suggest misdiagnosis of high-IQ youth may be frequent, but there clearly is a need for more study in this area. Children with a dual diagnosis of giftedness and a concurrent disability, or twice-exceptional (2e) learners, may be even less likely to receive an appropriate diagnosis.

Some of the drives and characteristics associated with high ability may also increase the likelihood of a mismatch between the child and the expectations of their environment. These include emotional intensity, idealism, different rates of social versus physical development (asynchrony; see also Chapter 2), and the drive to search for consistency and understanding. These may be misinterpreted as disorders rather than normal aspects of personality, and may be exacerbated by environmental factors or by perceptions or stereotypes in reaction to the student's background. Specific issues highlighted by Lein include difficulties related to asynchrony, social competence, self-concept, and the issues of perfectionism and underachievement also discussed elsewhere in this volume (e.g., in Chapter 7).

Chapter 9 concluded with a discussion of the mixed evidence regarding gifted and high-ability learners' overall psychological well-being, their susceptibility to psychiatric illness – the "mad genius" stereotype – and related forms of psychopathology, including mood disorders, suicide, and anxiety disorders. In some cases high academic ability may serve as a protective factor, but even if it does not, most authorities on these topics confirm that high-ability children appear no more susceptible to these issues than typically developing learners are; however, as Lein cautioned, this may not hold true within all sub-populations of high-ability or gifted children. Overall, it appears that the same kinds of preventative measures that are effective with the general population are also effective in minimizing mental health challenges among high-ability children. As other chapter authors in this volume have also said (e.g., Chapter 7), professional treatment is warranted if any of these issues begin to affect the child's ability to function effectively in daily life.

A few words about diversity. Throughout this book we have also presented several brief *Eye for Diversity* sidebars alongside chapters where the information or advice embedded might be affected by the race, gender, socioeconomic status, or English language proficiency of the students being served. Consistent with these sidebars, there are three areas where parents and school personnel can take action to increase the talent development opportunities for students from diverse backgrounds and make gifted education a more inclusive field. All three are centered around making learning environments more welcoming to students from diverse backgrounds and providing them with more opportunities to develop their talent. The first action is: *be open*. This is probably the most difficult of the three. Being open not only consists of being open to different perspectives, lived experiences, and circumstances but also to being wrong (i.e., having one's assumptions violated by their environment or the people in it). Being open is difficult because it is challenging to suppress one's assumptions about the world and consider that their lived experience might lead them to the wrong conclusion about a situation. However, to make a meaningful contribution toward making talent development more equitable, it is essential that parents and school personnel be open to new experiences, ideas, and perspectives. Openness is essential because the better one understands the circumstances of the "other" people (e.g., those from low and high socioeconomic backgrounds) in a system, the more likely the people who make up that system will empathize with each other and engage in action that make the system itself more equitable. In practice, being open entails a lot of introspection (i.e., thinking about one's experiences and how they may or may not be appropriate for the current situation), perspective-seeking (i.e., engaging relevant parties in conversation to better understand how their perspective might be different and more relevant to the current situation than one's own), and challenging assumptions (i.e., assuming that one is wrong and what being wrong might mean for the current situation). Although being open is not easy, it is a prerequisite to making gifted education more equitable. Moreover, if parents and school personnel put forth a consistent and concerted effort, it is easy to achieve with practice.

The second action is: *be intentional*. If one wishes to aid in the talent development of students from diverse backgrounds, it is imperative to have a plan. Diversity, advantage, disadvantage, and gifted education are interrelated in complex ways, and many well-intentioned parents and educators have unintentionally made matters worse for those they intended to help because they did not have a plan. Thus, to be an effective contributor to making talent development more equitable, parents and school personnel should: (a) familiarize themselves with evidenced-based ways that parents and school personnel can contribute (applying the principles from Chapter 1, this can be done by reading research articles or via a google search) and (b) create a plan for how they intend to contribute (with a focus on integrating this contribution within their interests, values, and daily life). The ideal plan integrates one's research, plan of action, and interests. For instance, it is easier–and more likely to persist and be effective long-term–if a teacher who loves teaching integrates a diversity section into every unit of his curriculum, than if a parent who has no interest in fund raising wishes to host a fund-raiser to increase access to gifted education services. The key is for the intentional contribution to be something you and others enjoy, so that it is more likely to be repeated and become effective in the long-term. One's plan provides a roadmap for how to turn intentions into a reality that is likely to make a difference. Relatedly, another part of being intentional is remaining constantly aware of the diversity of lived experiences. Awareness of different lived experiences, focusing particularly on those that are different from one's own, will aid in more equitable decision-making and actions.

The third action is: *act now*. It is imperative that parents and school personnel engage in behaviors that lead to more equitable talent development. Many people wish that talent development was more equitable, but to achieve this goal, more people need to take action. Moreover, it is equally imperative to be proactive rather than reactive: do not wait for a diversity-related problem to arise before taking action! Diversity-related disadvantages (e.g., racism) are a constant within the lives of students from diverse backgrounds and salient diversity-related issues (e.g., a single act of discrimination) arise frequently over the course of their talent development process. Thus, there is neither any shortage of ways to act, nor any single specific way that parents and school personnel should contribute to make gifted education more inclusive. For example, parents can check in frequently with their child(ren) to evaluate whether they are being appropriately challenged in their current learning placement (if their child is from a diverse background), or they can discuss the benefits (e.g., understanding that a situation can be viewed from multiple perspectives) of being friends with students from a background different than one's own (if their child is of the majority). Similarly, a teacher can develop their curriculum using material from a diverse set of cultures. The only requirements for an effective action is that it is evidenced-based and thoughtful. The action should be consistent with scientific evidence to increase the probability that it will be effective, and it should be thoughtful to ensure that it fits the specific situation to which it is applied. The more that parents and school personnel engage in effective action, the more equity in talent development will result. Overall, achieving a successful state of diversity is about understanding that despite differences, most people want to achieve the same things and that they are stronger together than they are divided.

Shared understanding is solidified with trust, which can be gained through open communication. McBee's discussion of credibility offers some helpful directions for future thought. As McBee observed, credibility arises from technical rigor, procedural rigor, and transparency. The programs that train scholars to conduct research increasingly are providing their graduates with strong training with regard to technical rigor, and many established researchers also are devoting increased attention to rigor in areas such as adequate sample size. Both transparency and procedural rigor are closely related, and the increasing emphasis on (and ready availability of) open science practices such as preregistration are a promising sign of the emergence of new, more thoughtful standards and expectations for evidence within the scientific community. Academic journals likewise have made some rapid initial progress toward editorial policies that encourage procedural transparency and openness, though it likely will take a generation or more for these changes to become widespread. However, the popular media that inform most parents and teachers may never reach this level of credibility. Parents and teachers alike can – and should – help children learn to think critically about the trustworthiness of what they watch or read, and should also apply these skills in their own learning. All too often the fads and exciting new ideas in education turn out to be unsubstantiated when one looks closer, but yet disproven or unsupported ideas like multiple intelligences, grit, and overexcitabilities remain popular long after they have been debunked.

Children who are identified as gifted in school, or who have high academic potential, are not the hothouse flowers that 100 years ago they were widely believed to be, but neither are they immune to the normal challenges that accompany growth and development. By addressing the details of their similarities and occasional differences from typically developing children and youth, we hope this book has provided readers with a clearer yet also more nuanced understanding of this specific group of learners, and further with the tools they need to learn about and evaluate future findings about them.

Index